Rollo Reuschel

The Knights of Industry

Revelations about Foreign Long-Firms in London

Rollo Reuschel

The Knights of Industry
Revelations about Foreign Long-Firms in London

ISBN/EAN: 9783337280727

Printed in Europe, USA, Canada, Australia, Japan

Cover: Foto ©Suzi / pixelio.de

More available books at **www.hansebooks.com**

THE

KNIGHTS OF INDUSTRY,

REVELATIONS

ABOUT

FOREIGN LONG-FIRMS in LONDON,

BY

ROLLO-REUSCHEL.

LONDON:
Published by THE AUTHOR at 142, Clerkenwell Road, E.C.

1895.

CONTENTS.

* These two articles, originally published in the 'Cologne People's Gazette,' led to the Libel-action brought against the author.

INTRODUCTION.

THE reason why this book was written, is in the first place to draw the attention of governments and the trading community, on the strength of documentary evidence, to certain crying evils that, as all and everything in our times, have grown to gigantic proportions, endangering the commerce in a most serious manner. The culminating point was reached, when a London enquiry-office, enjoying the absolute confidence, not only of their customers, but also of kindred trade-protecting institutions, entered into a conspiracy with a well organized gang of long-firm swindlers. Exporters and manufacturers were by this dangerous combination at the mercy of a gang of relentless robbers. Betrayed for years by those whom the victims considered their protectors, they were defrauded of goods to an incalculable value.

The material referring to this conspiracy is of *a most sensational character*. As soon as I had ascertained the facts, I opened my attack against the confederates in the columns of the "Kölnische Volkszeitung" *(The Cologne People's Gazette)*, a leading political, and, with regard to commercial matters, most important daily paper in Germany, to which I am for many years the London correspondent. But my warning voice was stiffled—for a time at least. The second article was in the press, when the proprietor of the said enquiry office, LOTHAR LEHNERT, of 46, Queen Victoria Street, London, E.C., and his so-called manager, but in fact partner, GUSTAV OPITZ, brought a criminal action for libel against me. Not to become guilty of contempt of court, I was obliged not to proceed further with my revelations. After prolonged proceedings in the police court, the matter reached finally the Central Criminal Court, where the case was tried on the 25th of March before Commissioner Kerr. I pleaded 'not guilty' and justification, but my hope, to find an opportunity at this occasion to disclose through my counsels in the public interest the existing conspiracy, and to make use of the damning material in my possession, was again frustrated. After hearing the opening part only of my evidence, and when Lehnert had been hardly one hour under cross-examination, the Jury stopped the case, declared justified what I had written, and found me 'Not Guilty'. The counsel of the other prosecutor, Gustav Opitz, intimated that he could not proceed with the action, and threw up his brief in disgust. A verdict of 'not guilty' was entered in this case too, and the Judge directed my solicitor to lay the documents referring to the case before the public prosecutor. I had gained the victory, and lost nearly two thousand pounds sterling, costs of the action, which certainly the prosecutors were ordered to pay, but of which, unfortunately, I shall never see a farthing again, with the exception of half of this amount, that has been refunded to me by the proprietors of my paper. A few days later the *par nobile fratrum*, Lehnert and Opitz, were arrested; the next day they were standing in the dock at the Lord Mayor's court to answer an indictment of fraud and conspiracy. The case was not gone into at this occasion, and to this regretable circumstance the defendants had to thank it that they were admitted to bail in a ridiculously small amount. At the next hearing Opitz only put in an appearance. Lehnert, when called upon, did not answer, and it became soon evident that he had transferred himself to another milder clime. Opitz was several times remanded and at last committed for trial, the result of which I shall deal with in another chapter.

But one thing was gained, I could speak out again, and show to the commercial world where the dangerous breakers are laying, on which the 'good ships' are coming to grief and sinking in the bottomless sea of bankruptcy. I consider it a public duty to do so. Before entering, however, on the principal part of my book, I think it advisable to point out a few differences in the organisation of trade in England and Germany, which are puzzling to many a merchant here and there, and seem to require a short explanation.

England is a free country. Everybody can come and settle here, without being troubled to produce papers, to give notice to the police, to say who he is, where he comes from, what profession he is following, what his means of existence, what his business. No questions are asked. He may choose what name he likes, he can start in business under what firm it pleases him. Nobody troubles about it, and he need not trouble too. There is no notification to the authorities, and no registration of firms, as in Germany and other continental countries, where every merchant and tradesman is bound by law to register his firm.

If someone opens a business in England, he can do so under any style he likes; he may call himself Liman & Co., even if his real 'honest name' be Lehnert, and Herr Hans Schulz may fly to-day from Germany, arrive the next morning as Mr. Robinson in London, and open in the afternoon as Messrs. Dumas, Grosvenor & Co., somewhere in a small back room in the city his business. Nobody troubles about it, and English liberty becomes thus the greatest protection to the swindling fraternity and to the guild of Knights of Industry. If Herr Schulz, alias Robinson has reasons of his own to get tired of his firm Dumas, Grosvenor & Co., then he buys for a penny white paint, and the beautiful long firm vanishes for all eternity; another pennyworth of paint, however, is sufficient to recompense the world for this loss, and under the deft hands of Herr Schulz alias Robinson, a new grand firm appears in the place of the vanished one. If the abode of this ever changing firm gets too hot for the proprietor, he simply leaves the premises, usually with some week's rent in arrear, and opens a new business under a new name a few streets farther off. Did not Mr. Gustav Opitz trade within a year under his name, and in quick succession as McEnti, John Mouat & Co., W. Arnold & Co., Bernard & Co., Lulu L. Clark & Co., within a radius of five minutes' walk? Nobody cares for it, the creditors excepted, and if one of these preying and disagreeable individuals happens by chance to find out the ever vanishing proprietor of the endless firms, and if he feels disposed to bring the swindler to bank and to help him to a few months of well-deserved hard labour, he may do so, if he does not mind a lot of personal trouble and heavy expenses. But let him beware that he be provided with conclusive proofs, else it may happen that he finds himself prosecuted, after an abortive trial, for wrongful imprisonment, slander, defamation of character, and a string of other inditable offences, carrying heavy damages with them. A public prosecutor who would take action on the strength of private information laid before him, as in Germany, France, Austria and other countries, does not exist in England, much to the relief of the international guild of long-firm swindlers, who honour this free country with their presence. Who wants to see justice done in England, must prosecute personally; he has first to pay a very heavy solicitor's bill, and when he attains his end and sees the person who defrauded him, sentenced, he will usually find, that the heavier punishment fell to his, the prosecutor's, lot. The fact is, that the law-costs are simply monstrous in England, that to go to law is really a luxury reserved for the rich. A short time ago, I had occasion to enquire from a manufacturer in Bohemia, how a law-suit he had instituted against a member of a gang of long-firm swindlers, had ended. The result was abortive, and the manufacturer wrote to me, he should not like to decide who was the greater rascal, the solicitor who conducted his case, or the swindler who committed the fraud.

In the proceedings of bankruptcy there are also great differences in existence. If somebody finds himself utterly stranded in England, he simply closes his office and leaves it to his creditors to look for him and to find him, if they can. And if such a defaulter is found, very little is gained indeed. If a fraud was committed, a great expense is required to bring the culprit before the proper tribunal. If there was no fraud, a civil action must first be taken to obtain judgement, and on the strength of this the creditor can make, at his costs, the debtor bankrupt. There, of course, the solicitors are standing again at the gate, and who has once gathered experiences with the English law, will be cautious not to burn his fingers a second time. I say at this point quite openly and candidly that even greater caution is to be observed at the choice of a solicitor than at that of an agent, and nobody ought to confide himself to the tender mercies of a solicitor who has not been specially recommended by a trustworthy person.

These are shortcomings which are quite incomprehensible to

foreign merchants, who in their own country have but to apply to the public prosecutor in order to secure, free of charge, the prosecution of a fraudulent debtor or long-firm swindler. As the prosecutor has besides to appear personally in England, most of the continental merchants and manufacturers abstain from bringing an action here for recovery of debts.

Under these circumstances the foreign consulates in this country can do but little for the protection of the commercial interests of the countries they are representing, and they also do not display great energies to exert themselves in this direction. All what is to be got from them are, as a rule, some general remarks and some indifferent advice, because they usually are not informed sufficiently to give a better one.

To my opinion this deplorable state of things could be ameliorated only, if

1. A law was passed, binding every foreigner who takes up his residence in England, to produce papers and to give notice of his presence and his address to the proper authorities; this would enable the police to watch in a more efficient manner the foreigners congregating in this country, and to prevent dubious characters to hide their identity.
2. If the compulsory registration of all commercial firms was introduced, where also the proprietor or proprietors of the firm were registered, and a considerable registration fee demanded, as in the case of limited companies.
3. If only such foreigners would be permitted to establish a firm in England, who had been established previously already in their native, or another country for at least two years under the same firm, and who can produce a 'clean bill' *i.e.* that they are neither defaulters or undischarged bankrupts. Of foreigners, who were not formerly in business for themselves, a residence of at least ten years in this country ought to be demanded, before permission is granted to them, to open here a firm.

At present the case stands thus, that foreign clerks, who are not able to find here a situation, enter the ranks of the long-firm swindlers ('sledge-drivers') as soon as their scanty means are exhausted and they find themselves driven to extremities; they become thus a disgrace to their countrymen and are not only discrediting them, but they grow also to a real terror of the foreign exporters and manufacturers.

Foreign governments ought also to take some steps to protect the export trade from the 'sledge-drivers' in foreign parts, and especially in 'modern Babylon'. I do not want to go so far as to say that enquiry-offices ought to become official institutions, but I maintain that the enquiry-agencies ought to be controlled by an official enquiry-department, connected with the consulates, where accredited firms could obtain against the payment of a reasonable fee, reliable commercial informations, in order to control by these means the informations received from other sources. The chambers of commerce ought to combine too, as a reader of the 'Cologne People's Gazette' remarks in his congratulatory letter to my victory, and the establishment of a central enquiry office at London on their part, would certainly prove a most useful and beneficial measure.

Finally the foreign press and the foreign governments ought to warn more often, yes, constantly and most urgently against an injudicious emigration to the United Kingdom. Perverse ideas of the wealth of England, and of the ease to earn here a good living, if not a fortune, are inducing great numbers of foreign clerks to transfer themselves to the shores of this country. Very few find their expectations realized; the great majority are soon cruelly undeceived and ship-wrecked in the streets of London town, not only materially but, worse still, morally too. Driven to despair, they soon swell the ranks of the swindling fraternity.

The name 'sledge-driver' *(Schlittenfahrer)* is the invention of German swindlers, who had chosen London for their field of activity. If Germans speak amongst themselves of an unprincipled man of business, they say: 'he is driving his sledge'. It is the generally accepted term for a long-firm swindler, otherwise a member of the 'black gang' *(schwarze Bande)*. A most important person in the sledge-driving conspiracy is the 'sharper', usually a 'respectable city firm', exporting goods to Australia, India, the Cape and other British colonies. He is nothing better than a receiver of stolen property, who disposes of the goods obtained by fraud and swindling from the manufacturers by the sledge-drivers. The sharpers are very careful to conduct their shady business in such a manner as not to come into conflict with the law. Whatever they pay for the goods, and if it be the tenth part only of the real value, they insist always on getting a receipt for an amount representing the current market prices of the commodity they buy, and they never make a payment in the presence of witnesses. They remain thus always on the safe side, and never being betrayed by the thieves, enjoy undisturbed the fame of most respectable firms. It is dangerous ground to tread upon, but I shall endeavour to pillory by and by these receivers in the same way as I have done with the swindling-enquiry-agents Opitz and Lehnert.

The History of the 'Sledge-driver' Articles in the 'Cologne People's Gazette'.

THE question was often put to me, why I persecuted so relentlessly and systematically, yes, even with undisguised hatred the sledge-driving fraternity. The answer is not far to seek. I wanted to put an effectual stop to the heartless and cruel frauds perpetrated continually on such manufacturers, who can least bear the loss inflicted upon them. Large and old-established firms do not easily become a prey to long-firm swindlers; this lot falls usually to the beginners who are anxious to get connections and are subject to the fascination that London, the centre of the world's commerce, exercises on the minds of all engaged in trade. To get a footing in this market, to do business with a 'London firm', is thus the pious wish of every German manufacturer, and in his ardour to see this realized, he forgets too often the simplest rules of caution and circumspection. This is well-known to the sledge-drivers, and they are choosing their victims principally amongst the young, struggling and inexperienced firms. One of the first cases of long-firm swindling that was brought to my notice, and actually gave rise to my hatred against this pest of the commercial life of our times, had reference to such a poor, young German manufacturer, an acquaintance of mine, who, after having worked hard for some years, was totally ruined by a gang of long-firm swindlers in England. He communicated with me, and I tried to recover for him at least a part of his claim and his goods, but all my endeavours were frustrated by the artfulness of the swindlers, who kept their prey and escaped also justice. The end of it was that my friend lost all he possessed, became a bankrupt, and found himself and his family in the most pityable position. I vowed to avenge him, and to this purpose

I commenced to study the tricks and dodges of the swindling fraternity, for I knew that by these means only their doings can be frustrated and justice meted out to them. Thus the study of the art of sledge-driving became my speciality—a kind of sport. Circumstances occured which strengthened me in my resolve, and these were my personal experiences. I must confess: I was swindled and defrauded too, and this so often, and to such an extent, that my former simplicity in trusting and taking everybody for an honest man has, to my great regret, given way to the ignoble principle to trust nobody and to regard everyone as a rogue, as long as I have no proofs to the contrary.

The first swindle to which I fell a victim is of particular interest to me, because a prince, a real prince, the descendant of a historic royal house, had a hand in it. H. R. H. was, of course, reduced in his circumstances, but, like his ancestors, he was an adept in squandering money, and living in grand style at other people's expenses. The noble prince introduced once to me a Mr. X who had been an officer in a Prussian regiment of Lancers. It seems hardly credible, but this quondam officer surpassed even the Prince in the art of borrowing. From the very beginning of our acquaintance, I felt an antipathy against this fellow, but, try as I might, I could not get rid of him. It did not take long, and both, the prince and the lieutenant, were in my debt. Once the prince came, quite broken-hearted, with the 'dreadful' news that his friend X had the broker in the house, and he assured me, in a very flattering manner, that I was the only man in the whole world and the surrounding villages, who would act as a Christian and save X from ruin. I informed the prince with great firmness that my modesty forbade me to aspire to such a distinction; I refused in fact point blank to render assistance, but, somehow, the prince prevailed upon me, and accepting him as security, I parted with my money, never to see it again! The week had passed, during which the prince had engaged himself to repay the loan, and when I went to remind him personally of his promise, I found him gone, and ascertained that his pityful story was a work of fiction from beginning to end, and that he had 'let me in'. However, after some time I discovered his address, and took the liberty to remind him of his unsettled 'debt of honour'. He answered by return of post, but instead of the letter he had written to me, the envelope contained a note, bearing in the left corner a ducal coronet, and informing 'my dear Prince' that the Duke of (*) has much pleasure to comply with his request and to forward to him a parcel of worn garments from the ducal wardrobe 'which may prove acceptable'. The letter had hardly reached me, when it was followed by H. R. H., who was anxious to prevent it falling into my hands; but, finding that the mischief was done, he tried to explain away the duke's gift, assuring me that it was destined for 'poor X'. But I knew enough, and he did not succeed to undo the impression this little incident had created in my mind.

For eighteen months I had the pleasure not to see either the prince or his lieutenant, and not to hear of them either.

The two rascals had nearly slipped from my memory, when, quite unexpectedly, Mr. X favoured me with a call. Did he come to repay his debt? Far from it. He had the impudence to ask for a new loan. All what he wanted were *only* £25. 'We are tired of our lazy life,' he declared. 'The Prince and I have resolved to start a new career, and to earn our living by honest work.' I assured him, I was glad to hear it. 'Would I give them a helping hand?' I enquired, of course, what kind of honest work the two 'gentlemen' intended to perform, and he then confided to me, that they intended to start in business. I laughed at the idea of two such men undertaking such a venture and this too with paltry twenty-five pounds. But he was quite in earnest, and declared they did not require more. It tickled my fancy to hear what kind of business they had in view. Was it a fried fish shop, or 'rags and bones'? No, the reply was: 'Export merchants.' All what we want is four week's rent for a small office, say twenty-shillings, second-hand furniture, a table and two chairs for ten shillings, printing of circulars and postage, say five pounds, some nice looking memo's, say ten shillings, and the rest for one month's living. That's all what we require. We can give capital references, the prince especially, and before the month is over 'our firm' will be supplied by the German, Austrian and French manufacturers with such a quantity of goods that we can repay you not only this twenty-five pounds, but all we owe you.'

I need not say that Mr. X did not get the money. At a committee-sitting of the German Society of Benevolence a few years hence, I heard a touching letter read from the same gentleman, and I came just in time to prevent a crying misapplication of the funds of this excellent institution. I hoped the rascals would not succeed to realize their commercial intentions, but they nevertheless succeeded to establish a 'sledge-driving' firm in Coleman Street, and before I discovered it and issued a warning, a considerable number of continental manufacturers had been victimised. However, acting for one of the defrauded firms, I succeeded to stop the game of H. R. H. and his *aid-de-camp*, who both left London to evade the proceedings instituted against them, and exported themselves with the proceeds of their robbery to America.

I commenced now (1886) the war against the German sledge-drivers in real earnest. Just before Christmas of the same year I helped one of their number, a man named Lewin, alias Popert, to eight months hard labour, much to the dismay of his friend, the notorious proprietor of one of the notorious German clubs, who at that time pleased himself to pose as the leader of the German social-democrats, and propagated 'the movement' with great success in London.

A short time afterwards, when hunting down with a detective of the City-police (Seething Lane Station) a sledge-driver, who had closed his office, we entered also a German public house in the Eastend. The proprietor called and calls himself the 'Sledge-driver' and claims the honour of having originated this significant name. He really was worthy of his title, and I admit readily that I am under the greatest obligation to this grand-master of the noble guild. Not suspecting our errand, and led on by us, he became quite confidential, and in course of time, he proved to me a living source of information. He initiated me in all the ins and outs of the noble craft, and into the mysteries of German 'low life' in London, and it is but paying a debt of gratitude if I acknowledge what I owe to this veteran of the noble fraternity. When he discovered that I would not become 'one of them,' and that I was an 'unprofitable investment' on which time, beer, exhortations, cigars, instructions and whisky were wasted, he tried 'to do me', but in spite of his many and varied trials to swindle me, the veteran 'sledge-driver', I must say so *to his shame*, did not succeed. But I do not bear him any grudge for that; I just took him for what he was, and remained thus safely guarded. The German manufacturers too, I am sure, will forgive him a great part of his many sins, if they consider that without this oracle many of those sensational revelations could not have been made in the 'Cologne People's Gazette', which proved so instructive and advantageous to them.

In 1887 the good old 'sledge-driver' sent a gentleman to me in whose interest it is if I do not mention his name. He submitted to me a volumnious paper dealing with the German sledge-drivers in London, and wished me to publish these revelations about their secret doings. I was decided already a long time ago to do so, because I knew it would be rendering a tremendous service to the commercial community to reveal the organisation and the *modus operandi* of the international gang of long-firm swindlers with their London head-quarters. What kept me back from starting my crusade in the 'Cologne People's Gazette' was a certain feeling that I had not yet studied the subject sufficiently, that the material collected was to fragmentary, with one word, that I was not competent for the responsible task of dealing efficiently with the matter. But the paper now laid before me, seemed to fill many of the gaps in my knowledge of the subject; it was evidently written by one thoroughly conversant with the matter, and when the gentleman said: 'If you publish what I am putting here in your hands, you will render a public service and earn the thanks of the whole commercial community,' I promised to consider it.

I read the manuscript carefully over and over again; the general drift was quite in accordance with my views and my experiences; but it contained many statements which I doubted, or which were not quite clear to me at that time, and then I set myself the task to verify it. It was an arduous labour; it involved visits to places where I did not like to go, intercourse with persons for whom I did not care, researches and inquiries, foreign and distasteful to my nature, involving great loss of time and great expenses. But all was overcome; the material was carefully sifted, and after many conferences with the gentleman in question.

I re-wrote the article, christened it 'The German Sledge-drivers in London,' and published it in the 'Cologne People's Gazette'. The article was published on September 30th, 1887, and with it was started the series of revelations, which created from the very beginning an extraordinary sensation and interest in Germany, Austria and Switzerland, the first, now concluded chapter, ending with the downfall of the stronghold of the German sledge-drivers in 46, Queen Victoria Street, the dispersion of the famous infamous trio Lehnert-Opitz-Zucker, and the destruction of the most dangerous conspiracy between a highly respected firm of enquiry-agents and long-firm swindlers, against whose combined action the most cautious manufacturer was powerless.

After the publication of the first article, the readers and subscribers of the 'Cologne People's Gazette' were demanding a continuation of the revelations, and valuable material reached the editor from parties who had been swindled by the London gang. About the same time, I heard of a personage who put even, as I was told, 'my oracle,' the nestor of the gang, quite in the shadow. He was described to me as the greatest rogue in existance, as the most inventive and artful sledge-driver, as a past master of his art. But I recoiled from coming into contact with such a depraved individual; at the same time I was very hard at work in business, and a year had nearly passed since the publication of the first article. The editor of the paper, however, kept on urging me to proceed with the articles, and he forwarded to me for that purpose a number of documents which had been sent to him by readers of the paper.. At this juncture a gentleman, Mr. B., with whom I was publishing a newspaper-correspondence, undertook for me to collect and arrange the material for the second article, which was then published by me in the 'Cologne People's Gazette', on August 31st, 1888. Mr. B. prepared after this two more articles on my behalf, and for these the mentioned arch-sledge-driver May, alias Päpke, supplied for a liberal consideration some material, proving clearly that there are exceptions to the rule of honesty amongst thieves. This supply of material gave rise to the ridiculous rumour, carefully propagated and circulated by May himself, that he was the author of the 'Sledge-driver' articles. It will be sufficient to state, that this man May is quite illiterate and not able to write even a letter, not to speak of a newspaper article. If in these first articles a few anecdotes were published, for which we would not have been able to produce proofs, then it was done for the internal value of these anecdotes, which were too good and too characteristic for the swindling fraternity to be omitted. But every item of information, sold to me by the arch-sledge-driver May, was carefully examined, a greater part rejected, and even where the truth was established, we did not mention names, because we could not trust to May, who cannot be trusted, and who had no documentary evidence for his assertions.

Since the publication of these two last-named articles, of which the second appeared on March 16th, 1890, I have written another sixteen 'Sledge-driver' articles for the 'Cologne People's Gazette'. The correctness of some of my sensational revelations was occasionally doubted; but events have proved the perfect truth of my assertions, every one of which I am able to prove by documentary evidence. In one case only I had to fall back for information on the arch-sledge-driver, and that was the occasion when I had to write about himself. He only could lift the veil of his doings in the past and present, and to a certain extent he did so with a pride and self-consciousness as if his swindles had been the best and noblest deeds, a moral degradation and a perversion of ideas, which I did not meet with in the case of this arch-rogue only. The whole guild seemed infected with this perverse conceit, and in their favourite clubs and taverns in the City Road and elsewhere, they could be heard boasting openly with their tricks and celebrating the heroes of 'special events' which often meant the ruin of an honest man and his family. When it leaked out that May had supplied some material 'for a consideration', other sledge-drivers approached me secretly and offered information. I did not hesitate to avail myself of their services, and many of the most sensational revelations, which proved very instructive and useful, and in some cases even frustrated well-laid schemes of the swindling fraternity, were obtained by these means. In fact for every article I examined now a considerable number of members of the fraternity, who came secretly and willing to earn 'an honest penny' by selling their comrades. 'Traitors in the camp!' was soon the general outcry amongst the 'sledge-driving' fraternity, and they lived in constant fear least I should hear too soon of some of their schemes and spoil their game—a fear, I am happy to say, that at more than one occasion was well founded. But the money thus saved to the endangered German manufacturers was lost to the German sledge-drivers, and it may be easily imagined that I soon became an object of terror and hatred to the whole fraternity. When they found that their threats to do me bodily harm, had not the desired effect and did not stop me from going on with my revelations in the 'Cologne People's Gazette', they tried other, more subtle and infamous means by putting into circulation slanderous reports, throwing doubts on the motives of my action, and discredit on my character. In these dealings, worthy of the noble swindling fraternity, they managed to secure the services of two German newspapers, who condescended and descended so far as to open willingly their columns to the attacks which the German sledge-drivers in London hurled against the 'Cologne People's Gazette' and 'their backers,' attacks for which the one surviving paper will have soon to answer before the proper German tribunals. In view of these perfidious attacks, however, it came to me as a relief when the enquiry-agents Lehnert and Opitz brought their libel action against me, and gave me the welcome opportunity to justify my assertions before an English jury, and to disprove and repudiate the calumnies to which I had been subjected.

Before entering on the history of this trial with its sensational conclusion, as mentioned in the introduction, I shall reprint some of the articles which threw such a lurid light on the doings of the German sledge-drivers in London, and I shall open this little picture-gallery of long-firm celebrities with an article I published in the '*Deutscher Hausschatz*' ('German Home-Treasures').

LONDON SWINDLING FIRMS.*

WHO has not heard of them, of the modern roving robbers, who are not attacking their victims openly with sword and pistol, as their colleagues did in olden times, but are doing so from their safe and secret ambuscade, from their London offices with ink, paper, pen and India rubber stamps.

There was a defence against the old roving thieves in arming one's self, in being cautious, in not rushing thoughtlessly into danger. But to escape the modern roving thieves, the 'sledge-drivers,' as they call themselves, the merchant has very little chance indeed; they are to be found in every branch of business and favoured by the English law, even the most cautious man of business can be defrauded with facility, if he relies on self-help only.

I said: the English law favours the swindlers. With this I did not mean to convey that England makes laws for swindlers, but that English institutions, liberty, free trade, which are all regulated by convenient laws, are favouring with the free citizen the swindler too.

The genii averse to labour, of whom there is in Germany, thanks to the increased general education, a greater abundance than anywhere else, need no further attraction for repairing to England, than the knowledge that London, the rich metropolis of the world's commerce, is the place to escape the stringent German laws and the punishments of justice.

Those good-for-nothings, who are possessed of some means, usually wend their way to the new world to start there, may be, a better life; but many escape justice at the skin of their teeth;

* From the 'Deutscher Hausschatz,' published in 1890.

they come to London without money and without introductions and hardly arrived, they are in distress, in the throws of misery, real London misery, which is specially hard to the German who is cut off here from all resources. To Germany he cannot look for help, for from there punishing justice is shaking her finger at him for the offences, and may be crimes, he has committed. The English he, being a foreigner, cannot address, because they have quite enough to do with their own lazy vagabonds.

These fugitive good-for-nothings are usually people with an excellent education, who could be useful members of society, if it were not surpassing their strength to be honest. For this reason they cannot claim assistance from the honest German men of letters, merchants, artisans, residing in England, because these have been swindled so often, that they draw back before every German who comes to ask them for support, and very often thus the innocent suffers with the guilty. The Societies of Benevolence are also not to be relied upon, because they are cautioned by experience, and not easily cheated.

The only refuge left are the low, notorious clubs with their constant customers, the sledge-drivers. These miserable abodes of crime, whose number is legion and who are usually kept by people of dubious character, are in fact nothing else but secret public houses, aiding and abetting gambling, thieving, swindling, and other vices. Yes, they are the hatching-bed of all vices, and in the first place the high schools of sledge-drivers. To this kind of persons also belong the 'sharpers,' who usually rise to this position from the ranks of the sledge-driving army. By fraud, crime and seduction they have gathered their harvest and become thus enabled to establish themselves in an apparently respectable business as shop-keepers, publicans, pawnbrokers or manufacturers. They buy stolen property only, and pay always cash. Because they never defraud a merchant or manufacturer, they enjoy the reputation of honest and respectable tradesmen, but in reality they are the most unscrupulous scoundrels living. All the goods obtained by fraud from continental manufacturers by the long-firm swindlers, go into the safe keeping of the 'sharpers' against the payment of a shameful price. They never pay in the presence of a third person, and they do not part with anything before receiving from the seller a proper invoice and a receipt for an amount representing the real market value of the sold article. I know cases where goods, invoiced with £150 by the German manufacturer, were sold to the 'sharper' for £5. Without the 'sharpers' the sledge-driving firms could not exist, because a respectable merchant buys from established firms only, and would refuse such offers as that just mentioned.

The sensational revelations of the 'Cologne People's Gazette' have opened the eyes of the commercial world to the secret doings of the German sledge-drivers in London; some of the articles were reprinted in hundreds of newspapers, even in those of America and Australia. But a retrospect may be in place, to bring once again to the memory of the readers the principal features of the dangerous guild.

About the origin of the sledge-drivers we are informed already. They are coming in shoals from the continent to London, and lead a thoughtless, gay and merry life as long as the coins are lasting which they brought with them. Already at their arrival in the docks and at the railway stations, the worthy elders of the noble guild are waiting for them to indroduce them to the proper branch of the craft.

Without this constant 'supply' the 'art' would soon die out, because the handwritings, the connections and references would become unserviceable.

The new comers without means are preferred by the old sledge-drivers to those who arrive possessed of money, for the latter are more independent, and for this reason not so easily managed. Who comes to London with sufficient means, good introductions and honest intentions, is no proper object for the 'Professors' of the sledge-driving art, and they leave him severely alone. An old sledge-driver told me once with regard to the young people who are coming here to perfect themselves in the English language and English business ways: 'These fellows are always running after clergymen, devout women and insolent capitalists, and they are for this reason no company for us respectable people.' With other words it could be said: Because these young people can dispose of money and of their time, they enjoy the opportunity to mix with good company; they are guarded against being mislead, and if they decide on settling in London, they become honest and highly respected merchants, a honour to Germany and an ornament to the German colony. For this reason it is also wrong to regard every German as a 'sledge-driver.'

Artisans likewise are as a rule not fit to become members of the 'guild', excepted they are hailing from a large town where they were corrupted. But there are, unfortunately, exceptions to the general rule, and also amongst the class of artisans people are to be found who, by sledge-driving, have made their pact with the devil.

The greatest pleasure to the heart of a veteran sledge-driver is to receive into the fold of the guild a clerk who fled in the company of his master's cash-box, and who trembles at the sight of his own shadow. They are the genuine material from which sledge-drivers are made, and they form the aristocracy of the German vagabonds in London. A German must feel ashamed if he hears such a demon in human shape boasting after a year's stay with his evil deeds.

Some time ago the clerk F. arrived in London. In Germany the fellow thought, he could dance merrily through life, without doing his duty. When he once 'by mistake' put one of his master's gold-coins into his own pocket, and then spent the money in a music-hall with a young damsel, he lost his situation and his honest name. In consequence he could not obtain another situation; to exert himself at honest work, he was too lazy, and so he resolved to emigrate. In England, he had heard, even idlers could earn a good living by doing nothing, and so he started for London.

Money he had none, but he was the possessor of two strong legs which carried him to Antwerp. Further he could not proceed because he discovered that there was no bridge to pass over to England, and so he had to turn to work, but he did so only after he had found out that the people of Antwerp could do very well without him. After having walked the streets for three nights, he went to an hotel and begged for some leavings, which were given him. One of the kitchen boys was ill, and he was offered to take, for the time being, his place. He accepted thankfully and stuck to his place for a whole week, until an opportunity offered itself to steal the purse and watch of his harsh task master, the cook, and half a dozen silver spoons of the hotel proprietor.

Twenty-four hours later he was playing billiards in a low German club with a very fine gentleman, who displayed an astounding wealth of diamonds. Later on they sat down together, and emptied one bottle of wine after the other. When they had nearly emptied the fourth bottle, the diamond-strewn gentleman said: 'I really do like your company. I suppose I am not mistaken, if I take you for a man of business?'—'Yes, I am a clerk out of employment, and I came here to-day to find a situation,' answered F. 'Well,' said the other pensively, 'I fear you will find it a difficult matter, because your English wants perfection. I hope you brought money enough with you not to be dependent on your earnings.' 'I have still two pounds left,' replied F., 'that is all what is left of the savings I made in Antwerp as book-keeper in an hotel.'

Three days later a garret in a large building near the Patent Office was taken by two gentlemen; to the 45 firms located in this house, a new, rather long firm was added, consisting of four names and an additional '& Co.' The proprietors of this firm were the two billiard players from the German club, whose names bore no similarity with any of the four names on their door.

The capital invested into the business were the remainder of the two pounds and the stolen watch and spoons of the thief, who had escaped from Antwerp. The diamonds of the fine gentleman were paste, unfit for business transactions at the pawnshop. They were in fact a keep-sake of X., who had obtained by fraud a parcel of imitation jewellery from a Swiss firm, and in memory of this transaction and the swindled manufacturer, he kept a few sets, which dazzled the greenhorns whom he wanted to catch.

Let us enter the office of the new firm. It is a small garret, eight feet by six. The only chair of the firm, bought for a shilling at an auction, is occupied by the 'pupil'. On a shaky table before him, bought for eighteen pence at a second-hand shop, are laying a hundred sheets of extremely luxurious note paper, bearing in elaborate letters the name and address of the firm, and an equal number of envelopes.

The 'master' is standing in a corner of the room dictating to the pupil, who is writing with a clear hand on the dainty paper, the letter having the appearance as if it came from one of the world's leading firms. The letters were destined for German manufacturers and their purport was, to induce the latter to execute orders for acceptances. It is hardly credible, but there are plenty of good firms in Germany who are easily deluded into sending goods on trust to dubious customers in London ; the one is mislead to do so by thoughtlessness, the other by the inspiring idea of doing business with a real London firm.

With great tension of feelings and eager with hunger, the half starved sledge-drivers were waiting for the first arrival of goods from Germany which finally came exactly four weeks after the firm had been established. One morning the advise was received by a forwarding agent that a box with hams and sausages from Germany would be delivered, and the two swindlers could have danced from sheer pleasure, if the room had been larger, when the parcel really arrived. The carman asked for a few coppers, and the elder partner of the firm was so overcome by joy, that he rushed to the house-keeper and borrowed two pence to reward the bringer of the good things from Germany.

No time was lost to open and to unpack the large packing case. On the top was a thick layer of shavings, then came some objects wrapt up in paper, which were carefully laid aside. The sausages were certainly put in the lowest layer, and to reach them the quicker, the sledge-drivers turned the chest over. What a heap of things! But what cruel deception! All the carefully wrapped up packages contained but old bones of horses and two skinned cats, and to complete the joke, the heartless sausage-manufacturer had enclosed in a large envelope a number of the 'Cologne People's Gazette,' containing the article 'Sledge-drivers and no end of them.'

But this disappointment was followed soon by better days. Bales and large cases full of goods arrived now in quick succession, and when the swindlers' eyes met with the blessed words 'Made in Germany' they were near crying with pleasure.

The only customer who patronized this celebrated firm was a sharper who called every day, and left the office regularly with a contended smile on his lips. His warehouse was filling rapidly with a great variety of valuable goods, which he bought at a twentieth of their real value.

Another kind of sledge-drivers are the 'Professors of Music' to whose doings a special article shall be devoted.

The 'Lager Beer Sledge-drivers' are rather on the vane, for the brewers are more cautious and careful in the choice of their agents. But sometimes a haul is still made, and only a few months ago many thousand bottles of genuine German Lager Beer were sold to the clubs at a shilling the dozen.

A very interesting beer-hauling case is the following:

A firm of sledge-drivers had entered into a contract with a large brewery in Germany, by which the latter was bound to ship every week for two years a certain quantity of bottled beer to the 'branch of the firm' in India. This 'branch of the London house' was another sledge-driver, a confederate of the London swindlers, who stayed in India for the sole purpose to receive the goods, and to sell them, the beer included, by auction directly after their arrival. When the brewers could not receive any payment after the first six shipments had been made, they stopped the further supply and appointed their own agent in India. The incensed sledge-drivers would not bear 'their loss' without protest, and they demanded damages for breach of contract. The brewers, of course, declined to pay a single farthing, and the swindlers threatened now through a solicitor to bring in an action if the matter was not settled amicably and damages, amounting to more than the value of the beer delivered, were promptly paid. The brewers, however, were not so easily frightened. They answered: If anyone has a right to bring in an action, then we have it with regard to our unpaid account. And there the matter ended. The brewers had lost their money, but it was very fortunate for them that the Queen's writ does not run in Germany. An English court of justice would have decided for the swindlers and against the brewers for breach of contract; for according to English law a contract must be carried through, even if the first deliveries are not paid for and the debtor be notoriously unable to fulfill his obligations.

Sometimes it happens too that the sledge-drivers actually do not know where and how to dispose of the 'hauled' goods.

Thus for example a gang had obtained some time ago some gross of artificial eyes from Germany. Nobody would buy the stuff, and finally a sharper took it over against a consideration of a few pence for postage expenses. Glue was at one time offered at such low prices and in such quantities, that the earth, if it had gone to pieces, could have been glued together again. Gruyère cheese was offered freely at 3 to 4 pence per pound, and was hardly saleable, and sausages had often to be buried by tons, because they went bad before they could be disposed of.

To the most dishonest scoundrels the world knows, must be reckoned the 'bill-haulers', who are accepting bills to any amount for 'a tip' of half-a-crown for every hundred pounds sterling. Of course they do not accept in their own name, but in the name of firms who may exist in the moon. The bills are accepted by imaginary firms of St. Petersburg, New York, Vienna, Naples, Paris or Brussels, and are put into circulation in London.

The simplest and cheapest way for the swindlers is to oblige one the other with their signatures. If a 'bill-manufacturer' gets an order from the continent for a bill of exchange of, say 300 pounds sterling, then he goes to one of the clubs where the bill-jobbers are meeting, 'stands' a number of glasses, inquires after the firms whom he intends to use for his purpose, supports too, may be, one or the other 'suffering houses' with a gift of a shilling, and obtains then as many signatures as he requires. To give the bill a proper commercial appearance, the acceptor and the indorsers of the bill bring out the India-rubber stamps of their 'firm' (the sledge-driver would think just as little to go out without his rubber stamp and his ink in his pocket, as a Prussian soldier would think of going out without his sword) and within a few minutes the bill is covered with fine names and still finer imprints. The 'acceptance' is after this sent travelling, and is never seen again by the 'sledge-drivers.'

Once the professional acceptors striked for an increase of the customary fee to four shillings instead of half-a-crown for every hundred pounds sterling, but the bill-manufacturers did not give in and engaged some young girls from 14 to 16 years, who did the work for four shillings a week, and this broke the back of the strike, the acceptors returning to their duties at the old wages.

This scandal could not exist if there were no manufacturers and merchants in Germany, who are still thinking that they can save themselves by such a jobbery in bills of exchange. If such unfortunate people would resign themselves to their fate, if there is no chance left to avert it, and if they would not send to the roving thieves of our times good money for notoriously bad and fraudulent bills, then the swindlers would soon cease advertising their 'London Discount Agencies' in the continental press, and millions of worthless bills would not pass year after year into circulation.

Twice a year the London sledge-drivers hold their 'International Congress', and the worthy proprietors of the leading long-firms decide upon their common action for the coming season. From time to time they visit Germany too in order to get connections. Their honest mien, their manners and appearance, their liberality in spending money on good dinners and champagne, dazzle their chosen victims, who do not wake from their trance, until they are taught by a heavy loss, that their amiable visitor and new customer, the proprietor of 'that leading London firm' was nothing more nor less than a—German sledge-driver!

GERMAN BEGGARS IN LONDON.*

LONDON, a town, that in many regards has no equal in the world, exercises such an attraction on many minds, that even the strongest warnings are insufficient to put a stop to the thoughtless immigration which, like an ever moving stream, is continually drifting thousands upon thousands of human beings within the walls of modern Babylon. Who does not know the many and urgent warnings published periodically by the German press? Who has not read such appeals? Were they of any avail? Did they attain their end? No. The senseless immigration continues, and with it grows here the misery in quite appalling and gigantic proportions. No earthly power can banish to-day the wretchedness, the cares and sufferings, or dry the tears flowing from the misery that reigns supreme in this vast town.

The many societies and the large number of magnanimous private individuals who are trying to alleviate the prevailing distress, are powerless against the hosts of mankind's old enemy dire poverty. Benevolence has a home in English hearts; it has a shrine in London; but the numbers of those stricken by poverty and requiring help are so great, that all benevolence is but a drop in the boundless sea. Hundred thousands of men can hardly earn a bare living, and equal numbers are constantly in actual want. Only he, who has seen something of London misery will comprehend what it means to walk the streets without friends, without money, without a shelter, without food, forsaken, homeless, hungry, cold and shivering. How many young men and young girls are visited by this fate, victims of misery, who came to

* Reprinted from the 'Cologne People's Gazette' (Koelnische Volkszeitung), August 17th, 1890, No. 226.

London with the idea of finding the streets paved with gold, a home of plenty. Full of hopes and pleasant expectations they set out, only to find themselves cruelly deceived. The gold is nowhere to be found; they are strangers in a strange land; their scanty means dwindle away as by magic; with growing anxiety they are looking out for work or a situation, and do not obtain it; soon they have to part with their trinkets, then with their cloths, and finally they cannot pay their rent and are sent adrift into the streets. The number of vagrant beggars is increased by one—a human wreck more, physically and morally.

Fate has no regard for age, sex, beauty, descent, knowledge, but treats one and all equally with its iron grip. What strange company do we find in the sediment of society! I know of many German officers, teachers, artists and aristocrats who arrived here on the free English soil as 'gentlemen', and soon walked the streets in rags and tatters.

Volumes could be written about such wrecked existences, and facts could be reported, stranger than fiction. We shall just give a few examples to show what thoughtless immigration to London means.

A young governess, a woman of high education and of prepossessing appearance, went, against the wishes of her parents, to London, 'to make her fortune.' Directly after her arrival she got rid of her large travelling trunk with all her worldly possessions. A German, apparently a porter, had offered her his services at the entrance to the docks, and she, glad to find a countryman directly at her arrival, asked him to conduct her to a respectable and not expensive German hotel. He was only too willing to do so, shouldered her trunk, and told her to follow him. After a mile's walk through crowded streets with a bewildering traffic, he stopped at the door of a large building. 'That's the hotel,' he said and asked her to wait that he may bring the trunk to her room and call the hostess. The unsuspecting girl did as she was told. She waited; but when a quarter of an hour passed, and nobody came to inquire after her, she entered the 'hotel', and ascending the stairs she met a boy, of whom she heard to her surprise, that the building was not an hotel but a city house, used for offices only and possessing two different entrances. The thief had availed himself of this circumstance, and entering at one door, had left by the other, taking with him the trunk.

The poor girl had but little money in her possession, and, detained by a false pride to appeal to her parents, she felt herself soon forsaken. She had drifted somehow to the Eastend, and when her few marks had gone, she was turned out from her lodgings. For two days and two nights she wandered about in the streets, homeless, hungry, aimless. And then she commenced to listen to temptation, and succumbed. The pride of a happy German home, became one of the lost women of London town. The degradation became insufferable to her, and to escape the dreadful life she was forced to lead, she accepted a common English labourer as suitor and married him. The fellow was a drunkard and a brute, and what her life is may be imagined.

Baron (*), a smart lieutenant in the Prussian guards, took the fancy to elope with an actress to England, at which romantic expedition his faithful valet was one of the company. When the money had gone, and no further supplies came from Germany, the young lady repented and, assisted by a benevolent society, returned to Berlin. The lieutenant was in sore straits, but his valet did not leave him, and having been lucky enough to find work, supported his master for a long time. Finding, however, a chance to emigrate with some relations to America, he left London and his former master had now to shift for himself. He was for a long time without shelter, living on the crusts of bread and crumbs of food which he picked up in the streets, and underwent untold privations. He dropped his title, forswore his former life, and is now happy of having found work in a tanning yard with nine shillings a week.

I could give examples without end. Just a few 'London careers' I know of. There is the former captain of cavalry, now a 'bus driver; a town-clerk, bottle cleaner; a solicitor, navvy; a Berlin banker, street vendor and sledge-driver; an architect, shoe-black. Clerks without number, sons of respectable parents, become swindlers, girls unfortunates. Many parents think their children happy, prosperous and respected in London, and have not the slightest suspicion that they are leading a life of the worst degradation. Beware of London! Many a father, a teacher, a clergyman could have prevented by a judicious word a thoughtless emigration, and omitted to do so. The word was not spoken, and a young life ruined. Why not listen to the warning : Beware of modern Babylon !

Who is not coming to London to acquire a knowledge of the language, of the country, or to gain commercial experiences, with sufficient means in his pocket to keep himself for the time of his stay, without depending on earning here anything, does much better to remain in Germany, where, taken all in all, life is not such a struggle for existence as in England.

THE MUSICAL SLEDGE-DRIVERS IN LONDON.*

IN my last article on the noble guild of sledge-drivers, I trod some gentlemen a little on their toes; they spoke accordingly of judicial proceedings against the 'Cologne People's Gazette' and their London correspondent, because, as they said, a man had been attacked in the article, who declares he had been honest already for six years! Of course the good fellow would have been pleased if we had found ourselves obliged to appear as defendants at the Old Bailey for libelling an arch-rogue, who is driving to-day, as he did six or ten years ago, his sledge with its merrily jingling bells. To 'ruin us', in December of last year a company was formed, to 'take it up' with those 'newspaper scribblers'. They think to frighten us, but for such an attack the weapons of defence are lying ready, clean and shining. We are prepared and can prove everyone of our statements in black on white.

Before making further revelations, I remark, that by principle I do not mention names, except I have written documentary evidence for my assertions, and I do not do so even then, if I cannot produce trustworthy witnesses. But to-day I shall mention names, as I did before, because I consider this a duty which has to be performed even in the face of the danger that all the sledge-drivers of London should be seized by the rage of writing, and try to save something of their reputation by the humour of the gallows.

As we mentioned already repeatedly on former occasions, the sledge-drivers do not disdain anything, be it trouser-buttons, glass-eyes, liver-sausage, whole flocks of sheep, ship-loads of timber, organs, or violins—all is fish what comes to their net. They obtain everything, and they find buyers for everything.

* From the 'Koelnische Volkszeitung', No. 175 (360), Sunday June 28th, 1891.

The editor informs me that amongst others a Mr. X. applied to him and confided to him, that he often came into contact with the sledge-drivers during his residence in London. I should think he did! A firm in Saxony has certainly not yet forgotten to this day the homœopathic medicine chest which they sent to Mr. X., at that time in London, only to become aware some time afterwards that they had been swindled by a sledge-driver. The former cigar merchant N., who kept a shop in the City-road, certainly often remembers too with sadness the fine cigars, of which he was cheated by Mr. X. Was not this loss the cause, that he was forced to stop his payments, which at that time were made already rather slowly? But what are medicines and cigars in comparison with a complete equipment of an orchestra of forty musicians, which a German firm sent to the very same Mr. X., who declares now that he too came into contact with these wicked sledge-drivers. Be the defrauded firm informed that the whole of the instruments are in the safe keeping of a 'dear uncle' in the city for 120 pounds sterling. The pawnbroker is a former waiter. I heard that the instruments spoken of were invoiced with 875 pounds sterling. Well, the defrauded firm, very likely, can bear such a great loss, but the same cannot be said of the victims of the '*fiddle-marten*' *Arnstein.* This swindler was a few years hence in constant company with a certain *Lewin.* The latter once obtained by fraud some parcels of cigars; his friend Arnstein assisted in selling them to a club in the neighbourhood of Finsbury-square. Lewin was run in, and he pleaded 'guilty', and the Lord Mayor sentenced him for two proved cases to eight months 'hard labour'. When he had served his term, he took the name of *Popert* and got employment in a world-renowned furniture manufactory on the condition, that he would be an honest man in future. But after six months, when he had hardly become a little warm in his berth, his old nature broke through again, and this betrayed itself by the fact, that all kinds of goods were sold in the factory at conspicuously low prices. Amongst other things he is said to have sold within a short time 15 gross of neck-ties, and 52 watches, which he had obtained by swindle from a German and a Swiss firm. For this reason he was dismissed at once, but before it became known amongst the workmen that he had been dismissed, he induced a joiner, employed in the factory, to entrust to him for sale three gold watch-chains, which the former had retained from a boarder in lieu of payment.

He had hardly left the factory, when an officer of police appeared with a warrant to take Popert into custody for a heavy theft which he had committed in Hamburg a week before he had entered his situation. Now he was to be extradited. How fortune is favouring such people! If he had been dismissed one hour later, he would have been caught. The police watched in the evening the house were Popert-Lewin was living, and they thought they had their bird, for he was in his room grinding on an ariston, one of six which he had got on the very same day from Germany, one dance after the other, enjoying his life. He was just adjusting the 'Blue Danube' valse on the roll, when he heard the police officer asking in the passage, whether he could see Mr. Popert. He 'smelled a rat', gained somehow the roof, entered the neighbouring house, escaped through it and some court-yards to a house in the adjoining street, through which he passed into the open road. From that time he was not seen again, excepted in the club of Mr. Daubenspeck.

Arnstein had lived some time in Prescot-street, but he returned some years ago to his old haunt in Clifton-street, where we find him at present in his full glory. An idea of this personage the readers will gain by the following. On January 16, of the present year, the musician X., from Cologne, wrote the following letter to the publisher of the 'Cologne People's Gazette': 'The most obedient writer of this letter, by his profession a musician, asks you kindly to insert free of charge the enclosed advertisement. In support I mention the following: A certain professor Arnstein of London asked me to send to him my valuable Amati-violin; he offered to give me 1000 marks for it. As Mr. A. had gained my confidence by his high-sounding title, I forwarded to him without misgivings my instrument. But I did not hear more from him and he did not answer my letters. An inquiry at the German consul made me still more suspicious. By applying to the London police I succeeded, that A. was forbidden to sell my violin (but he has done it nevertheless; the police had also no power at all to prevent him from doing so), but he demands for giving it up 52 marks. But I, being a poor man, must seek someone through the newspapers who would lend me the 52 marks. I assure you that my life is depending on this fiddle, which is a last dear family token. I can furnish you with proofs from the Imperial German Consulate.'

On January 20th, the same poor man writes again: 'Your kind letter of the 20th inst. has filled me with new hopes. The address you are inquiring for is: Professor Arnstein, 15, Clifton-street, Finsbury-square, London. But I must tell you that it is of no use to write to the professor, it be then that somebody would hand him over the 52 marks he demands, and receives in exchange the violin. If I have my violin again, I have earnings too. Enclosed the consul's report.'

These letters I received from the publisher of the 'Cologne People's Gazette' to look into the matter. From the report of the Consul General of the German Empire in London, I take the following points:—1. The Consul General was willing to help Mr. X. as well as he could, if Mr. X. would send to him the money demanded by Arnstein, and if he would release him of all responsibility that the violin, which Arnstein would deliver against payment of that amount, be the real one. 2. Should Mr. X. intend to proceed criminally against Arnstein, he would be bound to come to London.

I put the matter into the hands of the enquiry-department of the Casino 14, Upper Woburn-place, who wrote to Cologne, that they would take up the matter, and asked that Mr. X. may communicate direct to the committee. With this request Mr. X. complied by return of post, and he wrote: 'Professor Arnstein had advertised in newspapers of this town and also of Berlin, that he wants to buy old violins for which he is prepared to pay 800 marks. After some correspondence, I sent him my old and most valuable violin, but only for view. This was in June 1890; since then, I did not hear anything more of the professor. Inquiries which I made at the Imperial German Consul were answered to the effect that A. is a swindler who has carried on for years already the fraud with violins. Now the fine gentleman says the violin is not genuine; he also demands, as the consul informs me, 52 marks for custom duties. (In England instruments are not subject to any custom duty.) Now I am a poor musician, and I have spent already 20 marks in advertising, postage, &c., and I must ask myself: Is there nobody in the whole world to give the 52 marks, that I may get back my violin? I beg of you to help me!'

The Casino got also the original letters which Arnstein had written to Mr. X. One of these runs as follows: 'Professor Arnstein's Philanthropic School of Music, founded 1882.—15, Clifton-street, Finsbury-square, London, E.C., May 31st, 1890. Dear Sir,—I just received your post-card with which you are offering me for sale an old violin. I inform you that I often require good violins, and if you will send me yours, as you propose in your letter, I shall let you know soon after receipt, whether I shall keep it or not. Expecting your esteemed reply, I am, yours respectfully, A. Arnstein. N.B.—Please pay attention to above address. 1223/90.'

I wonder whether the figure 1223/90, means that 1223 violins were obtained by fraud in the course of the year 1890? This is not impossible. By the style and the school-boyish hand-writing Mr. X. certainly ought to have known with what kind of professor he was dealing. From Germany no orders can be given to the English police; they must act in accordance with the laws peculiar to the country. The Casino offered to pay the 52 marks, demanded by Mr. Arnstein, but the 'Professor' and proprietor of the 'Philanthropic School of Music,' declined the offer, and poor Mr. X. never saw his violin again.

Arnstein was also successful in receiving a number of violins from a head school-master in Silesia. The following letter of the teacher says quite enough about this matter:

'To the most honourable Casino, London. I am obliged to Mr. A. Gyigyi in Trieste for your address, and through this gentleman a new ray of hope has arisen to me. I beseech you to render me your help in the following matter: I am a Catholic teacher, I have seven children living, and I am poor. The education of my children, many misfortunes, and a small income, placed me into the necessity to part with the only possession which was left to me, and of which to part was very hard to me, namely, five violins, among them was a *genuine* Rauch, and an excellent old Tyrolese one. These two violins alone represented a real value of 1200 marks; besides these two were still three other good violins my property, which had also a value of 75, 75 and 100 marks. In answer to my advertisement in the 'New Musical Gazette,' a Professor Arnstein from London wrote to me, and his note-paper and envelopes bore the following firm: 'Professor Arnstein's Philanthropic School of Music, founded 1882, 15, Clifton-treet, Finsbury-square, London, E.C.' This gentleman wrote to me, I should send to him as soon as possible a few pupil's violins at the price of about 75 marks each, and one master-violin *for selection*, because he bought only what he had seen. Firmly believing in the honesty of the professor, and feeling convinced that he would buy and pay soon, if I made him a price below the real value of the instruments—*and in my distress*—I made him the really low price of 1050 marks (for the five violins). Arnstein wrote to me that he would keep and buy all the instruments at the price mentioned, and this he wrote on March 4th, 1890. He promised to pay in instalments, viz.: on March 16th and April 16th, 1890. But I received neither an instalment, nor could I get back the instruments. I appealed to the German Consul-General, and he put the matter in the hands of the solicitors of the Consulate. These gentlemen wrote to me, that as far as they had been engaged in the matter, nothing could be done, if I did not come personally to London. But this I unfortunately cannot do for want of means. In my great distress I address myself to you with confidence, and I beg of you urgently, to help me to recover the 1050 marks, which are for me under my circumstances, a large sum, and to take the matter up for me, for which I give you herewith full power. Pray, pray, take pity on me and on my seven children. I should not know how to show you my gratitude.'

An organist from Hanover also appealed in a letter of some length to the President of the Casino for help. This poor man sent to Arnstein three violoncelloes and one violin, representing a total value of 1550 marks. He says in his letter: 'Through the musical newspapers I heard, unfortunately too late, that Professor Arnstein is quite a common swindler, to whom such frauds can be proved in masses.' A violin-master in Rostock lost through Arnstein 1500 marks in the same manner as the other victims, and a gentleman in Lubeck, 750 marks. The latter succeeded to procure through an action attachment, but the broker did not find anything worth seizing, excepting a fiddle, the value of which did not cover the costs of the proceedings. Arnstein brought a counter-action because his 'tool' had been seized, but his action was dismissed.

Professor Gyigyi from Trieste, it appears, was the first victim of Arnstein; but he recovered the two violins which he had sent to Arnstein through the intercession of the Austrian Consulate. But as soon as Arnstein had given up the violins, he was very sorry for his 'foolishness.' On the very same day he rushed off to the solicitors, Messrs. Peters and Morris, and enquired whether he could be prosecuted criminally if he bought goods and did not pay for them. He received, of course, the answer, that he could not be prosecuted, and since then some hundreds of violins were obtained fraudulently by him, and all of them sold by auction through a well-known firm. But just this circumstance has rendered him criminally liable, and now but this is required, that one or more of the defrauded persons repair to London and proceed against this arch-swindler. The chief of the London police is quite willing to help, but one of the victims must appear personally as plaintiff. Characteristic are the words of the commissioner of police; he knew, he said, Arnstein a long time, and the police knew quite well Arnstein to be everything else, but not 'a clean potatoe.'

The 'professors of music,' as the gentlemen call themselves, are running quite in shoals all over London, and many of their number are not over particular as far as honesty is concerned. It is quite certain that at least one-third of their class belong to the guild of musical sledge-drivers, and they are not for an atom inferior to their colleagues, the commercial sledge-drivers. The one deals in pianos, the other in zithers, a third one in barrel-organs, but all of them take whatever they can get. Two of those gentlemen are keeping for years already a so-called 'school of music' in Tottenham Court-road; they have an excellent clientél and enjoy accordingly a good reputation. But they have also offices in Trafalgar-square, and Leadenhall-street. From these offices they are sending circulars to exporters on the continent and try to gain business-connections after the manner used in these latter days by sledge-driving firms, of which I shall have to say a word by-and-by. For the present I shall just mention with regard to this subject, that the firm, Jacob Marcus, 65, Fore-street, has been effaced (from the door-post) and that the proprietor is cautious not to be found, to avoid presentation of bills for advertisements which he had inserted in German newspapers. This firm was formerly known under the name of Jaques Marcus, Paris and London. The name of this firm was written on the wall in the same handwriting as the name of a neighbouring firm on the wall of the entrance-hall. Both firms were sending out bragging circulars, by which means they tried to obtain goods. I hear that Marcus intends to establish himself in Leadenhall-street. My attention was drawn to the office in the neighbourhood of Trafalgar-square, and I paid a short time ago a visit to this 'shop,' where the gang receives (from the continent) musical instruments, objects of art, etc., of course without ever paying for them. I found the office occupied by a little boy who represents the whole staff. Asking in a friendly and unconcerned manner, I heard from the boy that the proprietors made their appearance on every Saturday only for a few minutes. He had to bring all the letters to the 'institute' (he meant the 'school of music'), and the boy from the other office had to do the same. By some more questions, I got possession of the other addresses, and went first to Leadenhall-street. There too the gentlemen had in a tiny office on the third floor a boy of fourteen years only, who had to bring all their letters to their lodgings. The office in Leadenhall-street receives wines, hams, sausages, dress materials and what else can be made loose in the fatherland.

One evening I paid also a visit to the 'institute' and recognised in the two 'professors of music' a pair of most experienced sledge-drivers who were residing already for many years in London. About a year ago the two fellows visited the best city restaurants, played the fine gentlemen, and drank nothing but champagne. They pretended they were wine-merchants on a short stay in London. As they were spending money most liberally, some of the restaurant-proprietors found themselves induced to give large orders for wine at extraordinary low prices, and for this they were soon after let in by the following manœuvre. The two swindlers made their customery appearance, finished a few bottles of champagne, and went hammer and tongs about the sledge-drivers until the attention of the hosts was attracted. They enquired, of course, how the gentlemen had been defrauded, and they told them a tale how they had sold to a firm a parcel of wines for 50 pounds sterling for cash; the wine had arrived and was laying in the docks, but the 'sledge-drivers' declined now to take it, if cash was demanded before they had received the wine, and this caused the two gentlemen some momentary pecuniary embarrassment. Most of the restaurant proprietors declared themselves willing to buy on delivery of the shipping documents (which entitled them to fetch the wine), and to pay the full amount in cash to oblige their customers. But they were not a little surprised when they found out later on, and too late, that they had transacted business with swindlers, and that the documents were forgeries. It is not long since these gentlemen had received from a German piano manufacturer six valuable instruments, and they thought to sell them by the aid of two accomplices. In the mean time, before the pianos were fetched from the docks, an information had been laid with the police regarding the wine swindle. But, when the police came to the 'institute,' the two accomplices only were present, and not the swindlers wanted. The former declared they were the 'professors' and did not object to be taken into custody, and to be brought to the police-station, where the defrauded publicans had to admit that the prisoners were not the swindlers who had cheated them out of their money. The prisoners had to be dismissed, and since then the police did not hear anything more of the musical sledge-drivers.

A nice little blossom, it seems, is also the former shop-assistant *Isaac Werthheimer*, of Berlin, seventeen years of age, and now 'professor of music, and conductor of the court-orchestra of Her Majesty, the Queen of England.' It is, of course, superfluous to state that he conferred this title upon himself, and that he has no connection with the court, or any other orchestra. The little imp has hardly the length of three loaves of cheese, but he surpasses in cunning many an old sledge-driver. He has his own office, and obtains principally musical instruments by swindling; but he does not despise other goods either, especially hams and sausages. It is to be hoped that this communication will prove sufficient to prevent master Werthheimer getting any more credit in Germany. It would be too scandalous if the German merchants would permit him to swindle them in future of a single penny-worth of goods; but it would be more scandalous if ever a single musician, teacher, organist, maker or seller of musical instruments would send his last possessions to these good-for-nothings in London.

SLEDGE-DRIVING AND NO END OF IT.*

I cannot turn my look aside,
 But ling'ring watch ye on the strand,
As ever busy ye confide
 Your goods to swindlers with open hand.

WHEN Freiligrath was writing these lines (the fourth, of course excepted, of which I claim the authorship), he did not know anything about sledge-drivers. As manager of a commercial house in London, he certainly made his unpleasant experiences with swindlers; but the name 'sledge-driver' was unknown to him, else he would have made poetical use of it.

The easy-going German manufacturers, and the impudent and vile sledge-drivers have now combined to help the new coined word to an undesirable renown. By the great number of letters, reaching the 'Cologne People's Gazette' and the author from all parts of the world, it is easily to be seen that greater attention is now being paid to the swindling fraternity as they, very likely, care for. But in spite of the repeated warnings, published in the newspapers, the shady figures try and try again from their unpregnable stronghold in London, to remind the manufacturers that they are still in existence and resolved not to be conquered.

I intend with the present article to show to our readers on some particular cases with what impudence the gang are throwing their lines, and how easily the enterprising exporters and manufacturers take to the bait. How this is possible, is a puzzle to me. But so much can be taken as granted: complaints, regarding the English laws, are of no avail. John Bull will not pass new laws to oblige the Germans and to protect German manufacturers; he even does not sweep before his own door. When a short time

* Reprinted from the 'Cologne People's Gazette', Nov. 8th, 1891, No. 307.

ago a bill was brought in to prosecute, in case of bankruptcy of a limited company, the promotors and directors at the expense of the exchequer, it was thrown out very unceremoniously; one of Her Majesty's ministers declared simply, that such a law could not be passed, for all speculators would, as soon as they lost money in some commercial venture, apply to the public prosecutor and demand his assistance. People who were so careless in investing their money did not deserve to be specially protected by law; they ought to be left to look after their own interests, and to pay their own costs if an action has to be brought. These may appear to German ideas strange views held by a minister of the crown. But was the Right Honourable wrong? I feel greatly inclined to agree with him. Only a few days ago I met a German sausage manufacturer, who had come to London to introduce here his savoury article, and to engage an 'energetic and honest agent.' He had made his choice already, and this had fallen on a notorious sledge-driver. In hearing this agent's name, I warned him and told him that he had fallen in the hands of a swindler. He smiled at me a smile of disdainful superiority, tempered by compassion with my ignorance, and remarked with great assurance and in a most dignified manner: 'Sir, I have lived with my eyes open; I know the world, I know men and things; I am a reader of character, and I need not fear to be cheated!' Poor man! Two days later he called very early at my office, and implored me in a most pityable manner to render him assistance. He had brought with him from Germany about three hundred weight of best sausages, and now they had disappeared with the agent. Did the man deserve to be assisted in recovering his property?

My last article dealing with the 'musical sledge-driver,' has caused quite a storm of indignation amongst the 'professors' of music. The respectable and honest professional men were rightly indignant with the 'black sheep' in the fold of their profession, and wished to be able to expel them from their temple. Others again said, I ought not to have published the disgraceful dealings of the 'professors' in the interest of the Germans in England. But the poor defrauded musicians in Germany certainly do not share the views of their London colleagues, and the reprint of my article in a number of other papers is a proof to me that public opinion has no pity for the damage inflicted on the nefarious trade of the heartless sledge-drivers, whether musical or not.

It is also not my intention to induce German manufacturers and merchants by the articles I am publishing in the 'Cologne People's Gazette', to restrict their connections with England. But what I intend to show is the absolute necessity to make the most thorough inquiries regarding a new customer, and to beware of entering into any transactions, if the information is not perfectly satisfactory. But this information must be above suspicion; the sources where it comes from must not be tainted! *Even in the choice of enquiry-offices great discretion must be used, for the sledge-drivers have their enquiry offices too—genuine mouse traps* (I may remark in this place that at that time I had already strong suspicions against the enquiry-office of L. Lehnert, but conclusive proofs, unfortunately, were still wanting, and I had to confine myself to this general remark. Had it been otherwise, and could I have said what I wrote three years later, at least *a million marks* would have been saved to the German manufacturers.)

On December 6th, 1890, was published in the 'Cologne People's Gazette' my article, 'The Declaration of War of the Sledge-drivers.' The aristocracy of the noble guild was quite startled. It was certainly a dangerous thing to find a member of the fraternity trying his hand as an author, and speaking with real humour of the gallows of things, which ought to have been held secret as the secret mysteries of the temples of Isis and Osiris. In consequence of my article regarding the 'declaration of war,' a German export manufacturer communicated with a German institution in London, and forwarded some original documents which were handed over to me to make use of them, as I thought best. I had to make sure, and the enquiries and investigations I had to institute, protracted the publication up to now. After sifting the material, I am finally enabled to publish the following about this case.

The first letter addressed to the German society is from the swindled manufacturer, he says:

I have read with great interest the articles, published in the 'Cologne People's Gazette.' I too was swindled in June, 1888, by an undoubtedly sledge-driving London firm, who styled themselves Kresher, Otto & Co., 46, Southampton-buildings, Chancery-lane, London, W.C. The people asked me for a sample-sheet of my inlays of mother-of-pearl, and consequently gave me an order, amounting to 250 marks. I made enquiries through a local and a London enquiry-office, and the informations I received were in substance the same and not unfavourable. (Both came from Lehnert, the one directly, the other indirectly, as he was the London correspondent of the 'local' enquiry office, and the address of the manufacturer's firm, whom he knew to be his and the other enquiry-office's subscriber, Lehnert supplied to the long firm). In spite of this I asked for cash in advance, but received a rather abrupt note informing me off-hand, 'that it was a custom of the firm to pay only after receipt of goods.' Considering the informations I had received, I sent the goods, and was now waiting for my money. It did not come, and I drew on the firm and advised them of it. But no answer arrived and my bill came back dishonoured.

I wrote again, and after a deal of trouble, they finally accepted a three month's bill, which, however, when due, was also not taken up. Further enquiries elicited the fact that the firm had closed their office, very likely to open it under another name in another street. My last letter, dated August 4th, remained without an answer, and I asked a friend of mine in London, to whom I forwarded the protested bill and other papers, to do what he thought best in the matter. He made inquiries and wrote to me, the birds had left their nest, and to look for them and to take proceedings would be a sheer waste of money.

Richer for an experience and poorer for 250 marks, I dropped the matter. To my great surprise I received at the beginning of 1890 a letter from a London firm, inquiring whether I should like to buy for cash in advance, the mother-of-pearl goods which I had sold to the late firm of Kresher, Otto & Co., of whom they (the firm who wrote to me), had taken the goods over. I laughed at this piece of impudence and entrusted the letter to my paper basket, an unconsidered act which I regret the more, as this letter very likely would have enabled me to inform you under which style Kresher, Otto & Co. are carrying on their long-firm swindle. I enclose the original letters the swindlers addressed to me. I do not object to the publication of my communication, but do not mention my name, if you please.'

As the original letters are but a confirmation of the manufacturer's statement, I need not reproduce them. But to the victims of Kresher, Otto & Co., numbering some hundreds, it will be of interest to hear who the swindlers were. Mr. Kresher first. His real name is very similar to his alias, but I do not mention it out of regard for his most respectable family. His year of military service saw him, as he alleges, in the regiment of guards at Berlin. When he arrived in London he fared very badly, and for a long time he was glad to earn his bread in the sweat of his brow in working at the factories, first of Siemens, in Woolwich, and later on at H. Hermann, Limehouse. In the latter factory he had the misfortune to loose by an accident the tip of a finger, and this marks the bird and renders him recognizable under any alias he may choose. Shortly afterwards he was so fortunate to obtain a situation as clerk in a merchant's office in Liverpool-street. But it surpassed his strength to be honest. Not three weeks had passed, when the old cash-box of his employer run away with the new clerk. A prosecution was instituted; but the police were not sharp enough in the case of Mr. Kresher; they could not find him, and he did not hide himself. May be that was the reason of his escape, for he could have been fetched any day from the German Exhibition, were he represented some German firms, having besides a very cosy sledge-driving office in the city.

The other partner of the vanished firm was the well-known swindler O. The third party to this triple-alliance was a certain W., who has not the courage to act independently in spite of his being a born general in the domain of long-firm swindling and a very experienced sledge-driver. He invents the schemes, but leaves it to the others to execute them. Once, I must admit, I did a great injustice to this gentleman in suspecting him to have made a regular sledge-driver haul at which stood penal servitude. I got possession of, what I thought, his address, and thought already I had caught the bird. I went to the police-inspector in whose hands the matter was placed, and it was agreed that a detective and I should go the next morning at four o'clock to the given address, and fetch the culprit out of his bed.

With the first cock's-crow we were standing before the house were the supposed culprit was living. We knocked, and soon afterwards the landlord opened the door and asked what we wanted. I thought of a plausible excuse, and finding in the man a general dealer, I asked for half a pound of cheese. This gained for us the way to the heart of the poor grocer whom we had disturbed in his night's rest. I took courage and inquired after 'my friend' X. He answered with a superior smile, that he was still fast asleep, having come home rather late and rather 'heavy laden,' and that he would hardly receive visitors of our kind—we were 'dressed up' for the occasion—but he would inquire. 'That the fellow may rush out through the window, you old sinner!' said the detective; 'he is certain to think the police is after him, and we don't want to frighten him; we better go ourselves, just show us the way!' When we reached the bed-room door the much wanted person appeared before us in his night-dress with an oil lamp in his hand, and asked in his turn what we wanted. I saw directly that we had not found the right man, and I was ready with an excuse. Speaking in German, I told him I wanted to do some business with the right Mr. X., and that I was sorry of not having found him. Looking at my shabby clothes, he said: 'Look here, my dear fellow, if you are possessed of thirty shillings, I shall put you into a nice way of business; you shall have a fine firm. I know a house in Kiel for smoked sprats, just in season. Have some note-paper printed with your firm, and you can have any quantity you like, and need never trouble yourself about paying. We go halves!' I stood dumb-foundered—'sledge-drivers' everywhere. With the excuse that my line of business was not in sprats, I wished him a good night, and we beat our retreat. Two days later the good man heard who his early visitors had been.

* * *

Mr. Wordpicker (I do not give his right name out of regard for a German newspaper that would be well advised in making inquiries first, before appointing people as correspondents) had tried his hand at many things in his life. He had a university education, but when he came to London he was soon in dire distress and, driven by circumstances, he chose begging for his profession. The members of the committee of our Benevolent Societies had much to suffer through this gentleman. When he found benevolence drying up and begging becoming rather unprofitable, he turned into a most devout and exemplary attendant of the Synagogue, and by this not uncommon means, he moved the hearts of two Jewish merchants, well known by their benevolence, to take pity on him. They furnished him with the means to start in business as newsagent. But the glory as a shop-keeper did not last but a few weeks, and he went amongst the poets. He wrote English and German poems by the yard, much to the dismay of editors and publishers whom he pestered with the production of his muse. Fortunately for the world, none of his poetical emanations were ever printed, but this did not restrain Mr. Wordpicker to call himself a poet on his visiting cards. But as men cannot live on poems and air, and as begging did not pay any longer, the gentleman had to strain his wits to start a new scheme, in which he succeeded. With the help of his generous patrons who had made him a newsvendor, he established now a 'Literary Agency,' and soon after this event he advertised in a great number of German and English newspapers: 'Authors, professionals and amateurs, wishing to dispose advantageously of their manuscripts, are requested to communicate with advertiser. All communications must be accompanied by a reading fee of 2s. 6d., and all letters addressed to the 'Literary Agency' (followed the address).

Business was flourishing, manuscripts and 'reading-fees' arrived by hundreds. The money went as easily as it had been earned, and, acting on celebrated precedents, the manuscripts were returned unpaid to the unhappy authors with the complimentary remark, that the work was very good and most promising, but far too long; short stories again were accompanied by a letter of condolence saying, that the story required expansion. In every case, however, the advise was given to re-write the manuscript and to submit it once more for consideration with the usual reading fee—an advise that was very often acted upon.

Finally, however, some professional authors addressed themselves in an evil hour to the 'Literary Agency', and finding out the swindle, they soon put an effective stop to Mr. Wordpicker's little game. He just managed to escape the police, and his next move was to a large building near Falcon-square, where he opened business as 'sledge-driver.' But to have two strings at his bow he addressed himself to some German newspapers, offering them his services, and mentioning his thorough knowledge of English politics, his influential connections and experiences, and giving some London correspondents as references, who knew him only as a very entertaining and agreeable companion. He was happy enough to find a Berlin paper willing to accept his offer. His former patrons supported him in this matter again, and so Mr. Wordpicker succeeded and became the London correspondent of an influential paper. If he had turned over a new leaf, no objection could have been taken, but unfortunately he remained the swindler he had been before, and divided his energies between literature and sledge-driving with equal zeal.

From Westphalia hams were sent to him, from Nuremberg toys, from Aix-la-Chapelle cloth, from Silesia linen, and, unfortunately, wine too, the celebrated 'Gruneberger', the name of which is sufficient to make the *connoisseur* shudder. This happened in the following manner. A Silesian manufacturer had been swindled once by some London sledge-drivers of two bales of linen, and he waited for an opportunity to have his revenge on the fraternity. When Messrs. *E. Anderson*, *Bartles*, *Anderson & Co.*, *Limited*—thus Wordpicker styled himself in his commercial capacity—inquired of him whether he would send them goods for sale on commission and appoint them his agents, the manufacturer made enquiries, and when he heard who Messrs. E. Anderson, Bartles, Anderson & Co., Limited, were, it took him not long to decide upon his action. He sat down, and wrote: 'Gentlemen, I am greatly obliged to you for your kind offer, but to my great regret I cannot avail myself of your services, the prices in the English market being so low as to prevent me from competing. However, I am a large wine-grower. Our 'Gruneberger', as you know, and as I must admit, is not a celebrated mark, but if also a little acidulous, it is nevertheless a healthy and pleasant light dinner wine. Should you feel disposed to sell my wines in London, I shall be happy to appoint you my sole agent. Most respectfully——. P.S. Shall I send you, free of charge and carriage paid, a small box with samples?'

Mr. Wordpicker was of course not slow to accept this generous offer. The samples, 24 bottles, arrived soon afterwards, and Mr. Wordpicker rubbed his hands with pleasure. He opened one bottle and found the wine better than he expected. Certainly it was a little sour, but it might improve by keeping, and one pound of sugar goes a long way to improve defective wines. He wrote at once to the Silesian that he would accept the agency, and asked him to forward a thousand bottles for a start.

The offer had not reached yet Germany when a well-known 'sharper', who kept a public-house, came to the office of the sledge-driver and inquired whether he could not help him to a parcel of cheap cigars. The swindler promised to do so and invited the publican to try a bottle of wine with him. The sharper thought the wine a little sour too, but that was to be remedied. The two honourable men struck a bargain, and the sharper bought 20 sample bottles and the thousand ordered by the 'sole agent,' at the price of four pence per bottle. He paid cash for the twenty bottles, and took them with him in his trap. Arrived at home he directly set to it to transform the 'Gruneberger' into real hock, special brand of 'Rudesheimer', and, having emptied the twenty bottles into a small washing-tub, he left the doctoring to his potman, telling him to add the sugar, to stir it, and when all was finished, to call him again. All was done in accordance with these instructions. When the 'sharper' was called, he filled a glass and tasted the mixture. His features became fearfully distorted, he spat and spat, and with a fearful oath he caught hold of the unhappy potman and nearly strangled him, accusing him of having doctored the wine in an undescribable manner. The poor fellow denied and protested his innocence, but he was dismissed nevertheless. The explanation is easily given, only the top layer of the sample-box was wine, which the Silesian had bought for the occasion; all the other bottles contained an infernal mixture, the ingredients of which are better not mentioned. The order of a thousand bottles was, of course, never executed, but after a time the manufacturer inquired of Messrs. E. Anderson, Bartles, Anderson & Co., Limited, how they had liked the samples, and to this day he laughs at the revenge he had taken.

Mr. Wordpicker's firm has ceased to exist; it disappeared with the proprietor, for whom London became too hot after the forgery of two bills of exchange.

SLEDGE-DRIVERS' MISFORTUNES.*

WHEN Zeus had created the world, Schiller tells us in one of his beautiful poems, he said to man: take it, let it be yours for all times to come, but divide my gift as brothers between you. There was a great rush, the German poet continues, and every one secured his share. When the partition was completed, the poet came from the lands of dream and demanded his share. But there was nothing left, and bitterly complaining he approached the god. Zeus took pity on him, and said, if there is nothing left for you on earth, you shall be welcome in heaven, whenever you come to me.

The 'sledge-drivers' were unfortunate too; they had tarried too long in their public-houses to hear in time of the partition of the world, and finding themselves empty-handed, they also brought their claim before Zeus, and demanded to be admitted to heaven too. 'What is right for the poet,' they said, 'is equally right for the genuine sledge-driver.' But Zeus would not hear of it. 'Learn to earn an honest living first,' he said, 'and you may inquire again.' But that was not to their taste. 'If you do not give us what we want,' they threatened, 'we shall take what we can get.' And so they did. They stepped into the world, mixed with men, and lived by fraud. They liked this life extremely, because the honest merchants were always willing to supply them with all they wanted, and the law-givers did not mind their doings. It was not surprising that the whole guild finally thought their occupation equally rightful as that of honest men. 'The Cologne People's Gazette' thought otherwise, and the merchants agreed with it, because the impudence of the swindling fraternity had commenced to surpass all

* From the 'Cologne People's Gazette', July 17th, 1892, No. 389.

bounds. There was no other way left to the poor and persecuted 'sledge-drivers' than to imitate all kinds of men, and to pose in the guise of honesty and respectability, for thus only they could gain admittance where they wanted it, and to revenge themselves on those who, to their idea, had fared better at the partition of the world than they had done.

The readers will understand, that we are not in great favour with the sledge-drivers. But they cannot accuse us of anything worse, than that we are ruining 'poor people', spoiling their business, and depriving them of their daily bread.

If the 'sledge-drivers' arrive at the conviction that in reality they are honest, hard-working fellows, I excuse them most willingly, knowing what weak creature man is, and how habit may lead to it to regard even crime as virtue. But if the gentlemen think I shall share their views and cover their misdeeds with the mantle of Christian neighbourly love, they are mistaken. I intend to speak out and protect honest trade after my fashion.

That the 'sledge-drivers' take all they can, is an established fact; it is their principle, and they adhere to it. But it may be new to many, that even our classical poets are not safe from them, and that they are robbed if a 'sledge-driver' wants to gain the favours of a lady.

> Former happiness lays so far—
> And my longings, they are burning,
> And my eyes, they are now turning
> To a heavenly golden star.
> But the star, so clear and bright,
> Is but glitter of the night.

Thus Schiller was singing to his Emmy, and, may Apollo forgive it, Rosenberg to his Helen. (As more than one Rosenberg are living in London, I beg to declare distinctly that Rosenberg, the 'sledge-driver' is meant). Schiller is not to be pardoned for having written these verses, which Rosenberg intended to compose a hundred years later. Mr. Rosenberg was by profession a herring-tamer (who does not know this expression, may be informed that it means a gentleman selling salted herrings); his education was a modest one, and that was all the modesty possessed by Mr. Rosenberg. In Germany he was very much in love with things belonging to his employer, and he had a special predilection for his master's wine and cash. Finally there was an elopement of cashbox and Rosenberg to London, the Dorado of all the German good-for-nothings. But here he learned something to know about the finiteness of things mundane; he found it out at the contents of the stolen cashbox; they came to an end too, and this sooner than Mr. Rosenberg expected. A few days of extravagant living had done it, and after a week's sojourn in London, the young hopeful was as poor as a church-mouse. But in the meantime two elders of the noble guild had discovered his talent. On the third day of their acquaintance they had been already cheated by their young friend. They were filled with admiration and confidence. He was an acquisition, and they took him as a partner in the business, which did not exist yet, but which they were resolved to establish. A few begging letters did it, and helped them to 27 shillings and 6 pence, and with this capital and the help of a friend, who permitted them to use his office near Blackfriars Bridge, the business was started. A printer supplied the indispensible note-paper with elaborately printed letter-headings on misplaced trust, and within one week the first offers of the new 'leading London firm' reached Germany.

Goods arrived freely and in large quantities. Cheese was followed by watches, then came shoes and boots, and as a novelty in 'sledge-driving', a hundred wheel-barrows. Business flourished to such an extent, that after the first two months already the partners thought it advisable to disappear, and to leave no trace behind them. The firm was dissolved and gone, but it soon rose from the dead and reappeared under another name in the heart of the city.

Rosenberg abstained now from writing the letters for the new firm. His hand-writing could have been recognised, and this could have led to the discovery of the old vanished firm. But, in spite of his young years and his short experience in 'sledge-driving', he remained the leading spirit of the firm, and, tired of having to share the profit with his confederates, he decided to start business on his own account in grand style. But for this he wanted some capital, and to obtain this he made up his mind to take a partner for life possessed of money, in other words Mr. Rosenberg decided on marriage. To attain as quickly as possible his aim of conjugal felicity, *plus* the make-weight of money, or at least the latter article, he took the short cut through the advertising columns of 'Hymen's Official Gazette', known to all *thus inclined*. He described himself in his advertisement as the proprietor of a flourishing business, and invited young domesticated ladies of agreeable appearance, sweet disposition, and possessed of 2000 or 3000 pounds sterling, to communicate with him, enclosing their photo at the same time, 'in strictest confidence,' under certain initials.

He received three answers. One came of a 'sweet seventeen', who betrayed great common sense, demanding a statement of his affairs, with balance-sheet and references 'to enable papa to make enquiries.' If these proved satisfactory, she would further communicate. That was too strong for the former herring-tamer, and in passing over 'sweet seventeen' without honouring her with an answer, he decided for the eldest of the three candidates for nuptial bliss. It is true that she admitted herself to have crossed the line of thirty summers, and that 'her photo represented her rather younger,' having been taken some time ago. But what has age to do with happiness? She asked no question, declared herself to be possessed of 5000 pounds sterling in her own rights, with 'expectations' of an inheritence. What more is required to madly enamour even the most apathic sledge-driver!

But caution was the watch-word of noble Rosenberg. He had to keep dark his past and his present until 'all was over', that is until the marriage knot was tied. Not considering whether it was proper or not, he invited the lady to meet him in Hyde Park, where he would be at a certain hour near the gate, with a red silk handkerchief in his hand.

At the appointed time our would-be bridegroom paced up and down like a sentinel near the principal entrance to the park. The sun was burning fiercely, and he was waiving his handkerchief like a signal-flag. The chosen-one kept him waiting; but he had the 'good luck' to attract the attention of two very nice-looking young ladies, who were pacing up and down too, passing and re-passing him. He felt flattered, and had liked to have addressed them, but the thought of his chosen-one detained him from following his inclinations. No, he was not to be seen addressing young ladies. What would *she* and her £5000 think of him? Everything could be spoïled. Besides the two young ladies had such mischievous looks; he really commenced to feel uncomfortable at the marked attention they were paying him, and felt relieved when he saw them leaving the park.

The next moment a lady addressed him with much shyness —it was his Helen. He felt something like a chill; yes, she was over thirty, she limped too, and a slight impediment in her speech and a cast in her eyes did not improve her general appearance. But she wore a lot of fine jewels, and Rosenberg felt conciliated. The meeting was of short duration; they did not exchange their names, but agreed to enter into a correspondence, addressing their letters to a stationer, who took in letters to be called for at the charge of a penny the piece, and in this exchange of love-letters she called herself Helen, and Rosenberg signed himself as her faithful and loving A. N.

After a week had passed, the would-be bridegroom decided to bring matters 'to a head'; he would woo and win. He went to the expense of buying an album, and on the first page he wrote the verse by Schiller, which we have quoted. In the letter accompanying his gift, he assured 'his angel' that the poetical inspiration which dictated him these lines, flowed from the thoughts on his chosen-one, and in dropping his anonimity and giving her his real name and address, he asked for an appointment. To his greatest surprise this letter was not answered, and the gift not acknowledged. Rosenberg did not know what to think of his Helen. But he had not long to wait for an explanation. One morning, when he was at breakfast, a gentleman called to see him. 'Her father'! it flashed through his mind, when the early visitor was ushered into the parlour, but poor Rosenberg was cruelly undeceived, when the gentleman turned out to be a watch manufacturer, who had been swindled by 'the old firm' for a considerable amount. He addressed Mr. Rosenberg very unceremoniously as swindler (we omit the adjective), said the day of reckoning had arrived, and if Rosenberg would not 'shell out,' he would have him arrested. Rosenberg saw the man was in earnest, and after a great deal of palavering, which made no impression on the irate manufacturer, he paid up. 'But now tell me,' the swindler asked, 'how you got hold of my address, which I have kept so secret?' The manufacturer, who looked awfully pleased, gave a loud laugh and said: 'Well, you have to thank it to your matrimonial intentions. How do you like your Helen?' Rosenberg stared at him. 'Do you remember also two young ladies who paid you marked attention when you had to meet, for the first time, your chosen one?' Rosenberg remained silent. 'Well, one of them was my daughter. We came on a visit to my sister, and I thought to use the opportunity to look out for you. Chance would have it that the servant-girl of my sister, Helen, picked up somewhere the 'Matrimonial News'; she showed it to the girls, and they induced her to answer 'for a lark' the advertisement which you inserted, as I know now. My daughter, as I must mention, is helping me at home with the correspondence, and when your letter came, she directly recognised your handwriting. I induced now Helen to meet you, and to manage so as to get your address, and thus I caught you. I hope you enjoy the joke as I do! If you want watches again, I shall be happy to execute your order at any time for cash in advance. Good morning, Mr. Rosenberg.'

* * *

Mrs. Agnes Sp., living in Kentish Town, and having offices near the Mansion House, is, as far as I know, the only female sledge-driver working on her own account. She is an ornament to the profession.

Her first husband was a manufacturer in a small way in Germany. Business was prospering, and he was anxious to extent it. To his delight, he received at this juncture an order from London to forward samples and price list, and looking at the note paper he had no doubt that the order came from a big firm. The name too inspired confidence. The wish of the manufacturer to extend his business over the frontiers of Germany, was soon realized. Orders were flowing in from this and other big London firms, and the manufacturer was busy as never before. Hundreds of large packing cases were sent away, and for their bulk he received in exchange some stamped pieces of paper, which he treasured more than cash, and paid in his bank, proud of his London connections. When the bills became due, not one was taken up. All came back protested. The most urgent letters written to the accepting firms, remained unanswered. The poor manufacturer was in a fearful plight, and went to London to obtain payment. His whole existence depended on it. He paid his first visit to the 'big firm' of whom the first big order had come. The offices, which they had occupied, were still in existence on the third floor of a house in Milk-street, but the firm had disappeared. In their stead was another new firm, risen like a phœnix from the ashes of the former one. The proprietor, a German, was quite willing to give any information in his possession to the unhappy manufacturer. 'I am sorry for you that you fell in the hands of these long-firm swindlers,' he said finally, and advised the manufacturer 'to go home and to forget his loss. Even if you should find the rascals, it will avail you nothing. They cannot pay, and if they could, they would not.' 'That is all very well for you to say,' the despairing manufacturer answered, 'but it spells ruin to me. I have to meet some heavy bills next month, and if I cannot take them up, I lose everything. And I was so cautious! I inquired at each of the firms they gave me as reference! It is awful.'

'You must not despair, my good man!' the sledge-driver said with well-played compassion. 'You were not up to the tricks of these rascals. The references were very likely long-firm swindlers too. May be you can open somewhere a credit to help you over this crisis. London is a wonderful place!'

Two days later the swindled manufacturer was on his way back to Germany, and at his arrival there he paid in at his bankers 800 pounds in bills, which he had brought with him from wonderful London.

He did not grow tired of telling his wife how lucky he had been to meet this fine and kind-hearted gentleman, who had given him such valuable informations about the sledge-drivers, and finally had helped him for a small commission to these acceptances.

But the losses the manufacturer had sustained, were irreparable. He could not save himself, and stave off the unavoidable.

'*Sauve qui peut!*' he called out with Napoleon, and, acting on the advice of his new friend, he sent his wife to London, where the gentleman from Milk-street promised to look after her. After her was sent to the same address a large quantity of goods, and when the whole stock was cleared out, the manufacturer followed his goods and his wife, leaving the ruins of his once flourishing business to his creditors. The vile sledge-driver, in the meantime, had made good use of his opportunities. He had ruined the business of a striving and hard-working man, he did not hesitate now to ruin too his domestic happiness. When the defaulter arrived in London, he found himself cheated of his goods and of his wife, and this new misfortune preyed so much on his mind, that he fell ill and died within a few weeks.

Sp. who is known here under at least ten *alias*, married the widow. The marriage did not turn out a happy one, and Sp. was rather glad when, two years later, he had to leave England abruptly, in consequence of a dangerous transaction. He went to Australia, making before his departure certain arrangements with his wife, which caused her to establish a business under the style of 'The General Export Agency.' Under the tuition of her second husband, Mrs. Sp. had become an expert in sledge-driving, and she made most admirable use of her knowledge. Waggon-loads of goods were obtained from the continental firms in exchange of worthless bills, and directly shipped to Australia, where Mr. Sp. sold them at advantageous prices.

An untoward incident, however, closed the brilliant career of the young firm at a comparatively early date. 'The General Export Agency' had existed only a few months, when Mrs. S. wrote to a German manufacturer for samples. Unfortunately, he had been warned by his brother-in-law, who had fallen a victim to the 'Agency,' and the rude fellow wrote and threatened: 'I shall come to London to break your miserable skeleton.' It is interesting, that he addressed Mrs. Sp. in his letter, of which a copy is in my possession as 'You scoundrel.' But who would suspect ladies being sledge-drivers?

Whether Mrs. Sledge-driver was concerned about her skeleton, I do not know. At any rate, the firm was blotted out of existence, and Mrs. Sp. tried to sail under a new flag. But her sex rendered it difficult to her to secure another office, and she had to associate herself with a former colleague of her husband. This man died twelve months later; but his wife, an Englishwoman, had also profited by his instructions, and was very well up in the art of sledge-driving. The two ladies went into partnership, and to overcome all obstacles, they engaged a disgraced clergyman as manager, who took the office in his name, and there the new firm was opened as 'Ernest & James Walker & Co., Export Agents.' Somehow this arrangement did not work to the satisfaction of the chief sledge-driver in Australia. He returned, therefore, secretly to London, and established the women as 'sharpers,' and their firm is now highly respected, because no goods are any longer obtained by sledge-driving.

Sp. returned to Australia, and the two women are now buying all and everything the sledge-drivers are bringing, if not more than the tenth part of the real value is demanded. No goods are sold in London; all is forwarded to Australia, and thus the stolen property cannot be traced. The police has no cause to interfere, as the ladies are always able to produce receipts, showing that the goods were bought from 'a firm' at the proper market value, and the firm remains highly respected in the City to this day. But should they once offend against the law, then strange revelations may be expected.

* * *

Only a short time ago a gentleman from England was travelling in Germany, and, drinking champagne with many merchants, he told them a great deal about his friends amongst the English nobility, to whom he could even count the Prince of Wales. According to his statements, he had been in all parts of the world, and had appointed agents everywhere, to look after his business, extending to all countries of the globe. Thanks to the revelations of the 'Cologne People's Gazette,' the fellow was usually taken for what he really was. Often too, people saw in him but a conceited fool and boaster, but sometimes he succeeded to enter into, to him valuable connections with manufacturers. In a small Bavarian town he boasted on the very evening of his arrival of his successful commercial career, and especially of his 'new grand undertaking in London.' The proprietor of the hotel where our gentleman was staying, had a new waiter, who, being engaged in the adjoining dining room, thought to recognise the voice of the 'Englander;' he could not help to open the door and to peep into the room where the conversation had grown rather animated, and when he had done so, he broke out into such a thundering peal of laughter, that the host rose in haste, and hurried to see 'what had befallen the fellow.' The waiter whispered something into the ear of his master, who commenced to laugh in his turn, and having given his servant some whispered instructions, returned to his guest and the other gentlemen. Champagne was flowing freely, and the stranger commenced just to describe a dinner party at 'his friend's the Prince of Wales,' when the new waiter entered, and tapping the speaker quite familiarly on the shoulder, said: 'Look here, Fritz, don't tell such tales, the gentlemen besides do not believe you. It is no use to try it on here, you will not swindle them!' The 'gentleman from London' rose, demanded who the fellow was who dared address him in such a manner, and demanded satisfaction. But the waiter was not disconcerted. Turning to the other gentlemen, he explained: 'Twelve months ago we were together waiters in a London hotel. At that time Fritz fell in with some swindlers and became a 'sledge-driver', and now he comes here and tries to do you, gentlemen; I feel bound to warn you.' The next moment the poor waiter thought he saw a flash of lightning. Fritz had dealt him a fearful box on the ear, for which act he was rather badly handled by those present, and with bag and baggage turned into the street. He departed hurriedly with the next train, and the waiter was liberally rewarded by the manufacturers, who were highly pleased with their experience with a real London sledge-driver.

* * *

A very sad sledge-driving experience is that of the master-tailor St. For many years he had kept himself and his family in ease and comfort by the honest work of his hands. Who passed his shop was certain to see him hard at work, a happy and contented man. By and by he had saved some hundred pounds, and this came to the knowledge of sledge-driver K. The honest tailor was in the habit to go on Sunday to a German club, and there K. sought and found an opportunity to become introduced to St. After having met three or four times, K. said to the tailor, he was surprised that such a clever craftsman did not try to extend his business ; it would be the easiest thing to obtain the material from Germany very cheap, and also the machinery for opening a business as mantle manufacturer. There was a fortune to be made. The tailor wavered, and expressed his doubts. He had no experience for such an undertaking. But K. knew how to overcome the poor man's scruples, and to secure for himself the handling of the whole matter. Business was started with K. as manager. St. having been established for many years, and known as a respectable and honest man, got good references, and on the strength of these, large orders for cloth and material were given and executed. Mantles were made, but there were no buyers, and when the demands for payment grew always more urgent on the part of the manufacturers, the harvest time for K. had come. He brought a confederate of his, the sharper X., and to him the whole stock was sold by and by for a fraction of its real value. By this means one of the threatened actions could be staved off, but there was nothing left to pay the other creditors, and when one of them threatened with bankruptcy proceedings, the scoundrel K. cooly stepped in and demanded a hundred pounds as his salary as manager for twenty weeks. St. implored the swindler not to ruin him ; but the fellow knew no mercy. 'You pay up, or I shall have you up for underselling the goods and defrauding your creditors.' Frightened out of his wits, and seeing everything lost, the poor tailor gave in and sold his house for 85 pounds sterling to the sharper X., who passed the money on to K. The fellow, who wanted to get rid of his victim, gave the tailor ten pounds sterling, telling him that a warrant was out against him, and that he had better escape to a safer clime. And this the tailor did. He fled to America, leaving his wife and four children quite destitute behind him.

But the unjust gain brought no luck to the swindler. He started directly on another scheme, by which he thought to make a big haul. But trying his art on an English Life-Insurance Company, instead of German manufacturers, he came to grief. His scheme was the following: He tried, of course under another alias, to induce an agent of the company to procure for him a lapsed policy, that could be revived by payment of the arrears. He promised the agent a share of the profits of the transaction he had in view, and the agent agreed to assist him. Secretly, however, he communicated with the manager of the company, and with the consent of this gentleman and the directors, he sold a lapsed policy on the name of a Miss L. to the swindler. The arrears were paid, and soon afterwards K., posing as the brother-in-law of Miss L., obtained on the strength of a forged doctor's certificate, a certificate of death from the public registrar. He presented this personally at the offices of the insurance-company, and was arrested. Criminal proceedings were taken. Miss L. appeared as witness and protested most emphatically, that she had never left this world in her whole life, repudiating at the same time any relationship with the scoundrel who had committed her to the dead. The 'profits' of this 'stroke of business' for the swindler were five years penal servitude, which he kept all to himself.

* * *

Instigated by some gentlemen of dubious character, an enquiry office (Lehnert's, as we state now) has made enquiries with a view to identify the person of the correspondent of the 'Cologne People's Gazette,' who dares to brand existing firms as swindling firms. This enquiry-office, I am told, is maintaining that enquiry-offices are the only places where merchants ought to, and can get, for a certain fee, reliable information about the character and commercial position of other firms. I have no reason why I should satisfy the curiosity of the said enquiry-office, but may it take the following from me: I have no intention to damage the enquiry-offices; they have great expenses and must be paid for their trouble. I likewise do not intend to attack all swindling firms, for the simple reason that I do not know all of them, and because, if I knew them, there would not be room enough in our columns to register them and their doings. I accordingly confine myself to point out, as a caution to the manufacturers, the different ways how swindles are perpetrated, in picking out some of the 'sledge-driving' firms for an illustration. But there is no cause for the gentlemen to disturb their peace of mind. I do not obtain my information through enquiry-offices, *because it is not sufficiently reliable to me*, I make the necessary researches myself, and I pay much more in cash for the material I am working upon, than the enquiry-offices are paying to their agents. Accordingly there can be no question of a 'mysterious publication of informations emanating from our office.' What use would it be to the German manufacturers if I would publish the usual indistinct informations of the average enquiry-office, saying either 'it is thought the firm is respectable,' or 'it is thought the firm is not possessed of large means.' I do not ask whether this or that beginner has 'a big mouth,' or 'a banking account,' but I ask what was he doing until now, what is his past? I value a good character higher than mountains of gold. The enquiry-office referred to gave, by the by, two months after I had nailed down the firm of Jacob Marcus, Fore-street, E.C., in the 'Cologne People's Gazette,' a most favourable information about these people, who had their letters addressed to a hair-dresser's shop. The consequence was, that a German firm lost 1,300 marks, and a number of other firms smaller amounts. To avoid such mistakes, how would it be for that enquiry-office to become a regular reader of the 'Cologne People's Gazette?'

THE JOLLY SLEDGE-DRIVERS.*

IT is ordained in this life that thesimpletons and the wise do grow up together, and that there is never a lack of the former ones. ' We cannot be cheated ' the simpletons declare, and hardly said, they are cheated already, because they will not understand that things in England are different to things in Germany. As soon as they find out their shortcomings, they swear vengeance, call after the police, and threaten with the public prosecutor, not knowing all the time what merriment they cause amongst the swindlers, who are quite aware that the cheated ones imagine they can proceed here as they do in Germany, and how sorely mistaken they are in this conviction. The poor simpletons do quite forget that the ' sledge-drivers ' are usually possessed of a commercial education superior to theirs, for a real sledge-driver cannot be formed from inferior material.

I intend, to-day, to depict the life of the sledge-drivers in a few short sketches, which must convince even the greatest simpleton of his shortcomings.

The 'sledge-driver' Y. combined with the 'arch-sledge-driver' J. to do, for once, some business in cotton goods. The two succeeded to swindle a large German cotton manufacturer of a considerable parcel of goods, and the two partners were greatly pleased at the result of their stratagem. The goods had arrived, Y. was sitting in a 'classical' club in City-road, thinking how he could cheat J. out of his share, and pocket the whole money for the sale of the 'haul.' J., again, was sitting in another club not very far off, occupied with exactly the same thoughts as his noble confederate—he wanted to cheat Y. of his share. Now there are

* Reprinted from the 'Cologne People's Gazette' April 23rd, 1893, No. 226.

existing in the City of London two highly respected firms, who are nothing more nor less than the principal 'sharpers,' and if these two firms could be 'removed,' I feel certain 'sledge-driving' could not be carried on to such an extent as at present. Their large warehouses are filled exclusively with goods, of which continental manufacturers had been defrauded. Everything is bought for cash on delivery. Everything must be invoiced and receipted at the proper value, and then only the selling 'sledge-drivers' get their wages of sin. All the goods are exported, as soon as possible, to Africa and Australia, and sold with a tremendous profit at their proper value. The proprietors of these *respectable* firms are shielded against all attacks by their high financial position, but they are not safe of being swindled in their turn too. They made this experience in the case of Y. and J. and how this happened I will tell. J., the elder of 'sledge-drivers,' was the first to be ready with his scheme. The bill of lading was in his possession, and he hurried to one of the mentioned firms, and obtained an advance of £80 in exchange of the shipping documents. Y. had decided on the same transaction and not having the bill of lading in his possession, he forged one. Thus armed he went to the other firm of 'sharpers,' and sold it to them right out. The first firm was rather slow in fetching the goods from the docks, and when they arrived there, the goods had been fetched already by the other firm. The swindled sharpers had reasons of their own to avoid publicity and to keep the matter dark. They did not prosecute, and put up with their loss; but they were determined to have their revenge on the competing firm, who declined to give up the goods.

To this purpose they induced some well-seasoned 'sledge-drivers' to play the following trick. Two of them went over to Paris and established 'a firm' there, two other sledge-drivers did the same in London, and the ball was set rolling. After a time, when some smaller transactions had been made to the satisfaction of the 'sharper,' the London 'firm' came to the 'sharper' who was to be swindled, and presented a bill of lading for some bales of valuable silks, which were insured for £3000. The 'sledge-drivers' explained they had not sufficient money to pay the expenses of transport and insurance, and declared themselves willing to sell the whole lot for £800. After much bargaining, the purchase price was agreed upon with £500. The bill of lading was handed over, a receipt for £3000 given, and in exchange the sledge-drivers received their money in a number of small cheques, which were easier to be disposed of. In this they succeeded, and value for the cheques was obtained within a few hours by themselves and their confederates. One of their obliging friends, a notorious club proprietor, receiver of stolen property and sledge-driver, was, however, too slow. When he presented his cheque at the bank (it was post-dated one day) 'something' had already happened; it had been stopped. The 'sharpers' had in the meantime fetched the bales from the docks. The weight was correct, but the contents were—rags. Magnanimous as these kind of people are, they also did not prosecute. They knew best why!

* * *

The former village schoolmaster John, from Saxony, came to London, and being warned against the 'sledge-drivers,' he said, with true Saxon self-confidence: 'No, I need not fear the swindlers, if they would cheat me, they cannot. I am too clever for them.'

Poor John! His whole life long he had had to do with schoolboys, books, the cane, notes, and bellows only, when in his old age he thought he discovered in himself a genius for business. He was certainly born for a commercial career. It was now rather late in the day, but he could make his fortune still.

He had an old friend in Dresden, a successful publisher, and John went now as his agent to modern Babylon. It is true he could not speak a single word of English, but he thought that of little consequence. Was his 'Redeemer,' as the books were called which he undertook to introduce to the English trade and public, was it not written and printed in English? All what he wanted was 'a little bit of luck,' as he said and thought. From his old friend, the publisher, John had the order to bless the English and Irish Catholics with the 'Redeemer,' and the Protestants with German war-pictures 'in oil.' People in Germany had had enough of it, and the stock had to be sold somewhere.

Well, how did modern Jonah fare in modern Babylon? In the first week of his stay in London, he had his watch and chain stolen from him in a German public-house, and he was rather roughly handled and quickly turned out when he complained about it, and passed a few insinuating remarks.

That was a very promising beginning ; but worse followed.

He had put up at a small German Hotel ; a guide and interpreter was introduced to wise John, and engaged by him. 'I am not here for pleasure,' John said, 'but for business. I expect you to go about with me and to introduce me to firms where I can sell my goods.' The guide promised to do so, and he was as good as his word.

When they went out on their errand together for the first time, by a 'lucky chance' they met a gentleman with whom, as the guide whispered to John, 'a fine business' could be done. John promised to his new friend 10 % commission on all sales, if he would introduce him, and bring about some business. And the guide succeeded. John was introduced, invited 'the gentleman,' at the guide's advice, to a glass, and after having spent some shillings and some hours with the two, he booked, to his delight, the first order, which nearly cleared out his stock of 'oil prints.' They were delivered the next day. John received in exchange a three-months' bill, and paid the guide his commission in cash. However, he knew London already so well, that he thought he could do without the guide, and save the commission. And so he did. He got on his own account an order for another 10,000 oil-prints. His former guide, however, followed him, and finding out that F. & Co. were the buyers, he went there and demanded a commission, or else he would 'upset the car,' and prevent the pictures being delivered. He got thirty shillings, and John got rid of his 10,000 oil prints. He had sold 'for cash' three weeks after delivery, and when he called for his money, the office of F. & Co. was closed, and 'the firm' had vanished, and was nowhere to be found. The other 'fine firm' had also disappeared when the bill became due, and thus John had got rid, in a surprisingly short time, of his whole stock—without seeing a single penny for it. He was recalled by the publisher, and returned to Germany a wiser and a sadder man.

* * *

If an elder of the noble guild of 'sledge-drivers' departs this life, then the hearts of his 'sons' are deeply moved, not with grief for the dear departed one who was driving his sledge so merrily, but with the desire that the mantle of the prophet, or what else he left, be it money, goods, or valuable connections, may remain in 'the family.' One of these late lamented ones was the German nobleman, Herr von R., who in his life-time was unsurpassed in all branches of the noble art of sledge-driving. Besides of the German benefactors in London, he gave also a deal of trouble to the merchants in Germany, and many a manufacturer was nicely 'wrapped up' by him. Even Count Herbert Bismarck, when at the Embassy in London, did not escape the general fate, and was lightened of twelve pounds by this expert beggar and swindler.

When R., laying in the German hospital, felt his career drawing to a close, he was meditating whether he had done anything laudable in his life, and he found that he could not accuse himself of a single good action. He felt somehow uncomfortable at this discovery, when, in short succession, two of his 'sons' stepped to his bed, anxious to grasp once more the hand of their dying friend. And there came R.'s opportunity: he did a good work for the first and last time in his life. The two 'sledge-drivers' had fallen out about a certain transaction, and their former friendship had turned into hatred. They were enemies, and R. reconciled them and breathed his last in saying: 'Be united, united, united!' leaving this classical warning as a bequest to the 'sledge-drivers' of whose guild he had been a real ornament.

* * *

Another 'sledge-driver', B., was still in the midst of a brilliant career, when the scythe of death mowed him down in the open street. With two pawn-tickets and nine pence in his pocket, he was on his way from a club in Houndsditch to the German hospital, when he fell down expiring; he had just enough breath left to give the policeman the address of that club, and all was over with him. An inquest being necessary, the police had to make enquiries and repaired, of course, to the address given.

As usually, at all hours of day and night, some 'sledge-drivers were sitting there enjoying themselves and scheming, and it was quite natural that they should speak of their departed friend, and consider, how they could turn his death to a profitable account. Just then the police-officers came, and finding the gentlemen willing and able to give information, they took notes of what the latter were saying. Finally one of the officers asked what confession the deceased professed. One of the sledge-drivers was ready with the answer. '*Schlittenfahrer*', he said in German (that means 'sledge-driver'). The officer, not knowing the meaning of the jaw-breaking word, asked what confession that was in English, and was told 'Schlittenfahrer' and Jew were the same. The consequence of this little joke was, that the deceased, an inveterate Jew-hater in his life-time, was buried in the Jewish cemetery.

But how to turn his death to earning an honest penny? That was the principal consideration for the rogues. They knew he had a well-to-do brother in Berlin, and to him they communicated the sad news and asked for twenty pounds to pay the expenses of a decent burial. The answer to this message was, however, very disappointing; it was a refusal to do anything for the dead man, who had only given trouble during his life-time, and was a disgrace to his family. This want of brotherly love incensed the honest 'sledge-drivers', who had felt quite sure of the twenty pounds, to such a degree, that they decided to have their revenge, and to punish the heartless monster of a brother. The matter was put into the hands of the 'chief sledge-driver', and the following day he wrote to Berlin, and said, that he was very sorry that nothing was done to give the deceased brother a decent burial. 'I regret it the more', he concluded, 'as I have ascertained that he left £170 which you are inheriting as the next of kin, no last will having been left, as the landlord of the deceased, who is trustee in the matter, has informed me.' By return of post an answer came, in which grief was expressed, that the 'dear brother' had been buried as a pauper, especially as he had left money, which the surviving brother declared he would come to fetch.

It is superfluous to remark that no money was left; quite to the contrary, the deceased was owing at his death £18 4s. 7½d. to his landlord for board and lodging, and the latter was greatly pleased to hear from the chief sledge-driver that the brother of the deceased would pay all debts and would come to London for this purpose.

Three days later the gentleman from Berlin actually arrived, and repaired, first of all, to the address his informant had given him—the club in Houndsditch. He met there the chief sledge-driver and some of his confederates, who were pleased to welcome the guest in drinking some bottles of wine to his health and at his expense. In the course of the conversation the 'lucky heir' declared, he would not touch a penny of his brother's money, before having visited his grave, and at his request the sledge-drivers brought him to the cemetery. In entering the sacred ground, he could not help saying, 'how strange these English cemeteries looked.' 'Strange? How so?' the chief sledge-driver remarked. 'I suppose Jewish cemeteries look alike the whole world over!'

'Jewish cemeteries!' the Berlin man exclaimed quite terrified. 'My brother was a Christian! I hope he is not buried here!?' 'He is,' was the answer, 'and he had to be buried here, for he was converted twelve months ago. He died a Jew, as the police will tell you.'

'He has afflicted us often,' the mourning brother said, 'but that is the worst of all he did; it will break his old mother's heart!'

With great sadness the brother stood awhile at the fresh grave, and they all went then together to the deceased's landlord. He had been advised of the visit, and had made great preparations for the reception of 'the brother who came to pay the debts.' The table was laid, an excellent dinner served, and wine was flowing freely. When coffee was served, the landlord came to 'business.' He commenced to speak of the 'poor dear one,' of his sufferings, and how kindly he had been treated, in spite that he had not paid for two months for his board and lodging, incurring thus a debt of nearly £18, as the bill showed, which he begged to present to the brother. 'I am quite certain it is in order, and I shall pay it most willingly,' the heir said; 'just deduct it, if you please.' 'Deduct?' the landlord exclaimed in surprise. 'Off what, pray?' 'Well, off the money my brother left in your keeping.' 'Left! in my keeping!' the landlord cried indignantly. 'All what he left was a bundle of dirty, miserable rags, which I had to destroy! You pay! You shall not swindle me as your brother did!' 'Look here,' the Berlin man said, 'you better give up the £170, else I shall call the police, and have you locked up!' '£170,' the host gasped, 'who told you so?' 'Well, these gentlemen have written it to me. I want my money! where is it?' 'In the moon, you fool,' the sledge-drivers cried. 'We wanted to punish you for your want of brotherly feeling. And now pay up!' They locked the door. The Berlin man felt uncomfortable, and would have paid if he could have done so. But, expecting to get the money his brother left, he had not taken more with him than he wanted for his travelling expenses, and thus it came to pass that he settled the debt of his brother, with the receipt of a sound hiding and being kicked out from the house of the irate landlord.

It is not hard to understand that it is not all honey with 'sledge driving,' and many a driver has to pass often through times of great hardships, when even hunger is not an unknown guest to him. In such bad and sad times, four members of the guild got tired of London, and decided on a tour of exploration to some 'unknown land' with fresh pastures and hunting grounds. Their choice fell on Hull. It being summer, and not able to pay the railway fare, they decided to have a nice walking tour, and to tramp it. It was quite a pleasant trip, and if they also had sometimes to rough it and to camp in the open without a tent over their heads, the experienced quartett nevertheless got on very well, and had not to complain of British benevolence and hospitality. The worst of all was, that they arrived in Hull without any capital worth mentioning, in fact they had not a penny in their possession. But having reconnoitred the territory, they discovered a small German hotel, to which they laid siege, and succeeded in investing it. Somehow they got the notion that poor Hull could do very well with a little more education, and that they could supply the want. They accordingly conferred on each other the dignity of 'professor,' and decided about founding an 'Academy of Modern Languages.' The idea was a good one. The four 'German and French professors,' as they were now, found support, and succeeded to beg so much money together, that a house could be taken, furnished on the hire system, and the 'Academy' opened. The four foreign 'professors' were a decided draw, and, thanks to the influential protection they found, pupils were not wanting.

The 'head-master' taught, as far as he was able, French and

German; the 'assistant master,' Italian, and did besides, the housework and the cooking; the other two 'professors' looked after business, and obtained for the 'Academy,' from London and Germany, so many pianos on trust, that they had a deal of trouble to dispose of them without rousing suspicion. One of the swindlers, a nice-looking and well-mannered young fellow, had the good luck to be engaged by a local banker as his private secretary, and through him the three other professors were introduced to the banker's house, who was rather fond of their highly entertaining and spirited company. Sometimes they talked business too, and the banker often marvelled at the great commercial experience of the learned professors. They also broached the subject of export of English live-stock to Germany, and depicted it in glowing colours as such a profitable business, that the banker felt inclined to embark in it. The summer term came to a close, and the 'head master' and his assistant went for their holidays to Germany, 'to visit their relations,' as they said. A week after their departure, the banker received a letter from a 'landed proprietor' in Swinemunde, inquiring whether he could supply four stud-horses and six pedigree shorthorn bulls; if so, he was asked to forward the animals to the forwarding agent X. in Hamburg, who was acting on behalf of the estate. As the 'landed gentleman' had referred to the 'two professors,' who had recommended to him the banker as the most reliable source for obtaining English cattle for breeding purposes, the banker did not entertain any distrust, and forwarded the animals. It need not be mentioned that the 'landed proprietor' in Swinemunde and the 'forwarding agent' in Hamburg were identical with the two holiday-making 'professors,' who sold the cattle as soon as it arrived to a dealer, and 'being highly satisfied with the quality of the breeding stock,' gave another order.

But in the meantime something had happened in Hull what had not entered into the calculations of the two swindlers. In the first place, the 'assistant master,' who had remained in Hull in care of the school, got tired of teaching. He accordingly sold 'the whole show' to a second-hand furniture dealer for cash, put the money into his pocket, and absconed. When the children came the next morning to school, they found the forms, boards, tables, and all the other furniture heaped up in the fore-garden of the establishment, and the sign-board with the inscription in big golden letters 'German High School' taken down, and thrown amongst the rubbish. The children did not know what to think of it; but when a furniture van came, and 'the school' was carted away, they knew their holidays had come, and run home with the joyous information to their not over-plĕased parents. At the very same time something else happened somewhere else. The niece of the banker had fallen in love with the private secretary of her uncle, the sledge-driver No. 4, and when the 'Academy' came to such an ignominious end, the two lovers found it advisable not to ask for the consent of the banker and cattle-merchant, but to get married secretly, and without delay. They eloped to Liverpool with the savings of the young lady, and from thence the private secretary wrote to the banker: 'Having married to-day your niece, with whom I am proceeding to America, I think it my duty to warn you, as my dear and honoured uncle, not to send any more live-stock to Germany, your customers there being swindlers, who will cheat you, if they have not cheated you already.' The banker did not trouble about his niece and heiress, and did not try to stop her, but rushed off to Hamburg, to save, if possible, his bulls and horses. But they had been sold two days previous to his arrival, and no forwarding-firm X., and no landed proprietor F., were to be found in Hamburg or Swinemunde, they had just escaped of being caught by the banker, who returned to Hull as a sworn enemy of áll 'German professors.'

* * *

The sledge-driver articles have done some good, no doubt, but they have done harm too, and this with regard to certain German bankrupts, who escape to England with the remains of their creditors' money, to do here a little 'sledge-driving,' after the example of others, as described in the columns of the 'Cologne Peoples' Gazette.'

Such a defaulter was Herr S. who arrived here with 'saved' 2,000 marks, to turn over a new leaf in his commercial career, and to start as 'sledge-driver.' He was a tiny hunch-backed man, with a quite disproportionately large, copper-coloured nose, and a pair of dark artful eyes, of which the right eye was always looking in a different direction to the left one. His red hair stood up like bristles on his head, and his bandy legs with their big feet in a pair of clumsy boots, further increased the charms of his person.

Twenty-four hours after his arrival in London, he was safely landed in a German club amongst a notorious gang of sledge-drivers, and the establishment of a new firm had been decided upon. A few days later an attic had been taken in the fifth floor of a house near Finsbury-square, and at the door-post was shining a brand-new brass plate, showing in black letters the name of the new firm as 'Herbert, Enders, and Co.' Within a fortnight a German manufacturer, dazzled by the 1,000 marks in cash, which Messrs. Herbert, Enders, and Co. had sent with their first order, obliged these gentlemen with thousand pounds worth of cloth. At the arrival of these goods, the five old sledge-drivers connected with the concern, considered how to get rid of the 'imp,' and soon arrived at a very satisfactory solution of the question. When they were storing away the goods under the direction of the tiny gentleman, one of their number came greatly excited into the office, and communicated to them in a mysterious manner that the 'German Trade Protection Society' had made some inquiries at the landlord's, and that now a detective was watching the house.

All the sledge-drivers evinced the greatest concern, and taking their hats, declared they would 'get out of it.' The proprietor of the firm was quite bewildered. He begged of them, not to leave him in the lurch, and gave it as his opinion, that there was no danger. 'With the police watching us!' one of the sledge-drivers cried. 'You do not know what it means,' he turned to the poor little fellow, who, quite frightened, asked them now to dispose at once of the goods at any price they might fetch, and then to close the firm. This advice seemed acceptable, and one of the confederates took a parcel of samples under his arm, and promised to sell the goods, before 'something dreadful happens.'

After a few minutes he returned quite out of breath, and called out. 'The police are coming! let us save ourselves as well as we can! I take refuge on the roof!' and opening the window he climbed out on the roof and hid himself in a convenient nook, not visible from the window. The tiny fellow followed his example, and shivering over and over, settled down at his side.

'What will happen to us if they find us?' he whispered. 'Hold your tongue! They must not hear us! Don't budge, or it means ten years penal servitude!'—'And for *this* I came to London!' the poor little fellow sighed. 'I could have had it cheaper, and with less trouble in Germany!' 'Quiet, or I kick you over the breast-wall into the street, you rascal! Don't you hear the police! The fellows are clearing out our stores!'

And so they did, but not the police, the other sledge-drivers did it, and it took them some hours. During the whole of the time, the two were sitting on the roof in a drizzling rain, not moving an inch, the one by fear, the other by calculation. When nothing was more in the attic, the sledge-driver said: 'I cannot stand it any longer. I must chance it and see, whether the air is clear.' Very cautiously they approached the window, and not seeing anybody in the office, they entered it. The room was quite empty, and the little man commenced to cry bitterly at the sight of his empty stores. The other swindler asked compassionately: 'Look here, have you any money left?' 'Yes, about a couple of pounds,' the other sobbed. 'Well, the best advice I can give you is, get out of the country as quickly as possible. You know, you have written the letters, you gave the order too, you received the goods; if we are arrested, then you will have to bear the brunt of the matter; we may get months, but you'll get years.' Two hours later the poor little man was parting from his 'friends' in London-Bridge station. He was on his way to Paris. 'Good-bye! I shall never come to London again!' were his last words. The five confederates looked after the train, and when it had disappeared, they looked smilingly at each other, and then shook warmly the hand of the chief sledge-driver, saying: 'Well done! a clean job indeed!'

I reprint, after these sketches of doings of the highway-men of our times, the two articles, that caused at their appearance such a sensation in the commercial circles of Germany, evoked such a wrath among the London 'sledge-drivers,' led to the libel action against me, and ended with the destruction of the conspiracy between Lehnert's Enquiry-office and the long-firm-swindlers, and the flight of my prosecutor.

THE 'SLEDGE-DRIVERS.'

IT is said that my articles on the highway-men of our times have caused a great increase in the ranks of the sledge-driving army in London. And, pray, who says so? The sledge-drivers themselves; they allege that, by my revelations, I instruct the young clerks, how the thing is done, and initiate them into the tricks and mysteries of the noble art. With equal right it might be said, man would not be sinning if he was not taught, what sin is. The simple fact is, the sledge-drivers do not like the attention I am paying to their guild; their threats did not stop me from doing, what I consider right and in the public interest, and so, in order to obtain their end, they try now to persuade me that I am doing harm. But, before I approach to-day the theme proper of my article, I must throw a glance at one of the contributing causes of sledge-driving, and in doing so, I shall have to add as a new class to the import swindlers of the English metropolis, the export swindlers of the German empire. It is an act of justice if I devote to this matter a few lines, before I enter on a fresh attack against the London sledge-drivers. My remarks, of course, do not reflect on the respectable exporters, and the poor manufacturers, who are now mourning over their reverses in London and the losses they sustained, must not misunderstand me. It is sad, very sad, that so many striving manufacturers fell victims to, and were ruined by these Knights of Industry, and what I have to say, I hope, will be taken to heart by those who have escaped being scorched until now.

In general it is a well-known fact that German exporters are prone to put the German measure on the conditions of English

* Reprinted from the 'Cologne People's Gazette.'

trade, and that they demand from the agents in England what they never dare ask from their agents in Germany. If a really good firm intends to introduce their manufactures in a foreign market, they certainly will first assure themselves that their produce is equal to what is demanded, and having ascertained so much, they will arrange with their appointed agent in such a manner that, in case of a success of the venture, he does not become reduced to poverty, when they are growing rich. In this regard many German firms are committing a great mistake. Bad trade in Germany causes them to look to foreign markets. There, to their imagination, the ground is paved with gold; there they can obtain any price they like. But they never think to make a trial at their own expense; their scheme is to look for, and to find an agent possessed of a few thousand marks, and to him they offer a commission of 2 or 3 per cent., that he, at his expense, may lay the foundation of a future 'world-renowned firm.' All what they offer him magnanimously with much boasting about their liberal terms are, besides of the commission, the *expenses for postage*, and then he can start the business and introduce the article. That they put 15 per cent. on their usual quotations, 'because the goods are destined for happy England and the English who can pay,' they are wise enough to suppress, but they assure him that his commission will be paid promptly *at the end of every half-year*.

The agent gets his samples, for which often a security of some hundred marks is demanded, and starts his work. From morning to night he is on his way, spends every day at least ten shillings in expenses, and when he returns home at night after a hard day's work, he finds his earnings amounting to a few shillings only. But he does not despair, he sees a possibility to work up a connection, and to build up what promises to become a profitable business. It is true, his savings are nearly exhausted, travelling in London, with its tremendous distances, is expensive, and the living still dearer; they have made an ugly inroad into his means. However, the six months are drawing to a close, and now his commission falls due. He is waiting, and waiting in vain; the remittance does not arrive. He writes letter after letter, and receives no answer. Finally the firm condescends to send him a reply, and invite him to take goods in settlement of his claim. He objects; they renew their offer. What is he to do? He is hard pushed already: he has no means any more; he is owing rent; to keep himself, his wife and children, he has to pay clandestine visits to certain shops adorned by three brass balls; his situation grows desperate, and finally he accepts what the firm is offering him in lieu of his commission: goods. But goods are not money; they must be sold for cash, and this he has to do at a great reduction. He is a loser by the transaction, and he does not like to bear the loss, and, may be, he cannot bear it. His commission was honestly earned; he will have what the manufacturers were bound to pay him; he, besides, wants the money badly, and seeing no other way to get it, he orders goods, and sells them as well as he can—far under price. To make up the first deficiency, he has to order more goods and undersell them again, and soon he finds himself involved in such a depth of debts that he cannot extricate himself any more. The guild of 'sledge-drivers' counts one member more, and the greedy manufacturers find out their mistake.

The following case within the experience of the author, throws a characteristic light on the ways of some German manufacturers. An envelope manufacturer engaged an agent in London, who succeeded within a few weeks to introduce the article to some of the leading English houses. Millions and millions of envelopes were ordered, delivered, and regularly paid for, and the agency proved, as an exception to the general rule, a paying one. After two months, the firm sent a traveller with the pretext and the request to the agent, to introduce the former at the customers, as it would be very advantageous if they became acquainted at the factory with the demands and wishes of the buyers. The agent, not suspecting any underhand dealings, complied willingly with this request, and after having done so, and the first three months of his agency being over, he wrote to the firm and asked for his well-earned commission. The answer was as usually, that the commission is paid half-yearly only. Just to think, the firm receiving their money regularly every month, and keeping the agent six months waiting for his comparatively small earnings. But the agent in this case was not dependent on his commission, and he submitted to these arbitrary terms. But before the six months came to an end, he received a letter from the manufacturers, informing him, that they think they do not require an agent any longer, that they prefer doing business directly, *and that they would pay him the commission he earned after other six months, if he engaged himself not to visit the customers for other firms engaged in the same trade.* That was his reward for having introduced the firm in the London market at a considerable expense, and a great deal of trouble. Such a mean action is nothing but swindling in *optima forma*, and if I do not disclose the name of these manufacturers, I do so, not out of regard for them, but out of consideration for some other persons. Such cheating sweaters well deserve to be cheated in their turn by agents whom they engage with the intention, to use them as their cat's paws. In the case just related, the German firm 'did' a man who could bear the loss, and was not driven by the perfidious action of his employers on the switch-board of 'sledge-driving;' but usually the cheated agent has no escape but to save himself by underselling goods confided to his care, or which he may order, and if no other manufacturers are defrauded than those who were employing him, then no injustice is done.

To introduce an article on the English market, and to secure customers, great sacrifices have to be made at the beginning. Who is not able to do so, shall not try and expect a poor fellow to do it for him. But if an agent does it, then it is a great shame to withhold to him his well-earned commission for a single day, and it is nothing but bare-faced 'sledge-driving' to deprive such a man of his agency, after he has spent time and money to introduce the firm and to secure a paying business.

There are, of course, whole flocks of professional swindlers in London, who cultivate their dishonourable profession from the love of it, and these I particularly wish to hit in my articles. I declare, to begin with, that all assertions made below can be proved by documents which are deposited with the solicitors Messrs. Osborn & Osborn of this city.

Let us first of all look more closely at the firm B. Arnold & Co., 3, Guildhall-chambers, Basinghall-street, London, E.C., a very fine firm, with smooth, easy manners. This 'house' applied exclusively to the subscribers of the Enquiry Office of *L. Lehnert*, 46, Queen Victoria-street, London, E.C.

What fine scent these B. Arnold & Co. had, to apply always to such firms only as received their information from one and the same office. The information regarding B. Arnold & Co. read as follows:

'February 28th, 1894.—This firm exists since last year, and is exporting goods of all kinds to East India. The proprietor, B. Arnold, is said to have been there with the following firms:—'*Ardeshire Hormusge & Co., Bombay, Mittree Ball & Co., Calcutta, Anomally Chitty & Co., Rangoon*, who have sent him to London as their buyer in Europe. He is said to draw *from each* of the firms a salary of £400 per annum and 2½% commission. The person enquired is a capable man who understands his business. He is believed to have some means. He has his banking account with the City Bank, Fore-street. B. Arnold & Co. have paid until now. Payments are made according to the terms usual in the East, that is cash against shipping documents, and as regards any eventual credit, it is strongly advised to insist upon these terms.

Of course no one insisted upon these terms after such an information, and B. Arnold, up to July 15th, received 120,000 marks credit from 30 manufacturers.

On this fatal July 15th Lehnert's enquiry-office wrote to all the creditors as follows: 'I have just heard that the firm's office is closed since this morning, and that Arnold had been obliged to leave for India suddenly. This of course looks very suspicious, and it would be well to look after the interests of creditors in time. If therefore, against my expectations, you should have a claim against the firm in question, I request you to put the matter into my hands to take soon further steps. I am now busy to ascertain his address in East India, and should then endeavour to trace him in that country. Anyhow this is only a preliminary report, and it will take several days before I get at the bottom of this affair.'

After this epistle the creditors received another circular with the demand, that each firm should remit 40 marks towards costs.

But from another side steps had already been taken in the matter, and I therefore fear that Mr. Lehnert did not receive 40 marks ahead, for the German Consul at Calcutta had already written to another person as follows:

'The address given at 92, Bow Bazaar does exist, but nothing is known there of the addressee. The numerous letters to hand could not be delivered, and therefore found their way to the chief post office, where they now remain. No firm called Mittree, Ball & Co. exists here, and the firms in Bombay and Rangoon may have no existence either. Very similar enquiries have come to hand here from several German firms, which remove every doubt that Arnold was a swindler. I am of opinion that Arnold never went to India, but took the route to America or the Continent, and that he had his letters addressed to Calcutta to gain time, and thus avoid an immediate pursuit.'

(Signed) 'The Imperial German Consul.'

Mr. Lehnert used to represent here several German Trade Protection Offices, and still to this day represents that of Lesser & Liman. Amongst the others he used to represent, I still mention the firm of Messrs. Wilh. Schmeisser & Co. of Berlin, and this firm writes:

'On account of a shameful trick which he, in conjunction with one of his confederates, tried to play against a German firm and ourselves two years ago, we were obliged to take a special journey to London, but we have caused him such a mighty stop, that his evidently declining position dates from that moment.'

In another place the same letter says: 'The person referred to, flooded Germany two years ago with circulars and subscription slips as proprietor of a Trade Protection Office at ridiculous prices. Thus he landed all the greenhorns, who took to low rates, and gave away their confidence by tender, and told us we were much too dear in comparison with our able competitors.'

Without entering upon Mr. Lehnert's antecedents at Vienna and Berlin, I mention that he formerly represented as agent the firm of *Jahnke & Foelsch*, Hamburg, who have their office at 14, Trinity Square, and to which Lehnert formerly attended. This is important to know, as I am going to refer to it presently. I have already mentioned the fact that he represented the firm Lesser & Liman (Trade Protection Office), and he also represented 'Creditschutz,' Maria Theresiagasse, Vienna, and the office 'Providence.' Gonzagagasse, Vienna.

In 1885 there appeared in London two men against whom warrants were out, and of whom one was called *Max Borchardt*, alias *Schütz*, and the other *Michael Zucker*, alias *Sugar*. Neither of them could speak English; they therefore took a third partner into the swindling business started by them, and his name was *Opitz*.

A fine trio indeed, that at once obtained a name of considerable notoriety as the terror of export merchants.

Of course this firm did not last long, but *Gustave Opitz* of Great St. Helens, may even to this day be a painful memory to many a manufacturer, for 'the house', in about two months, got by swindling great quantities of cloth, merinoes, colours, albums etc. Most of these goods were shipped by an English firm to India. Stupidly this gang had also taken liberties with English firms, and those soon put an end to them, about which Detective Inspector Downs of the Old Jewry is able to tell interesting tales.

Opitz, however, got away to Cardiff on board a coal ship, in which he fled to India, where we shall leave him in peace for a year, until we meet him in London again.

In the meantime the two gentlemen, Borchardt and Zucker, started the firm Bernhard & Co., Bury-street, St. Mary Axe. But on account of their past, they could not come forward, and so they took a clerk, and picked out a fine fellow in the person of the swindler Alexander Ovitsch. This happened in the year of grace, 1886.

The first robbery was perpetrated against an Italian firm, which became known to them through Mr. Lehnert. They cheated this firm out of £400 worth of felt hats, which they sold for £250 to a Mr. Cohn at Islington, and with the money they opened an account at the Continental Bank in the name of Ovitsch. Now, as swindlers like to cheat one another, so it happened too in the case of the firm Bernhardt & Co. Zucker, alias Sugar, conspired with Ovitsch, in whose name the money was standing at the Bank, and they withdrew the entire balance with the exception of three pence, so that their friend Borchardt had to go empty. But he soon got over his loss, and found another partner in the person of a certain Holm. This 'Trading Co.,' alas, made away with the property of English firms, and thereby came to grief. For after having swindled a firm, Jackson & Graham, out of a lot of silk, a warrant was taken out against Holm as proprietor of the firm

Bernhardt & Co. He was arrested, tried and sentenced to 9 months, and died in prison before he had served his term.

Borchardt, alias Schütz, got away with a passport made out in the name of Weichbrodt (and procured by a Mr. Lehnert) via Rotterdam to America, and thus closed the firm Bernhardt & Co., which caused many tears to many a manufacturer over his lost goods.

(In the meantime I have ascertained that Opitz not only had business transactions with Bernhardt & Co., but that he was a partner of this swindling firm, for he wrote himself a great number of the letters of this firm).

Almost simultaneously with the disappearance of Borchardt, Zucker, alias Sugar, appears again on the surface and establishes himself in Coleman-street as *Morris Brandt & Co.* At that time he was in constant communication with a Mr. Lehnert, and the mutual friendship appears to have been a profitable one for both parties, for it continues even up to the present day. Morris Brandt & Co. were not particular. Huge shipments of butter, eggs and other provisions were forwarded to them, and it is proved that from Hamburg alone over £400 worth of butter and eggs came through the forwarding agents, Messrs. Andree and Wilkerling, Hamburg, by the Great Eastern Railway.

Their principle was not to pay for anything. From the firm J. Wolf, 4, Kohlenhof-gasse, Vienna, a large shipment of boots was imported, and sold at half the cost price. A second shipment of boots from the same firm was on the way; but Morris Brandt & Co. could not wait any longer, because the ground had already become too hot for them, and thus the firm was closed, and a new firm opened as *M. Hart & Co.*, at 8, Lime-street, Leadenhall-street. With what effrontery these fellows proceeded may be seen from the fact, that this fresh firm applied at once to the same people who had just been plucked by Morris Brandt & Co. The fate of the firm of J. Wolf, Vienna, whose last shipment had not even arrived in London, is really tragic. Hart & Co., in the first letter of April 27th, 1888, to Mr. Wolf, say—'We have an export order for 50 dozen men's boots, calf, with flap lace, nine holes, English heels,' etc. J. Wolf had the article, and he was done out of this and several other lots. But before that, there was yet another by-play. The former confederate of Zucker, Ovitsch, whom we remember from Bernhardt and Co., had gone to Germany, and established himself at No. 31, Nicolai-strasse, Zwickau, in Saxony, to give ıeferences.

M. Hart and Co. referred to him, and they also referred to the firm Jahnke & Fölsch, 14, Trinity-square, London, whose agent Mr. Lehnert was. Also to the firm F. C. W. Wagner & Co., Water-lane, friends of Mr. Lehnert and of Mr. Sugar; further, to the firm Lesser & Liman, Vienna; Creditschutz, Vienna; Providence, Vienna—all being trade protection offices, who were supplied with reports from London by Mr. Lehnert.

In the meantime, the last shipment from J. Wolf to Morris Brandt & Co., had also arrived in London.

The following letter furnishes the explanation—'Mr. Joseph Wolf, Vienna.—Just now the carman of Schenker & Co. called with a case, No. 870, shoes, from Vienna, addressed to a firm, Brandt & Co. As no such firm exists in this building, he was unable to deliver the case. He also happened to call at our office, and as we are the only firm in this building, who expect shoes from Vienna, we ask you whether the shipment comes from you, and whether you have not made a mistake in the address. If such should be the case, please order Schenker & Co. at once to deliver the case to us. Yours truly, M. Hart & Co., (per Hasfeld).'

Thus the fellows actually received this lot too, besides the boots ordered by Hart & Co.

When Mr. J. Wolff saw the terrible loss, he cut his throat, and after his death his firm went into bankruptcy.

The official assignee, Dr. E. Friedmann, of Vienna, will confirm that he did not receive a single penny for the estate from Hart & Co.

Another swindle was perpetrated by Hart & Co. upon the firm W. Kührt & Schilling, at Mehlis in Thuringia. I cannot say whether the 'sledge-driver' Zucker was attracted by the sleigh-bells which this firm manufactures as a speciality. But as snow never remains laying in London, Hart & Co. considered it better to have a trial with cycle-bells. First a small sample order was given in November, 1888, the amount of which was remitted at once. Shortly after, an order for a lot, worth 2,700 marks, was given. The manufacturers consulted Lesser & Liman, who advised them to insist upon proper references. This was done; the references answered, and amongst them was one from C. A. Ovitsch, Chemnitz, who had been already referred to, and who wrote:

'I have received your letter of the 19th inst., and in reply I inform you that I have done business with Messrs. Hart & Co. for some time and they have paid me promptly, and that I continually give them credit. I have also had a good report about them from the enquiry office, W. Schmeisser & Co., Berlin, and I give them willingly such credit as they require.'

The credit asked for was given, a bill was drawn, which later on was protested, and thus the firm lost, including charges, 3000 marks. An enquiry made about the whereabouts of the firm from Mr. Lohmann, 22, Jewin-street, London, was answered by the latter to the effect, that Hart was incurably ill with consumption, and awaiting death in the south of France. But this information came from the same Mr. Lehnert, who also told the same tale to another man. But I can state that Mr. Zucker—formerly 'boss' of Hart & Co., is to-day well and hearty, and established as a diamond dealer in Hatton Garden as Sugar & Co. When the firm Hart & Co. had to be stopped after swindling a firm W. H. Moore of Rennes out of £200 worth of butter and eggs, Zucker established the firm of M. Freeman & Co. in Leadenhall Street, and especially distinguished himself by swindling gold paper from the firm Gebrueder Pauli of Nuremberg.

Now let us look back again to Mr. Gustav Opitz, who made his principal haul in the year 1887, at 22, St. Mary Axe. According to a list which was again made by Mr. L. Lehnert, Mr. Opitz's liabilities amount to £6377 1s. 6d. (I can furnish the names of all the creditors, together with the amounts).

But the principal thing is this: At present Mr. Opitz is, according to his own statements, a partner in the firm of L. Lehnert; according to other accounts, he is said to be only Lehnert's manager.

Be that as it may, one cannot help thinking that Mr. Opitz is not a fit person to save the German commerce from losses.

I advise the creditors of Arnold & Co. (Arnold's real name is De Groot) to take joint proceedings against the firm Arnold & Co., so as to ascertain by bankruptcy proceedings who really were the accomplices of B. Arnold. If the German merchants, on account of a few pounds, allow the swindlers to escape, because they suppose they will receive nothing, they commit a great wrong.

By proceedings in a Court of Justice most astounding revelations would come to light. The material required for this purpose is, as aforesaid, quite complete in the hands of the solicitors, Messrs. Osborn and Osborn, to whom application should be made.

I consider it my duty to expose these swindlers. The informations I am giving are dry reading, and I hope, therefore, the reader will be glad to hear a few things more 'spicy.'

*

* *

It is most amusing when sledge-drivers swindle one another. They then speak with such deep indignation of fraud, and of those who have 'done them,' that the uninitiated could admire them for their own moral principles, and pity them for the loss they sustained. An extraordinary skill to swindle his colleagues of the sledge-driving guild, possesses the former banker Pepke from Berlin, who is living here under the alias of Rayner, and swindling under the name of a beautiful month. His greatest pleasure is to rob his confederates of what they had robbed the German manufacturers, and afterwards to betray his colleagues for a consideration. Who does not know this old dilapidated fellow, who goes from one club or low public-house to the other, borrowing here two pence and somewhere else six pence 'until to-morrow,' which never dawns! A German merchant thought of giving him and some other sledge-drivers a chance of earning an honest living, but an old bear does not learn any more to dance, and an old sledge-driver is equally incapable with regard to honesty. He has now sunk lower than ever before, and the sooner the police takes care of him, the better; but this very likely will not happen until the terms of five and seven years penal servitude are served by some of his friends, who are paying the penalty for misdeeds, of which he drew a principal share of the profit, and whom he betrayed, in order to escape punishment himself.

Those 'in the swim' hate and despise him; but the 'sharpers' are constantly at his heels, because they know that he can help them very often to extremely cheap lots. A short time ago he got an order from a notorious hotel proprietor, to help him to swindle a well-known wine firm in the city of two hogsheads of wine. The firm having their suspicions, escaped being defrauded, and the swindler was baffled. But he is a man of many resources, and the order had to be executed. What did he do? He went to a well-known 'wine manufacturer' on the Surrey side of the river, and ordered from him two barrels of the brand 'vintage of 1878, that the hotel proprietor wished to procure 'cheap.' Next day the wine, 'vintage 1878,' was ready, and the old sledge-driver hired a car and delivered it personally. 'Got it,' he said, apparently highly pleased, and making the host believe the wine came from the proper firm. 'But it was hard work. They invoiced it to me at £31 10s. and I cannot let you have it under half price.' After some bargaining, and after the 'vintage of 1878' had been duly tested and approved, the swindlers agreed on a price of £13 which was paid in cash. The wine-manufacturer had to get £4, but not being able to get his money from Pepke, he sent his bill to the hotel proprietor, who thus learned to know where the wine had grown, and how he had been cheated. Was he more cautious the next time? Not at all. Two days later, Pepke who did not know what had happened, came and offered a barrel of 'genuine' margarine. First of all the cheated swindler gave the cheater a good talking to. It was fortunate that he had not suffered any loss, his customers not having found out that it was no vintage at all, let alone the celebrated vintage of 1878; but he hated crooked ways and would not stand such deception, especially if practised on him by a friend. Pepke was repenting and promised never to do such a thing again. 'To-day,' he declared, 'I am 'honest,' here I brought you a barrel of margarine, quite fresh from Germany, and you can have it at three pence the pound.' The host declined, saying, whatever his guests knew about wine, they would detect the margarine, and he was bound to serve them with butter. 'I can supply you too,' the sledge-driver fell in; 'I have at home two half-barrels of fine butter, which came together with the margarine; you can have it at eight pence.' The two gentlemen agreed on sevenpence, and the sledge-driver went home with his barrel of margarine. Soon afterwards he could be seen in his back-kitchen, sawing in half his barrel of margarine and turning the bottom of the firkin inside out. This done, he brought back the transformed margarine to the host, who liked the 'butter' very much and paid for it. But great was his surprise when the bottom of the first firkin was reached and showed in big red letters the treacherous inscription: 'Margarine, made in Germany.'

The inventive genius of sledge-drivers knows no bounds. I have shown them in different characters already, but it gives me special pleasure to be able to introduce one of their guild in the capacity of a medical doctor, as specialist for the cure of red and deformed noses.

As it sometimes happens in the career of mortal man, he finds himself oppressed by the want of funds. Sledge-drivers form no exception to the general rule, and B., an old member of the fraternity, found himself, for once again, at the bottom of the ladder, starving, homeless, absolutely penniless. He had not money enough for postage, this most important factor in sledge-driving, and business came thus to an absolute standstill. For how shall German manufacturers oblige with goods, if they do not know you want them? How shall they execute, if they get no orders? How shall they be informed where to get rid of their manufactures? It is always grievous to a patriotic heart to see a decline of the national export in the Board of Trade returns, and to contribute his share to the prevention of such an eventuality in the fatherland, B. was now firmly decided to get the money for the postage. He had tried already at many doors, but in vain, and he turned now to a public-house, the host of which was closely connected with sledge-drivers and sledge-driving. He was the man to lend a couple of 'tanners.' Now it must he mentioned that B. and the host had been companions in adversity. Both were possessed of olefactory organs not only of an extraordinary size, but of a still more extraordinary deep red and blue colouring, which made their noses quite a sight of London. Strange to say, the enforced period of abstinence and meagre diet, had quite changed the appearance of B.'s facial protuberance, and had given it its natural colour. When B. now entered 'the house,' the host looked at him most attentively, and B. was greatly pleased at the hearty manner in which his hand was shaken. That meant 'bobs' instead of 'tanners.'

'Look here,' said the host, 'you are just the man I want.' The sledge-driver was delighted to hear it. 'I want to marry.'—'Right, my dear fellow!' cried B. in slapping cordially the host's shoulder. 'Do you want me to procure for you a bride?'—'No, no, thank you,' the host interrupted him, 'I look after that myself, I have, in fact somebody in sight; I have chosen. But there is an obstacle—my nose, this really *blooming* nose! Now, your nose was a sight too, worse than mine, may be, and now it looks quite decent. What have you done? Do you know a remedy?' That was an opening for our sledge-driver! He answered without delay: 'Do I? What do you think? Do you think such an alteration is brought about without a remedy? Of course, I have a remedy, and I had to pay for it dear enough.'—'Well, how much?' 'Twenty-five shillings.' 'Well, I do not mind to pay that; here is the money, fetch it at once for me, and there are five shillings extra for your trouble. Have another glass before you go?'

B. went to the chemist and asked whether he had a remedy for the redness of noses, and he was sorry of the negative answer he got. But a sledge-driver is a man of quick wit and many resources. A remedy he had to bring, and nothing was left to him, but to invent it. A cure was, to his idea, not impossible; he had his own theory, and if it succeeded, it meant a fortune. There was a chance to try it on someone, and B. made soon afterwards a mixture of chlorate of lime, carbolic acid, chalk and mustard, and labelled it: 'for outward application only—twice daily.' He brought it to his patient, and after having been treated to some more glasses, he left him with the ointment and the instructions how to use it. When he called the next day to see how his patient was going on, he found the host with a dreadfully swollen nose. 'I hope the ointment is all right,' the sufferer asked, 'but look how the nose is swollen, it peels too, and the pain is quite unbearable!' 'Yes, I know,' said B., 'it is painful. But you need not concern yourself. The ointment is all right. The skin must peel off. Just have a little patience, and you will see what fine white skin will replace the old one. Go on using the remedy, and be careful to rub it in properly.' The host did so once more, but an hour later he had to call a medical man to alleviate his pains, and it took a long time before his nose was healed. The colour of the new skin was into the bargain redder than the former skin had been, and the host complained bitterly to B. about the 'infernal remedy' he had brought him. 'Well,' said B., 'it is not my fault. You ought to have gone on for a week painting your nose twice daily, when a new white skin would have grown.' 'Well,' said the host, 'this matter costs me now £5, but I rather keep my red nose, that pain can only stand a sledge-driver.'

I cannot make use of all the material at my disposition; but I cannot omit to warn before a new kind of swindle.

Induced by an advertisement, a young gentleman came from Paris to London, and applied to a Mr. M. Jokel, 29, Buckland-street, New North-road, for a loan of 6000 francs with which he intended to purchase a most profitable going concern in the French capital. Mr. Jokel was quite willing to let him have the loan, but the securities not being all what was desired, he told his customer it would be an indispensable condition to insure his life with the 'National Mutual Insurance Company,' and he had better see the 'Director,' Mr. Charles Walz, 51, Baker-street, King's Cross-road, W.C., to whom Mr. Jokel introduced the young man by letter. The Parisian duly paid the premium of 558 francs, and was waiting for the Policy to raise the loan, but he was waiting in vain. He never heard and saw anything more of Jokel or Walz: a noble pair of common swindlers.

* * *

(The preceding article caused a tremendous sensation. I was just in Germany, and had an opportunity to hear with my own ears, and incognito, what was said for and against my action. Reports from London informed me of the great excitement which my disclosures had caused, and that Lehnert and Opitz were preparing a reply. I did not want a controversy, what I wanted was to induce Lehnert and Opitz to take proceedings against me, and to give me thus an opportunity to destroy with one stroke the dangerous conspiracy of the gang of enquiry-agents and long-firm swindlers. For this purpose I wrote at once the following article, which was published in the 'Cologne People's Gazette' on the 11th of November, 1894, and which led to the desired end).

MORE ABOUT THE SLEDGE-DRIVERS.*

LIKE a thunder-bolt from a cloudless sky came to the concerned parties the revelations about the 'sledge-drivers' in the previous number of the weekly edition of the 'Cologne People's Gazette.'

Never before did our articles create such a sensation, and such an excitement amongst the London 'sledge-drivers.' The entire fraternity, usually as cool as cucumbers, became quite frantic, and could be seen running from one friend, and from one 'pub' to the other, to give vent to their enraged feelings, and to drown their sorrow in large bumpers of 'Lager,' much to the delight of 'my hosts' of City-road. In a quiet hotel, not far from Finsbury-square, two German commercial travellers came at logger-heads about this article, and the altercation rose to such a pitch as to end in a cross-action for slander and defamation of character. I, as a man of peace, regret this incident, and wish my friends would moderate themselves, and leave it to me to fight the battle.

It goes by itself that in the general wail of the 'sledge-drivers,' *that dreadful fellow of the 'Cologne People's Gazette'* came in for a good deal of abuse. The legends about his person were multiplied by scores, but, in spite of their variety, bearing witness to the fertility of the sledge-drivers' imaginative powers, the moral of all these tales for rather big than good children, was with touching unanimity, that this *fellow* is the ruin of *the trade*, and the cause of the calamitous miscarriage of the most carefully planned actions, by throwing such a fierce light on the dark doings and dealings of the honourable guild of London sledge-drivers.

* Reprinted from the 'Cologne People's Gazette', Nov., 1894.

I was rather surprised at the disclaimers and alleged rectifications that were addressed to the chief editor in Cologne by some of the firms mentioned in my article. The 'Cologne People's Gazette' was asked to revoke what was never said. But I state with pleasure, that I never thought of casting doubts on honest and respectable firms, whom I could not avoid mentioning in connection with the shady fraternity. I did not sustain, for example, that the Vienna Enquiry Agencies I mentioned, and some other firms, *had given* good reports about Hart & Co., or that they were requested to do so, but I said that Hart & Co. *referred to them*, and for this assertion I have undeniable evidence in my possession. The swindlers gave simply the names of these firms as references, of course without being authorised to do so, a piece of cheek which need not surprise anybody. I sustain, therefore, every sentence I wrote in my preceding article. However, I feel bound to correct a few clerical errors. Thus I stated that Mr. Zucker, after his resurrection from the dead, whom he had joined in the 'south of France,' as was alleged, a victim to his *consumption* (very likely of liquors in Brixton), had established himself anew as Sugar & Co., in Hatton-garden. I was mistaken, and I crave the pardon of this gentleman, for Mr. Martin Zucker from Berlin (late Morris Brandt & Co., Hart & Co., Freeman & Co., etc.), styles his new long-firm simply M. Sugar. I have, likewise, to apologise to Mr. Päpke, the former Berlin banker, from *Unter den Linden*, whom I christened Pepke, and who may complain too, of the suppression of the fact that he was, at the time of his glorious departure from the German capital, the proprietor of the fashionable 'Officers' Gazette.' Those anxious to see the effigy of this great celebrity, may find in the files of some leading German papers his likeness attached to a curious piece of literature, known by the name of '*Warrant*,' the indescreet authors of which never obtained their end to secure his much wanted person. His departure from Berlin was, as report has it, of a most interesting, and even romantic and touching character. A number of his creditors, amongst them a jeweller from the immediate neighbourhood of the royal castle, saw him off. It was a joyous occasion, for their debtor was going to Hanover to be *betrothed to an heiress*, as he said. He was equipped for the occassion: brand new suits, linen, hats, boots, umbrella, travelling bags, diamond studs, rings, all furnished to the 'lucky dog' by credulous tradesmen, and a lot of jewellery and other costly presents, supplied at the same terms, and filling his portmanteau for 'his bride' (she turned out later a London pawnbroker). Amidst the hearty congratulations and cheering of his creditors, he steamed out of Berlin never to return again, concluding thus his career in the fatherland in a manner worthy of his swindling genius. I wonder whether his cheated friends would recognize him again if they would meet him by chance in the streets of London? Hardly, he is no longer himself. Even his likeness, affixed to the said piece of official literature does no longer betray the original, for Päpke is but the shadow of his former self.

I obtained a well-deserved satisfaction from the applause which greeted my revelations respecting the inquiry office of L. Lehnert. The proprietor of another enquiry office, who, however, is at loggerheads with Lehnert, expressed the opinion that a statue should be erected to the writer of the articles, because he raised the curtain which covered this kind of enquiry traffic with the Continent. I agree with him, provided however, that Mr. Lehnert contributes the 1000 sovereigns in gold, which he offered by his emissary, Mr. Rewman, for the documents mentioned in the last article. If I am allowed to say a word, I might suggest that a few interesting scenes should be recorded on the four sides of the pedestal. On one side should be carved the scene which the astonished observer beholds on arriving on the 4th floor of 46, Queen Victoria-street. There, under the roof, Lehnert has his office, trading as 'L. Lehnert,' and 'Liman & Co.' It consists of three low garrets with two entrance doors. On the one appears the name of the firm, L. Lehnert, on the other that of Liman & Co; both enquiry offices, who, when enquired about, are giving the most excellent reports one about the other, although both are conducted in the same rooms, and by the same persons, and belong to the same individuals. After the appearance of the last article, another office on the Continent, to whom Lehnert acted as agent, broke off the connection. Simply shake him off, that would be exactly the right thing. It is very easy to accuse the correspondent of the 'Cologne People's Gazette' of having written the untruth. One party declares, 'we never had anything to do with 'Lehnert.' But I can prove the contrary, for people who wrote to Liman & Co., wrote in fact, without knowing it, to Lehnert. The address is different, but the house, the office and the man are the same. The house has two entrances from different streets. If you want Liman & Co., you go to the three garrets from Pancras Lane. If you want L. Lehnert, you go there from 46, Queen Victoria-street. This is how it is done. (I refer to the plan on another page for the situation of this famous double office).

Thus, for example, the firm Hermann Gunther of Kirchberg makes an enquiry at L. Lehnert's 46, Queen Victoria-street, and another enquiry at Liman & Co., St. Pancras Lane, believing them to be two different firms, and thinking that the reports received in reply are coming from two different enquiry offices. (On the following page I reproduce the signatures of Opitz and Lehnert as Liman & Co., also Opitz's signature as L. Lehnert, and G. Opitz.) The same was done without suspicion by the association 'Credit Reform' in Germany and Austria, as also by the Agence Probitas of Paris and other towns. My list contains no less than 23 offices who were served by either L. Lehnert or Liman & Co., although Lehnert addressed a direct circular to the merchants in Germany, in which he says that he, as correspondent of the office, was supplying for the last six years, all the reports which referred to London. A German manufacturer felt quite indignant that the report about Arnold & Co. furnished by Lehnert had been incorrect and misleading, but he did not complain, because a Berlin office had supplied a nearly identical report. He will know now why he had almost the same report from Berlin and London. If the German commerce is served with reports in the same way in future, very peculiar circumstances must arise, to which I shall perhaps apply the lancet one of these days. I shall do so at the risk of causing the disappearance of a dozen offices. On the second side of the statue's pedestal there should be represented the scene when Mr. Opitz arrived in January, 1894, at the hotel 'Prince Regent,' at Hof in Bavaria, under the name of Lehnert. But the artist who does the work must not forget to show the tears of joy of the stout red-haired 'gentleman,' which he shed, because he was able to travel in Germany without danger, under the assumed name of his friend. Some Bavarian and Bohemian firms no doubt remember

Yours faithfully
G. Opitz

(Opitz's handwriting.)

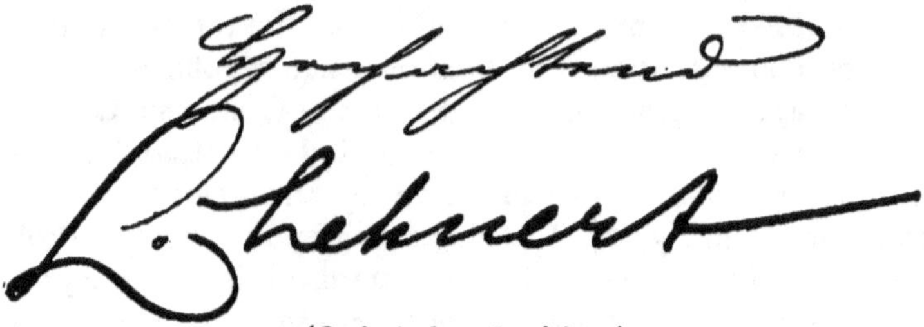
L. Lehnert

(Opitz's handwriting.)

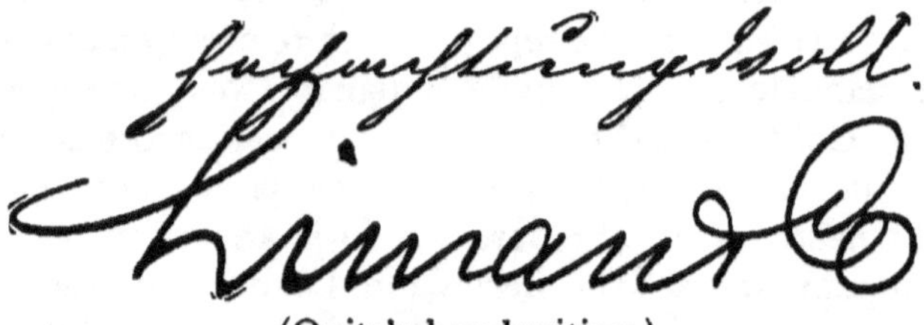

(Opitz's handwriting.)

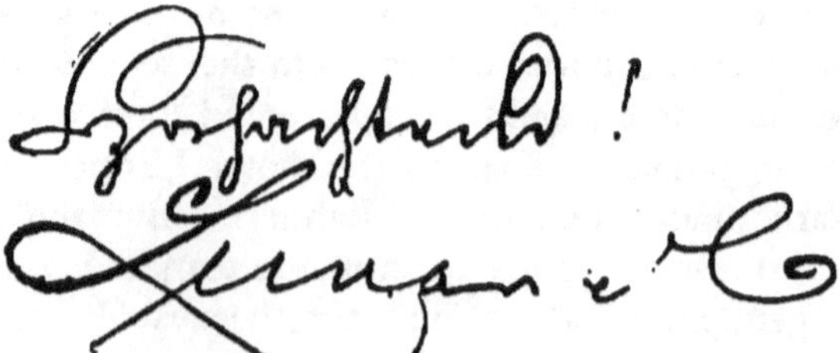

(Lehnert's handwriting.)

still to-day with sorrow the days of pseudo-Lehnert's visit. As to the third picture, I propose the scene in which an emissary of Mr. L. Lehnert, a Mr. Kinderlin, tells at the offices of the Solicitors, Messrs. Osborn & Osborn the lie, that he is coming on behalf of the firm of Goldschmidt in Vienna, and wanted to see the documents which were mentioned in the 'Cologne People's Gazette.' When Messrs. Osborn & Osborn asked the ambassador to make an affidavit that he came by order of the firm Goldschmidt (whose correct address he did not know), and when he was told that he might be prosecuted for perjury, he admitted, trembling, that he had been sent by Lothar Lehnert. As fourth picture, I propose the scene when Lehnert, rubbing his hands in a manner peculiar to him, and smiling by moving his lower jaw, orders his clerk to write about De Groot the report already partly published, remarking: 'There we have a report provided with back-doors and traps, for when the crash comes, there will be a mighty explosion.' And his prophetic mind saw it already coming, and the correspondent of the 'Cologne People's Gazette,' furraging amongst his papers. I beg to remark that Mr. Lehnert, respectively Liman & Co., gave nearly 300 reports about De Groot, alias B. Arnold & Co.; further, that these reports were not confined to Germany, but that a large number also went to France. The French reports contained a sentence which I miss in Mr. Lehnert's German reports about B. Arnold & Co., namely: 'The only known proprietor is Mr. Bernard Arnold.' (This letter on the following page is a facsimile of the report in Lehnert's writing, the corrections in same are in Opitz's handwriting.) How dare he say that, since he knew that Bernard Arnold's real name was De Groot? However, I am going to speak about that later on.

These are my proposals for the four sides of the statue to be erected, but if an octagon should be desired, the missing scenes may be selected from the other parts of this article. For example, it would not be bad to illustrate a visit of Mrs. Opitz at 46, Queen Victoria-street, when one day the honest Messrs. Lehnert and Opitz had for a German firm recovered a case of stockings and other woollen goods from a doubtful importer. Mr. Opitz ordered a clerk, after looking at the things himself, to compare the goods with the list from the German firm

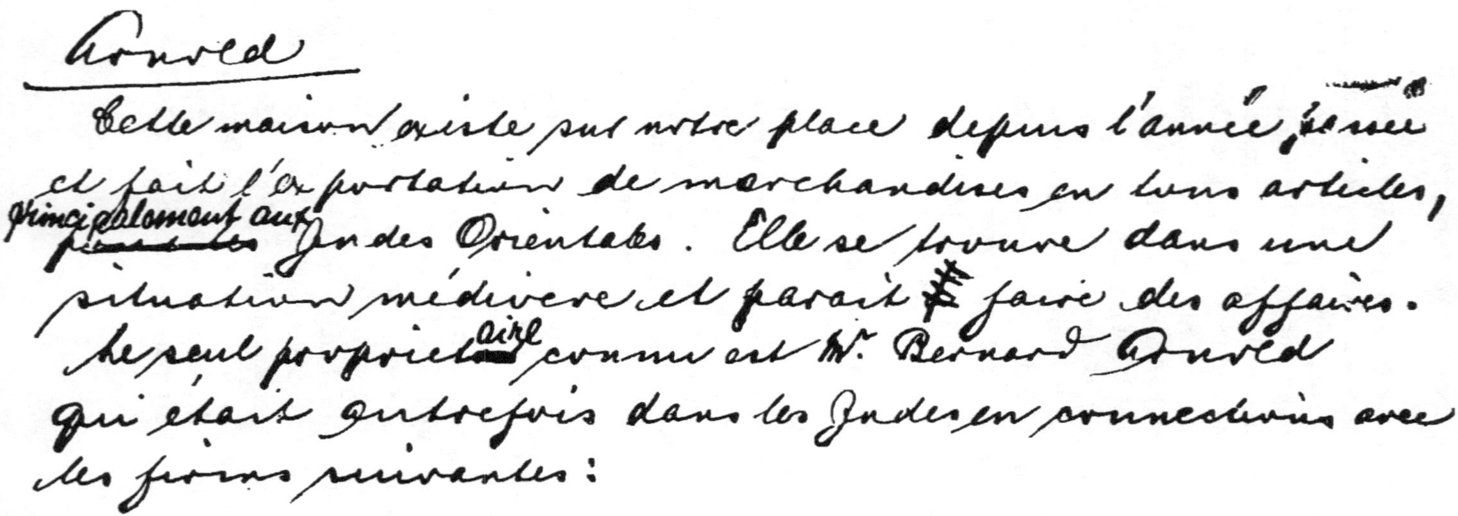

Arnold

Cette maison existe sur notre place depuis l'année [illegible] et fait l'exportation de marchandises en tous articles, principalement aux Indes Orientales. Elle se trouve dans une situation médiocre et paraît faire des affaires. Le seul propriétaire connu est Mr. Bernard Arnold qui était autrefois dans les Indes en connection avec les firmes suivantes:

(Lehnert's handwriting, corrections by Opitz.)

The young man found that several articles were missing, and reported this to Mr. Opitz. The latter said unconcernedly, 'that does not matter; to-morrow *Mrs.* Opitz is coming here, and then still more things will be missing.' Now, reverting again to B. Arnold & Co., I must put a new firm into the field, namely, Messrs. Payne & Co., Coleman-street. The proprietor's name is *Schreck,* and he is a constant visitor at Messrs. Lehnert & Opitz. When this gentleman arrives at 46, Queen Victoria-street, the doors of the principals are closed as soon as Mr. Schreck has entered, so that the clerks should not hear anything. To make the thing quite plain for the reader, I herewith give a plan of Lehnert's celebrated office, in the three garrets of Queen Victoria-street. *D.* means door, and *W.* means window.

The Garrets of the Office Lehnert & Liman.

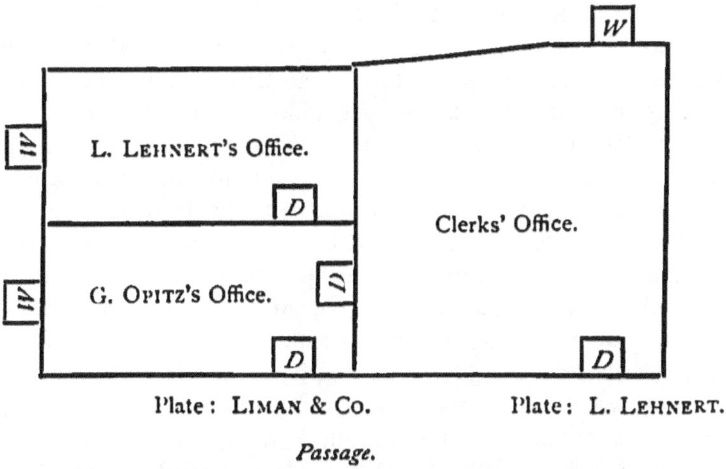

I cannot give any information about the things which happen there after Schreck enters, I only know that on such occasions the clerks say to one another, 'there somebody is to be slaughtered again,' or 'there someone else is going to be blackmailed.'

I cannot say much about Mr. Schreck's past, I only know so much, that this faithful friend of Messrs. Lehnert & Opitz looked last year with De Groot at the office in Guildhall Chambers, which the latter afterwards took. When £75 rent was demanded, which appeared too much to De Groot, alias B. Arnold & Co., Schreck said, 'never mind, let us take it immediately.' B. Arnold & Co. opened an account at the City Bank, in Fore-street, and Lehnert's report says with regard to this matter, word for word: 'Not much is known here in town about his own means, only that when starting his business, he opened an account with the City Bank, Fore-street, with good recommendations. Until now his account has been kept in order. He pretends to settle his purchases in the manner usual in the East Indian trade, and as long as he adheres to these terms, the execution of orders up to a few £100 offers little or no danger.' Then with good recommendations B. Arnold & Co. opened their banking account? Who gave him these good recommendations? Ernest Schreck, alias Payne & Co., a friend of Lehnert and G. Opitz, a friend of De Groot. Opitz even took the trouble, as already mentioned, to travel to Germany in Lehnert's name. This was in the first week of the month of January, 1894. At that time already some of the creditors were getting impatient, and yet Lehnert, still in February, was induced to give reports 'with trap-doors' about B. Arnold & Co., and later on emphasized this. When a further information was demanded, he wrote word for word: 'After having given you already a full report about the firm, I have only little to add to-day in reply to your renewed enquiry. The purchases made by the firm have all been settled by cheque, and I have not yet heard anything unfavourable about their mode of payment.' How did he know that all the payments had been made by cheque? Was he not aware that a long, long time before De Groot bolted, the City Bank had closed the account of B. Arnold & Co., and that already months before this the goods, obtained by swindle from Germany and France, had been sent to Amsterdam in 180 cases? And when later on De Groot himself bolted on the 15th of July to Amsterdam, to be where his booty was, why did Lehnert take occasion to write to those who had been swindled, that B. Arnold had gone to India? And why did he tell this only to those firms who had really supplied Arnold with goods? Why not to all the 300 firms who had made enquiries from Lehnert? How did he know the firms who had been swindled? He admits he might have judged the position of B. Arnold & Co. too 'rosy,' but this was not his habit though. Let us look at Lehnert's or Liman & Co.'s reports about such firms, who declined to have anything to do with him, and against whom he had a spite. Take, for example, the following report:

'This former swindler has started now afresh some nine months ago, and has joined the 'exporters.' He has now become a decidedly steady man. Favoured by the same luck with which he used to make havock among the mercantile world, he has now conquered the heart of a maiden, and on the 15th November, 1890, he married the niece of one of the first magnates in England. He is said to have received a very handsome dowry. Anyhow, it is a fact that he has opened an account with the London and Westminster Bank. After these remarks, I must leave it to you whether you will trust him with £400 to £500, I should not do it.' This report speaks for itself. The gentleman in question will certainly be grateful to me for having called his attention to what is thought of him at 46, Queen Victoria-street. Lehnert also gives a fine title to Mr. Edward Carey, to whom he sold the bells already mentioned in the last article, and from whom he obtained in settlement a bill which he tried to discount with a gentleman in Finsbury. He says about this former friend: 'Edward Carey is an arch-humbug, who is as full of debts as a dog is of fleas. To me personally he owes still £5.' Was this the balance of the bells?

As Lehnert is ready to blacken everybody's character, it will easily be understood that he abused in a shameful manner the agent of a German firm, who had blamed him for the loss the firm suffered at B. Arnold & Co. These letters have brought him a libel action, which was heard in the City of London Court, and settled by Lehnert paying costs and £20 damages.

In the Leipsic paper of the association 'Credit-reform', I read a notice a few years ago, in which the contents of my articles were called 'lies.' Intending to lessen the merit of these articles, the writer mentioned as the inspirers of these articles certain persons, who were not known even by name to the 'Cologne People's Gazette.' My only reason for reverting to this to-day is to show that Lehnert or Liman & Co. supply some of the 'Credit-reform' branches in Germany with reports. I therefore need not look far for the writer of that notice. I understand that Lehnert and Opitz intend to publish in Germany a reply to the article in No. 596 of the 'Cologne People's Gazette;' but that will be of no great avail to the two gentlemen. We demand something more than empty excuses. We demand from Mr. Lehnert to take proceedings against us. This only can satisfy us. With regard to the proposed rebutting article against the 'Cologne People's Gazette'; I must state that we are awaiting it with great interest. It is to be produced on the one hand by Lehnert and on the other by Opitz, with the kind assistance of a certain Stein, alias Semansky, a painter called Winter from Berlin, and of the above-mentioned former banker Päpke.

As medium for their emanation they intend to have a Leipsic paper, for which the Israelite Stein sometimes concocts something as 'Christian correspondent' (so he calls himself). It will suffice when I state that this Stein-Semansky used to be secretary to the notorious 'professor' Arnstein, who was frequently mentioned in my articles of former years as swindler of musical instruments. The readers of the 'Cologne People's Gazette' will remember him. Stein's friend, the journeyman painter Winter, is not allowed to return to Berlin, as he is wanted there, and Päpke we already know on account of his deeds. When a short time ago he bragged in a den that he would shoot the correspondent of the 'Cologne People's Gazette,' a witty person went up to him and offered him a pea shooter. We see thus, that the elements of swindledom that brood revenge, are not very selected. I take this opportunity of repeating that this article is also written for the purpose to again call the attention of the German as well as the foreign trade to the dangerous doings of the expatiated swindlers in London.

With regard to enquiry-offices I should like to submit to the German Government, to make the commercial enquiry-business a state affair and to entrust with it the consulates in foreign parts. If this is not done, associations should be formed who make the protection of honest trade their task. Although it is certain that some of the better enquiry-offices are well organized and their proprietors are honest men above suspicion, still they have mostly to rely upon agents, who, badly paid as they are, cannot resist the frequent temptations put by dishonest firms into their way.

In order to be enabled to write on this point with authority, I caused enquiries to be made through friendly firms from different offices about good and bad firms. The reports showed that one enquiry-office gave a perfectly unintelligible report about a swindler, and another office gave a splendid report about the same man. In another case I have a report about a man who already lives 12 years at the same address, and whom I have known 10 years, and the information stated that he had only lived a few months at that address, and that every connection with him was to be avoided. When I addressed a protest to the office, they answered that the former report was wrong, and the gentleman enquired after was good for the credit named.

In conclusion I must once more refer to the last article on sledge-drivers. I repeat, I did not assert that the offices and firms mentioned in the article, had given references to the swindling firm 'Hart & Co;' but what I said was, that Hart & Co. gave these offices as references. This also applies to the mercantile firms mentioned. I declare emphatically that I only mentioned these firms and had to mention them, to punish the irresponsible actions of the guilty persons. The firm of Jahnke & Fölsch of Hamburg, about whose respectability I have no doubt whatever, appeared to have taken the matter particularly to heart, and they wrote a long letter to the 'Cologne People's Gazette,' from which I reproduce some parts as follows: 'In No. 42 of the said paper, of Thursday, October 18th, we find a long article, headed "The Sledge-drivers.' We have a particular interest in your revelations, regarding Mr. Lehnert of London. We presume that after you have mentioned our firm in this matter, you will also publish the following explanation, so as to clear the matter up as far as we are concerned (I willingly comply with this request, as the explanation in itself is interesting). The enquiry-agent Mr. L. Lehnert, who is prominently mentioned, was, as far as we know, employed by the forwarding agents, Brasch & Rothenstein, up to about 1885, and as we saw from his offer to us, he was finally one of the managers of the London office. We then engaged him, thinking he was a clever forwarding agent, at a yearly salary of 4000 marks, for the purpose of obtaining London connection for our forwarding business. But we soon found that his results did not correspond with our expectations and with the salary paid, and after one year we had to reduce his salary to one-half, or 2000 marks. He accepted this most readily, but on condition that, whilst acting as our canvasser, he might at the same time establish an enquiry-office of his own as L. Lehnert, to which we had not the slightest objection. All we have known of Lehnert since then is, that he has done less and less for us, that his salary was reduced correspondingly, until his enquiry-office induced him to take offices of his own, and after this we received only occasionally a letter from him. We repeat the request that you will explain our connection with Mr. Lehnert in your paper, and hope that the other papers which have reprinted your article will also publish our reply.' It is clear that these lines are a confirmation of my first article. The name of the firm of Jahnke & Fölsch is still painted at Lehnert's garret at 46, Queen Victoria-street. The London Directory also still shows the firm of Jahnke & Fölsch at 46, Queen Victoria-street; and the same address is still to be found on the Hamburg letter-headings of the firm, which therefore does not yet appear to be sufficiently convinced of Lehnert's real character, as the firm pays a yearly contribution towards the rent of Lehnert's office. One thing more. I have discovered that most of the German firms who took their information direct from Lehnert, referred to C. Regenhardt's Business Almanack, where they had seen the address.

Up to 1892 L. Lehnert was put down as the only enquiry-office in London. I state with satisfaction that the address has disappeared in the edition of 1895.

* * *

In consequence of these articles, Lehnert sent out a 'Reply,' which was circulated broadcast all over Germany. The 'Reply,' however, did not refute any of my direct and implied accusations; it was, in fact, no answer at all, but simply a denial in general terms, full of untrue statements, and of defamations of 'Rollo.' Lehnert and Opitz had also hired a so-called journalist, viz. Stein, alias

Semansky, alias Winter, whose shady character and former experience as private secretary to the notorious 'Professor' Arnstein, mentioned in the article on 'Musical Sledge-drivers,' rendered him an extremely worthy person to do service to Messrs. Lehnert and Opitz. Two German newspapers were also found willing, from motives pretty well known in Germany, to open their columns to the defence of the noble fraternity of sledge-drivers, and to the calumnies and vituperations hurled against the 'Cologne People's Gazette,' and their hateful London correspondent.

The following article of the 'Cologne People's Gazette' will throw all the light on this matter which is required for the purpose of this book :

THE GERMAN SLEDGE-DRIVERS IN LONDON,

AND

THE 'COLOGNE PEOPLE'S GAZETTE.'

'It is generally known that a newspaper in Essen, and in an abbreviated form, a Cologne paper, have opened their columns to a London letter, emanating, nominally, from 'Herbert Winter,' and describing all our sledge-driver articles, from beginning to end, as a fearful 'web of lies.' We have answered already by the publication of the last article of our London correspondent, who replied at the same time with a few words to this letter. The really insane contradictions it contained were quite sufficient to raise, even with the most believing readers, grave doubts into the reliability of this 'Herbert Winter.' We are now enabled to furnish some further contributions, which are throwing a really glorious light at the veracity of this gentleman and those who are standing at his back.

'Herbert Winter' tried his best to connect Mr. Henry Joachim Gehlsen in London, with our articles. This gentleman now writes to us :

'In London and elsewhere, the assertion is made that I am the author of your sensational article of the 7th of October, against the excrescences of so-called Enquiry-Offices.

Permit me to state publicly that I had nothing whatever to do with the publication of this article, neither directly, nor indirectly, and that I first became aware of its existence when I read it printed in your paper. I do not make this statement because the untrue assertion could be detracting from me, but for the reason that I do not want to appropriate the merit of those who had the courage to attack these infamous parasites of commerce, a veritable modern *Vehmgericht* (a secret tribunal of justice in Westphalia, similar to the Spanish Inquisition).'

Another letter reaches us from Mr. E. Hesse, in London, to whom Mr. Herbert Winter ascribes, without a vestige of truth, a great share in the two last-published sledge-driver articles in our paper.

We take the following from Mr. Hesse's letter. 'It is a fact that Mr. Lothar Lehnert appeared on the 3rd of November before the Magistrate, and swore that I am the author and publisher of the sledge-driver article in the 'Cologne People's Gazette'—a false and untrue declaration. Michael Zucker, alias Martin Sugar, the former confederate of Mr. Opitz, has left on Saturday last, the 3rd of November, his office in Hatton Garden and also his private lodgings. An old man is sitting in the cleared-out office, and informs visitors that Mr. Zucker has gone abroad and will return in four or five weeks time; similar information is given by his landlady. But 'Rollo' will be able to find him in London, in case he should require his attendance. Zucker drew on Saturday all the balance in his favour at the Union Bank, Hatton-Garden branch, all in all £3 10s.—and such an amount does not carry a traveller very far.

It is true that I had to stop payments eight years ago. But the principal loser was I, who lost all what I had earned by many years hard and honest work (I am already 28 years in England), and the next losers were my relatives. But permit me to state now, that great losses in business were the cause of my misfortune. I will but mention three of their number:

As stated in your paper of the 7th and 18th of October, there existed a gang of commercial robbers, consisting of Gustave Opitz, Michael Zucker and Max Borchardt. They pretended to ship goods to India, and to pay for their purchases 'in accordance with the customs of the Indian trade,' exactly as the celebrated enquiry-office of Lehnert said in its information about B. Arnold & Co. Two small invoices were paid promptly, but for the third and fourth invoice, amounting to £800, I received bills and post-dated cheques, which were all dishonoured, and I lost every farthing.

Another 'Indian house', Messrs. Grieslich & Co., friends of Opitz, ordered at about the same time goods for £1500. I executed the order on a Tuesday and was promised to get my money on the following Friday. My goods were shipped directly, and when I called on Friday at the 'Agra Bank', where Grieslichs kept their accounts, I was informed that the Bank would not make any more payments on account of Messrs. Grieslich, and I never got a penny!

A third 'Indian house', also connected with Opitz, and styling himself 'Jehanger Mular Framjee', cheated me for £300 in accordance with the customs of the Indian trade, and I did not receive any payment in this case too. I have at least the poor consolation that the noble Indian is still kept in penal servitude in one of her Majesty's prisons. I mention these three Indian cases only, but I could add quite a list of similar losses.

But Opitz speaks for once the truth, when he says that after my bankruptcy I was not possessed of a single penny, and that to this day I am not a rich man. But it is *untrue* that I ever traded under another name as my own; it is *untrue* that I ever intended to buy or bought pianos, excepted the one which I possess for the last twenty years; it is *untrue* that I was declared a bankrupt in 1893 again, or that bankruptcy proceedings were taken against me; *untrue* that I had a levy for a debt of £11; *untrue* that the firm of C. D. Nicoll & Co. in Sunderland, whom I had to sue for the recovery of a debt, which was paid before the action came on, can say anything to my disadvantage; *untrue* that I have written an apology to Mr. Lehnert, as was suggested by his solicitor; to the contrary, I do hold in my possession an apology of Mr. Sugar, which is certainly valueless in itself, but is so far interesting as it bears an autograph of Mr. Lehnert (the documents in question are on pages 106 and 107), which read as follows: 'In witness of the hand-writing of Mr. Zucker (not Sugar), L. Lehnert. It is finally *untrue* that I have my office 'in a cellar,' and that I am a manufacturer of accommodation bills. (Signed) E. Hesse.'

Very significant with regard to the persecution instituted in the press against our correspondent, is the following letter of the 'General Advertiser' in Leipsic:

L. HESSE & Co

MANUFACTURERS OF

Buttons & Bodice Steels.

82, FORE STREET,

London, ________ 18

E.C.

Mr Emil Hesse

82 fore street

Ich habe mich gegen meine bessern Wissen zu Bemerkungen & lügenhaften Äußerungen hinreißen lassen, die jeder wahren Basis entbehren. Ich erkläre hiermit daß mir nicht das Geringste gegen Ihren Character bekannt ist & daß ich aufs tiefste bedauere Sie direct oder

indirect beleidigt zu haben. Gleichzeitig verpflichte
ich mich diese als unwahren Beschuldigungen
allerwärts zurückzunehmen + hoffe ich
dass Sie nun von gesetzlichen Maßregeln gegen
mich Abstand nehmen.

Mit Achtung:
M. Sugar

Als Zeugen für die Unterschrift
und M. Zucker
L. Lehner

'To the Editor of the 'Cologne People's Gazette.' In the No. 670 of your paper, of the 11th November, you have published under the heading 'More about the Sledge-drivers,' an article of your London correspondent, containing the following passage:

This important reply, it is said, will be floated by Lehnert, by Opitz, and by a certain Stein, 'with the kind assistance' of the journeyman painter Winter from Berlin, and the former banker Päpke, whom we had occasion to mention before. As sewer for this emanation a Leipsic paper is taken in view, for which the Jew Stein as Christian correspondent (as he dubbs himself) is committing occasional articles.

Referring to this, we beg to communicate to you the following:

A few months ago, a certain Adolph Stein from London, whom we do not know personally, addressed himself to us with the inquiry, whether he could supply us with telegrams and articles from London. We left it to him to submit us his articles, and we published some of them, principally translations from English papers on political incidents in Germany.

These articles were absolutely harmless. But far from harmless appeared to us a private letter of Mr. Semansky, in which he informed us a few weeks ago, that he would open a campaign against the sledge-driver revelations of the 'Cologne People's Gazette.' A short time afterwards a voluminous manuscript was submitted to us, and carefully read, with the result of speedy return of the manuscript to the author. At the same time the Chief-editor made inquiries in London at a highly respected author about the person of Mr. Semansky. The answer was received a day ago, and caused the name of Semansky being struck at once from the roll of the contributors to the 'General Advertiser.'

You will see by this declaration that nothing was farther from our intentions than to put at the disposal of that Semansky our paper 'as sewer' for his suspicious journalistic activity. The article we mentioned before, was submitted by Semansky a second time, with an explanatory letter, and was entrusted, without further ceremonies to the care of the waste-paper basket.

There are certainly very few papers who do not publish contributions from occasional correspondents, for whose private character or literary qualifications they cannot vouchsafe, because these contributors are not personally known to them, especially if they are living in foreign parts.

With the request to bring this letter to the knowledge of your readers, we are, etc., 'The General Advertiser' for Leipsic and suburbs. (Signed) Otto Friedr. Koch, Chief-editor.

Leipsic, November 12, 1894.'

It will be seen that this letter confirms fully our correspondent's statements with regard to the journalistic activity of the firm Stein-Semansky-Winter.

After Stein-Semansky, who writes now under the alias of Herbert Winter, had been dismissed by the Leipsic paper, the leaders of the noble sledge-driver guild turned to Essen and Cologne, where they found willing helpers. These, the two papers referred to, improved on the occasion in publishing a false and malicious report about certain preliminary proceedings in the Guildhall Police-court on the 7th inst.

The firm of L. Lehnert, enquiry-agent in London, are preparing now, as it is reported, to take action against our London correspondent, Rollo, for the articles against the German long-firm swindlers in the English metropolis, published in the Nos. 596 and 670 of the 'Cologne People's Gazette.' We shall welcome such proceedings, which we hoped to see taken during the last seven years, because such a law-suit would widen the field of our battle against the nuisance of German sledge-drivers in London. The interest in the sledge-driver articles has constantly increased in Germany and England, since their first appearance in the year 1887. Until now, not one of our correspondent's actual statements and accusations against swindling firms has been contradicted or refuted. On the other hand, numerous letters of German manufacturers, who were either swindled by the sledge-drivers, or guarded from loss by our articles, have proved to us the reliability of Rollo's assertions. Every day is bringing us letters from persons who suffered losses, and hearty thanks are said to us for our action in this matter. We shall publish to-day just one letter only, to show how accurately informed our correspondent was with regard to one of the more serious accusations raised in our paper. The letter runs as follows:

'To the Editor of the 'Cologne People's Gazette.' The late Mr. Joseph Wolf supplied at his life-time in 1888, goods amounting to 1442 florins to the firm of Hart & Co. In settlement I received, after Mr. Wolf had ended his life by suicide, an acceptance to the same amount of the firm of Hart & Co. At the same time the firm inquired whether I would be disposed to let them have a parcel of boots and shoes, which was laying at the forwarding-agents, Schenker & Co., because the firm which had given the order could not be found, and actually did not exist. I declared to be willing to do so, for cash, an offer which was refused by Hart & Co. I submitted the matter to the creditors, and they decided, against my advice, to let Hart & Co. have the goods against acceptance. Both bills were made payable at the Credit-Bank of Vienna. When due, it transpired that no cover had been received, and that the acceptor was quite unknown at the bank.

I put now the matter into the hands of the solicitor Mr. Schweder, in London, to take proceedings, but the only result was that I had to pay expenses amounting to £25. It was discovered at this occasion, that a certain Zucker represented the firm of Hart & Co. as sole proprietor. *Zucker is a swindler;* he has a small city office, furnished with a single table and a single chair, and from there he is swindling continental manufacturers, under the style of Hart & Co. I even suspect that Zucker himself ordered the goods which could not be delivered by Schenker & Co., and that he did so for the purpose to obtain them easier, knowing that goods sent to foreign parts are not easily ordered back, because of the expense of transport, and rather sold on credit if there is a chance for it.

You would greatly oblige me if you would let me know the result of your researches regarding this swindler. Should proceedings be taken against him, I should join in the action.

Yours, etc., Dr. E. Friedman,
Solicitor to the Imperial Court in Vienna.'

* * *

I, personally, have nothing to say to the knavish attacks of the 'Rhenish Westphalian Gazette,' and the deceased Cologne paper, for the best answer is the glorious victory which I gained in my actions over the London sledge-drivers. But, for the better understanding, I must remark that the attacks of those papers, who took so manly the part of sledge-drivers, were directed far more against the 'Cologne People's Gazette,' than against my person. The ridiculous nonsense of the sledge-drivers in their articles of the above-mentioned papers, I have already scourged in the chapter 'More about the Sledge-drivers.' I content myself to remark that a knowledge of the tricks of the 'black gang' cannot be gained in royal palaces, but at the proper address, that is, the sledge-drivers themselves. A child will undertand that it was no pleasure to me to have to mix with these tattered scoundrels; the editors of the mentioned papers only did not understand it, and tried, therefore, to prove the existence of a very close friendship between myself and the swindlers. They would not understand that there is also such a thing as duty, which a journalist has to perform in the public interest. To be enabled to inform the readers of my labours in a thorough manner, I have done many things that would have even amazed the night-watchmen of Essen, if they had been present. I have passed many a night in the streets, that I might be able to feel with these ill-fortunates, and then to write an article about it. Once, when in the guise of a genuine tramp, I was nearly arrested by the police, and only my visiting card as correspondent of the 'Cologne People's Gazette,' saved me from being 'run in.' But, was there a necessity for me to court danger? No, I could have slept at my residence comfortably on my pillows of soft downs, instead of running the streets like a vagabond. But, was I for that a vagabond? Then I convinced myself, personally, about the nature of the lodging houses. One night, in the shelter of the Salvation Army, huddled together with 170 persons in one room; one night in 'Wildermuth House'; one night in the 'Christian Shelter' (the German 'Deutsche Herberge.') Was there a necessity for me do it? No, I could have slept again on my pillows of downs, instead of sleeping together with dirty scamps from all parts of the world. But I had my good cause for doing it, for my publications about these matters have brought about changes for the better of really scandalous conditions, which otherwise, very likely, would have remained in existence to this day. Nobody thinks of upbraiding me for this cause from having kept company with homeless people, beggars and vagabonds. I like such adventures. Many a reader finds a pleasure in my experiences, and if I am not very much mistaken, the editors and publishers of the 'Rhenish Westphalian Gazette' too. I do not think any adventure could be detrimental to my honour, even if I should have one with the editor of the Essen paper.

On the other hand, it is no honour for the papers mentioned, that they have associated with the sledge-drivers, and that they are publishing libellous articles, emanating from this fraternity and dictated by their desire to avenge themselves for the defeats inflicted on them. People who are going about with down-trodden heels and torn trousers, who are constant visitors of low German public houses, frequented by sledge-drivers and scoundrels; who engage a bed for 3s. a week, and finally are not able to pay even these 3s.; who were secretary to notorious sledge-drivers; who fled from Germany to escape the constant visits of the brokers, such people have no right to make the slanderous assertion of a man of consequence that he is an associate of swindlers, because he had been seen in their company.

THE SLEDGE-DRIVERS OF NAPLES.

ONE of the greatest long-firm swindles recorded, is certainly that perpetrated in Naples in the year 1886. By rights, I ought to say, enacted in Naples, for the scene of action extended from Italy to Germany, Bohemia, London, and finally America.

As one of the 'heroes' of my sledge-driver articles, which led to the sensational trial, is also the leading 'hero' of that great Neapolitan sledge-driving transaction, I think it not out of place to publish too the history of this most remarkable gigantic swindle. I am not doing this to cause a sensation, but for the sole and exclusive purpose to show the international character of sledge-driving, and to caution manufacturers and merchants how careful they must be, if they do not want to fall victims to the fraternity of long-firm swindlers.

In England credit is not so easily given and obtained as in other countries. But here, as elsewhere, the small manufacturer and the beginner are far more disposed to open a credit to customers than old established firms in a large way of business, who have greater experience, and who may dare to demand from new customers cash at the first, second and third transaction. But the small manufacturer and small merchant should also not be tempted to entertain whatever business comes, just for the sake of doing business, if he is not absolutely certain that he will receive the money for his goods. If he does not use every precaution, he will not only lose his goods, but undermine his own credit into the bargain, and finally find himself ruined.

The actors in the following chapter are: 1. a certain Ernst Schreck, who was established under the firm of Geremiah & Schreck as commercial agent in Naples; 2. his brother Arfest

Schreck; 3. Louis Listmann, the brother-in-law of the two Schrecks. —a beautiful shamrock, grown up on the German soil of Itzehoe. But their 'activity' was transferred, as we shall see presently, to such countries, where milder laws permitted them to trespass to their hearts desire. At present the two Schrecks are living in London, the Eldorado of the German swindlers, and I consider it my duty to reveal their past career, in spite of the intercession of a German firm, who say they had been dealt with honestly, and I should therefore cover the past of Ernest Schreck with the mantle of Christian love. I regret, but I cannot extend Christian, Mahommedan or Jewish love to these gentlemen, and still less can I cover their past with any mantle whatever. I do not do so from any motives of hatred or vengeance; I do so for the sole purpose of drawing the attention of the commercial world to these people, and, at the same time, to give a deterrent example. By the statements I am making, the reader will, however, be able to judge for himself whether such people deserve to be spared. At any rate, they did not take any regard, and spoke of their victims as of 'dogs who must not be treated with a forbearing hand.' The three scoundrels did not consider what cares and troubles arose from their dealings to the hard-working, honest manufacturers. They felt no pangs of conscience if other people were ruined by their frauds, and they thought still less of 'Christian neighbourly love,' when they delivered coolly their victims to beggary. And towards such people I shall act with 'Christian neighbourly love,' that they may go on with their doings!

The case created at the time it happened, that is about ten years ago, considerable sensation, and many papers reported upon the matter. One of these reports in the 'Hamburger Fremdenblatt,' dated Altona, September 7th, 1886, says:

'The matters of the so-called 'black gang,' are gaining quite gigantic dimensions. At a book-keeper in Ottensen, who is already arrested, 30,000 marks in cash were seized. At present the following is ascertained: A merchant, named Listmann, from Mecklenburg, established at the end of last year a business as commission-agent in Naples, and engaged his two brothers-in-law, Ernest and Arfest Schreck as travellers. These three persons acted in concert with a whole gang in England, especially in

London, and the swindlers perpetrated wholesale swindles all over Germany, and caused great losses to manufacturers in Bavaria, Saxony and Austria. Altogether a sum of quite 1,500,000 francs is involved. First a small order was given and promptly paid, and after that the swindle was enacted in great dimensions by giving bills of London firms in payment, who, if existing at all, were no guarantee for the bills being taken up. As soon as the goods were obtained, they were directly sold far under price. When matters commenced to look suspicious, the three relations, Listmann and the two Schrecks, decamped. Ernest Schreck went to London, Arfest Schreck came to this town, and secured a place as clerk at the firm of Bauermeister & Jantzen at Ottensen, with a salary of 75 marks (£3 15s.) a month. There he was discovered and arrested, and at his lodgings were not only found the letters which disclosed the whole swindle, but the clues for the discovery of the other two fugitive men, and 30,000 marks in cash. Italian and English police-officers are already on their way to arrest the fugitives. The Schreck who is detained here in prison, intended to emigrate to America (where Listmann had gone), and 13 large boxes and travelling trunks filled with goods were seized. In the course of these days further 67,000 marks were discovered and seized, which Schreck had deposited at the 'Hamburg Vereinsbank.' Schreck will be brought now in the custody of the Police-inspector to Bautzen, where the judicial inquiry is taking place, as the greatest number of the victims are living in Saxony.'

On the strength of inquiries I made in this matter at the just-mentioned inspector of Police, Mr. Rüschel, at the Vereinsbank in Hamburg, the German Consulate in Naples, the Public Prosecutor at Bautzen, and all the firms who had been swindled by these knights of industry, I can say beforehand that the statements of the Hamburg paper are correct in principle. A few minor errors will be rectified, when the depositions of the proceedings are given. But before proceeding further, I shall quote, for the better understanding of the matter, another newspaper report, from the Neapolitan 'Il Commercio.' I mentioned already that Ernest Schreck was trading at a time as 'Geremiah & Schreck' in Naples. I must now add in explanation, that in this business Ernest Schreck was the principal; Arfest Schreck acted as book-keeper; and Listmann as traveller. When this firm came to a premature end, after having come to arrangements with the creditors, who received hardly anything, the new firm of Listmann was established, and the parts changed. Now Listmann advanced to the position of principal, Ernest Schreck contented himself with the place of book-keeper, and Arfest Schreck became traveller. The name of the new firm was Louis Listmann; its career was short and 'brilliant.' After a few months it 'died out,' and 'Il Commercio' dedicates to this 'great house' the following appropriate necrolog.

THE BLACK GANG.*

'I directed public attention already to a certain moral disease which is affecting our market in a very serious manner. I spoke of the dishonesty raised to the height of a principle by so-called commercial representatives, and of the want of penetration on the part of the firms they are representing. I regret to be able to prove to-day my assertion by some examples, but to give truth its due, I must state, and I do so with pleasure, that the principal part of these swindlers flock into our town from foreign parts like smuggled goods. This time we have to deal with a regularly organized gang, a gang of intelligent rogues, having a chief and a staff and a carefully preconcerted plan, that is put into execution to its fullest extent by using the names of well-known and highly respected firms. Large quantities of goods are thus obtained by fraud, forged bills put into circulation, letters of advice of forwarding agents intercepted, and finally the goods sold 60 per cent. under their proper value. As leader of this gang appears before our eyes the imposing figure of the German Louis Listmann, one of those strange characters, those inexhaustible intelligences, those extra-ordinary genius, who are possessed of a craving to exercise their faculties on a field of boundless expanse, and who find it the easiest to satisfy their desire, in giving play to their faculties on the marshes of roguery. Next to him we find a certain Chêren (recte Schreck),

* From the 'Giornale di Commercio, Naples, May 26th, 1886.

immortalized in the records of famous bankrupts of Naples, and as third confederate we must not forget to mention a certain Hisninger (the name is, as in the instance of Schreck, given incorrectly, and really is Keisslinger). In these three persons we have the principal elements of that remarkable association, reinforced by a host of bribed custom-house officers, post officials, railway clerks, and even employees of the defrauded firms. To cut it short, it is a question of 800,000 lires (£32,000), of which a number of foreign firms were swindled in the short space of 40 days, and to obtain this result extensive use was made of the names of many highly respected Neapolitan merchants.

'There is, and always was, at such an occasion a great outburst of indignation and execration against these rogues, but there is also a lack of perseverance to secure their punishment, and to make a deterring example. At the beginning all are incensed, the swindlers ought, at least, to be hanged. But this feeling cools down very soon; a more lenient view is taken, if a proposition is made, a composition of 10 or 20 per cent. is accepted, and finally the debtors are rehabilitated. But where is the conscience of honest people? Where are the men who have an understanding for the important social and moral bearing of such matters, who have the courage to speak the truth, openly and plainly, who will unmask these swindlers, and call white white, and black black. In the cowardice of the just roots the courage of the wicked.'

The author of this article has really written my mind. Yes, to call a spate a spate! that is what I am doing. I do not intend to give the 'sledge-drivers' further scope by 'timidity,' but to spoil their game where and whenever I can by out-spoken writing. It would be wrong to cover the past of a sledge-driver by any kind of mantle, except in those exceptional cases where such a Knight of Industry has really broken with his past, turned over a new leaf, and has become an honest man. But it is, to my belief, a good work to warn constantly those who escaped being victimised, and to avenge the poor manufacturers who have lost what they earned by hard and honest work through these modern highway-men, to bring the latter to justice, also to protect the English trade by keeping out of this country stolen goods. No English manufacturer can compete against thieves, who do not pay for their goods, and who, therefore, can sell them at any price.

THE SLEDGE-DRIVERS OF NAPLES AT WORK.

I HAVE made it my task to confront the modern highway-men, because, as I could observe for many years, the manufacturers and exporters never dare to set an example. It is not difficult to understand the reason of this backwardness. In the first instance nobody cares to throw good money after bad, and for the second a business man shuns publicity and does not like to see it proclaimed that he was swindled; it means undermining one's own credit, if such losses are paraded before the public. We have no such regards to take, because we have not to study the advantage of individuals, but the interests of the whole commercial community, and we confess that we do not think of the German trade alone, but also of that of other countries. German trade is losing every year incalculable sums through the doings of the 'sledge-drivers.' But this loss does not concern Germany only; its effects are felt outside the frontiers of the German Empire too. As soon as the 'sledge-driver' has obtained possession of the goods, he disposes of them at any price he can realize, and sells very often at a nominal price only. This has a depressing influence on the market in two directions, as mentioned already: prices are unfairly lowered, and a part of the necessary supply being covered by these swindled goods, the demand draws in.

Looking at England, we are confronted with the fact that German competition is severely felt in many branches of industry, as well as in the export-trade. How is this? Any article may be produced in England in as good a quality as in Germany, and if we consider the carriage and other expenses connected with the exportation, it may be said that most articles can be produced equally as cheap in England as in Germany. But there appears the 'sledge-driver' on the scene, and defrauds the German manufacturer of his goods, to undersell them in England, and against such villainous competition the English manufacturer is, of course, powerless. He has to pay his hands, and he has to pay for the material and all the other costs of production; he cannot sell as cheap as the German sledge-driver is selling the German goods, for which he never pays anything, and English and German manufacturers are suffering thus alike.

It is sad, very sad indeed, that the greatest part of these long-firm swindlers are Germans. For the 'why' of this phenomenon I have no explanation. To a certain extent the cause might be found, perhaps, in the abundance of educated men in Germany, who are not able to find a suitable occupation; to do a common labourer's work they are too lazy, and thus they turn to easy sledge-driving. I hear that my out-spoken language is giving offence to the circles of the sledge-drivers, and that the reproach is raised against me, of discrediting the Germans in England. It is said, I am no German, else I would not do it. These reproaches are really ridiculous. It is true, I am a naturalized British subject, but nothing is further from me than to discredit the Germans in London. I consider it my duty to cut down the remaining swindling-brotherhood in London, in order that the English, whose hospitality the Germans in England are enjoying, can respect the Germans.

It is, therefore, necessary not to confound the Germans with the German swindling-brotherhood, and I raise a protest, in the name of the Germans, that the sledge-drivers consider themselves as belonging to the German colony. They are excluded from German company and from Germany, and they are not accepted as British citizens; they are without home, and their domicile ought to be the tread-mill. The greater the severity of the English law against these people, the greater the rejoicings of the honest Germans. The 'Cologne People's Gazette' has gone with me together to the expense to prove before an English Court of Justice the assertions we made for many years past, and we shall keep up our hostile attitude against the excrescences of commerce, the sledge-drivers, also in future. We expect with confidence to find in this matter the support of the English and German trading communities, and I beg to thank at this occasion all who have helped me with their informations, in one way or the other, directly or indirectly, to establish the truth. In this way only I was enabled to find out the really astounding and sensational matters, to the number of which this chapter also is belonging. We are now engaged with the sledge-drivers of Naples and, without disclosing the names of the victims, I shall follow closely the official documents in my possession.

The goods which the firm Louis Listmann in Naples obtained by their fraudulent manipulations, came, as far as officially established, from thirteen firms. The value is given with 280,434 marks 99 pf., but there is no doubt that the losses sustained by the manufacturers were much larger.

The manner in which Louis Listmann entered into connection with his victims, and how he gained their confidence, is most instructive. We shall just go through the thirteen cases, giving only the initials of the defrauded manufacturers.

1. W.T., a manufacturer of flannels. In December, 1884, Louis Listmann wrote from Naples to W.T., offering himself as agent for Italy, and giving some references in Germany. W.T. was induced to appoint him his sole agent for Italy. All business transactions, the correspondence and invoices, it was agreed upon, were to pass through the hands of Listmann, and he was to receive a commission of 3 per cent. of all transactions.

But, instead of transcribing the orders, and to give the names of the customers, Listmann ordered 400 pieces of flannel, to be delivered at the end of July, 1885, in his own name, and explained, he would first see how the firm kept the time of delivery before giving the names of the customers.

Soon after this order, Listmann induced W.T. to deliver 600 instead of 400 pieces. But W.T. was not able to deliver the whole lot at the appointed time, and an arrangement was come to, according to which W.T. supplied 250 pieces. Listmann acknowledged receipt of goods, but commenced at the same time a correspondence, complaining about the quality, and raising other objections. This exchange of letters lasted some months and resulted in Listmann obtaining a reduction of the invoiced price. But nothing was paid. Finally W.T. asked to settle the matter with a four months' acceptance. Listmann declared in his answer, 'it was an impudence to ask for payment at all for such goods,' but he condescended to permit the manufacturer to draw on him three bills at the dates of April 15th, 30th, and May 31st, 1886. No other settlement being obtainable, W.T. did so, but the bills were not taken up. All the letters referring to this matter are in the handwriting of Louis Listmann and Ernést Schreck, and the latter made it a practice to sign all letters in a disguised handwriting, and writing the body of the letters in his proper hand, a manœuvre employed also in the case of other firms, and evidently to the purpose to make the people believe that the firm of Louis Listmann was employing a large staff. The result of the connection with Louis Listmann was for W.T. a loss of 9,256 marks. Strange to say, this manufacturer was done by Lehnert too, in 1894-95. W.T. lost £70, which Lehnert obtained by false pretences. This transaction was started by Opitz, when he was on Schreck's behalf in Germany, introducing himself as L. Lehnert, on January 7th, 1894.

---

2. T.B. is a manufacturer of cotton coatings and trouserings. He also entrusted Louis Listmann, in 1885, with the sale of his manufactures in Italy. On the 15th of December Listmann gave an order for 120 pieces of trouserings for the firm of Giovanni Malatesta in Naples, to be delivered at the end of January, 1886. When the goods were being manufactured, Listmann wrote he had come to certain arrangements with his forwarding agent, Mr. Francesco Parisi, in Trieste, who made such advantageous terms that all the goods had to be sent to him for further forwarding. The invoice too should be sent to him (Listmann), that he may obtain from Malatesta the promised acceptances, which he would get discounted, and this would enable him to send T.B. cash by return.

On the part of the manufacturer everything was done in accordance with these instructions, but Listmann failed to comply with his promises. A prolonged correspondence ensued, with the result that T.B. received on the 7th of May three remittances of £75, £75, and £74 6s., payable in London on the 31st of May. The bills were accepted by 'Cory & Leo' in New York, and endorsed by 'W. Moll' of Hull. The bills had hardly reached the manufacturer, when he received a letter from the solicitor Dr. Wex in Hamburg, who asked him, in the name of Listmann, to withdraw the bills from circulation, as they would not be taken up. A fresh exchange of letters followed, conducted by Listmann and by Ernest Schreck. Inquiries made disclosed the fact, that the acceptances were bogus bills. Result of the transaction: loss to the manufacturer of 4,855 marks 39 pf.

---

3. J. P. was the third victim of Louis Listmann and his confederates Schreck. J. P. is a cotton-spinner and weaver. He transferred likewise the agency for Italy to Listmann. In the month of December, 1885, J. P. transmitted to Listmann a bill of 350 francs for collection. Listmann did so, but he omitted to deliver the money. About the same time Listmann took over in lieu of payment for J. P. a parcel of goods to the value of 2039 francs from Messrs. Mazzano & Co., and his order was to keep these goods at the disposal of J. P. But Listmann sold these goods, contrary to his instructions, and without informing the owner, and kept the money for himself. Not enough with this, Listmann favoured the manufacturer with an order of Signor Pietro Menegozzi at Bovino for not less than 564 pieces of flannel. Inquiries made by the manufacturer disclosed the fact, that the firm in whose name the order was given, was no 'firm' at all, but a poor servant in the employ of a certain Zorzi. Having received this information, the manufacturer declined to execute the order. In consequence of this Listmann wired: 'Information absolutely wrong, go on working.' This telegram was followed by a letter in which Listmann described Menegozzi as a rich man, and to prove his confidence, Listmann promised to become responsible for the amount of the order against a compensation of 1%, and he added, he took orders from substantial firms only.

J. P. accepted this proposition, and Listmann wrote now to him: 'Please write out the order in my name, that I might invoice the goods to Menegozzi, and he may make payable his acceptances to my order. I should not like Menegozzi to perceive that you were suspicious with regard to his trustworthiness, and this will be avoided, if I forward and invoice the goods to him in the name of my firm.'

In the meantime a further information in regard to Menegozzi had reached the manufacturer, in consequence of which he declined to part with his goods on other terms as cash in advance. Listmann contradicted again the unfavourable report and declared, that he had sufficient credit to discount directly Menegozzi's acceptances, and thus to forward cash to J. P. on receipt of the goods. The unhappy manufacturer was deluded into accepting this proposition and forwarded on the 3rd of February 558 pieces of flannel to Louis Listmann. At the same time he wrote to the latter: 'I could not get a satisfactory information regarding Menegozzi, but I put all my confidence in you, and rely on it that you will fully justify my trust. In accordance with your promise, I expect your remittance in cash directly after the arrival of the goods. The 30,000 yards of flannel reached Naples in safety, but no return was made for them. When the money did not come, J. P. reminded Listmann of his promise. In answer to this refresher of a sometimes weak memory, Listmann wrote he would send remittance in a few days; he explained that a disagreement with Menegozzi caused him to sell the goods to another firm. That was true enough, very likely, but the manufacturer never received a penny for his goods and lost by his connection with Listmann and Schreck 12,042 marks 72 pf.

---

4. The fourth victim was G. H., a glass manufacturer, who had also named Listmann his sole agent for Italy. It is a long story of most artful frauds and swindles as disclosed by the official documents; but we shall just lift a corner of the veil only. When Listmann had got as much goods as he possibly could obtain, he sent a set of ten acceptances to G. H., all made payable to the order of Listmann, and domiciled at the Banca Nazionale at Bari, Salerno, Caserta and Leno. The whole of these remittances came back protested, with a bill of costs amounting to about £16.

Listmann, being informed of this little occurrence, somehow 'explained away' this 'unexpected little mishap,' and consoled the manufacturer with another set of ten acceptances, ranging from 700 to 1000 francs, and bearing as acceptors the nice-sounding names of

Luigi Langirosi, Ludovico Guerri, Luigi di Domenico, Frederico Asio, Eugenio Parletti, Michelo Zottola, Marabim Giso, Emilio Curci, Leopoldo Leposi, Santorio Genaro. All the bills fell due in June and July. Listmann prolonged thus the settlement for another two months, and *après nous le déluge!*

It is needless to say that all the bills were again absolutely worthless. But the experiences of the Notary who protested them, were interesting. Strange places that where the bills were domiciled! The lowest quarters of the town had to be visited, narrow streets climbed, where no carriage could enter. One of the domiciles was a church *(Santa Maria Merconiolia)*, another was a cellar, a third a watchman's box, the remainder low taps, and actually notorious resorts of *banditti!* Half of the acceptors could not be found at all; of the remainder, one was a cook out of work, who did not know Listmann at all, another a lad of seventeen, a notorious good-for-nothing, a third a real and genuine Neapolitan *lazzaroni*. All the bills were signed for a small consideration, and it is needless to say that not one of them was taken up.

In this case too the greater part of the business letters of the firm of Listmann was written by Ernest Schreck, and signed by him in a disguised hand by procuration. G. H. had made inquiries about Ernest Schreck, and the informations he received gave Schreck a very bad character. In the summer of 1885, Listmann visited the manufacturer personally, and G. H. told him in plain language that it did not inspire great confidence to a firm, if its procurist was a notorious swindler, and if such a character was employed at all. Listmann assured G. H., that he had not known the career of Schreck at the time he engaged him, but that in consequence of certain things which had come to his knowledge, he had dismissed the man, and severed every connection with him; a statement which was proved untrue, as letters and the endorsement of the bills received later on by G. H. from Listmann were in Schreck's handwriting. The total loss in this case amounted to 14,565 marks 49 pf.

---

5. G. F., a handkerchief-weaver, became the fifth victim. As all the preceding manufacturers, he named Listmann his agent for

Italy, and was soon favoured with sample-orders, which were executed to the 'perfect satisfaction of the Italian firms,' and led to some considerable orders. The manufacturer, however, had made some inquiries, and this led to a refusal on his part to execute, unless some more satisfactory references were given. A protracted correspondence ensued, conducted on the part of the swindlers by Ernest Schreck; the manufacturer, however, had made some more inquiries, and these induced him to declare finally, that he would only send the goods for 'cash in advance.' Now the head of the great Naples firm, Mr. Louis Listmann, stepped in personally, and told the manufacturer his style of writing and his conditions might do for Polish Jews, but a respectable firm could not accept such disgraceful terms. The righteous indignation of this most respectable firm of Listmann impressed the manager to such a degree, that he forwarded the goods without delay. Listmann sold them directly far below the invoiced price, never paying the manufacturer a single penny.

---

6. The woollen manufacturer, Mr. F. F., was induced to follow the example of other firms, and to appoint Listmann his agent for Italy. Mr. F. F., however, seemed a little more cautious and less confident, and Listmann, perceiving this, thought it advisable to give at first a few sample orders and pay for them in cash, calculating quite correctly that this would alay the distrust of his new customer. As soon as he felt firm ground under his feet, he wrote to the manufacturer on the 23rd December, 1885, in way of a Christmas-present, that he had succeeded to secure for him the custom of 20 firms, who gave a small trial-order of 400 dozen shawls with fringes (lively patterns). For the present, however, the firms did not want to enter for this small trial orders into direct communication with the manufacturer, but wished to receive the goods from the agent for cash on delivery. For this reason, Listmann explained, he gave a cumulative order, and asked for careful execution, as a tremendous sale might be secured. The customers paying cash, Listmann was pleased, as he wrote, to be able to let the manufacturer have a remittance on Berlin or Frankfurt after receipt of goods. The discount demanded by Listmann for this 'cash transaction' was rather high, and the manufacturer declared

he could not accept the terms, and declined to execute the order. A correspondence ensued and magnanimous Listmann declared 'he would waive for once his commission, in order to secure the customers.' That settled the matter. The manufacturer sent the goods, Listmann acknowledged the receipt, and said cheque would follow within a few days. Days and weeks and months and years rolled by, but the promised cheque never followed—an awful slow travelling, if we consider that since then ten years have passed. Whether Mr. F. F. still expects to get his 7755 marks 73 pf. for his 'lively patterned' shawls, we do not want to decide.

---

7. Another firm represented in Italy by Listmann were A. & P. These people were also too cautious for the liking of the Neapolitan sledge-drivers, but not cautious enough for their artfulness. When Listmann gave his first large order, they had made already inquiries, which turned out far from satisfactory, and they wrote accordingly an explanatory letter to Listmann, dwelling on their 'principles in business,' which led to the demand of 'cover on delivery.' Listmann answered with an equally long and apparently straightforward letter, saying:

'To your principles and your open language no exception can be taken. Your views are also my views, and I shall give you an open and honest answer. I am not a rich man, but, for my circumstances, fairly well situated. My last balance-sheet closed with 52,000 francs in cash on the right side of the ledger, and I hope that the next balancing at the close of 1886 will prove still more satisfactory. At present I have advanced 40,000 francs for customs-dues, which I shall not receive back before the Leipsic Easter-market, but it is a nice round sum for an agent to advance. I have a number of friends who are always willing to discount for me good bills from my customers with my indorsement, and often too without it. This enables me to oblige my friends in foreign parts with cash instead of acceptances, if they desire it. To give you encouragement and to facilitate to you the business, I offered you this way of settlement, for—candour for candour—I made inquiries about you too, and from the enclosed information you will see, that I knew you were beginners and I, as experienced man of business, know what this means. You will understand that a cautious man of business does not make promises which he is not able to keep. . . . I sold a lot of your velvets after samples, and I can discount all the acceptances which I receive in exchange from my customers. This enables me to promise to you, for certain, cheque within 30 days after receipt of goods.'

This letter, as most of the correspondence with this firm. was written by Ernest Schreck, and signed in a disguised handwriting in his name *per procura*, as he personated the procurator in the intercourse with foreign parts. But A. & P. were cautious; they were not deceived by the bragging missile of Signor Ernest Schreck, and another similar letter failed also to produce the effect the swindlers desired. Now Listmann entered personally into the action. He wrote with his own hand 'a private letter' to the firm, bragged again a good deal, but gave as references two well-accredited German manufacturers, who played in the whole affair *a very strange part* indeed, and one of whom is to this day in the same *very strange* relationship to Schreck in his present capacity as London 'City merchant.' In consequence of the references given by these two firms, A. & P. decided on executing half the order, and became thus losers to the tune of 4734 marks 12 pf.

---

8. In this case we find Listmann again the sole agent for J. G. P., a cotton manufacturer. The first act ot the 'honest agent' was to represent to the manufacturer some of his former customers as 'quite rotten,' and thus to get hold of some small parcels designated for them, which Listmann pretended to 'keep in stock,' but actually sold to his own profit for 1366 francs 40 c., of which J. G. P. never saw a farthing. Listmann obtained further, by fraudulent pretences, from the same manufacturer, 17 parcels of goods, collected and embezzled moneys belonging to the firm, and caused to J. G. P. quite a disastrous loss of 58,784 marks 96 pf. The correspondence in this case was conducted throughout by Ernest Schreck.

---

9. C. G. H. is a manufacturer of dress materials, and he also entrusted to Listmann the sale of articles for Italy. After the fashion followed in the preceding cases, 'Louis' acted also

against this new victim of his and his confederates. Not trusting to give an order in his own name, he transmitted to the manufacturer an order purporting to come from the old established firm of Giovanni Malatesta, but declared, the firm had stipulated to get the goods duty-free, and to arrange matters with the Custom-house, Listmann directed the goods and the invoice to be forwarded to him for delivery to Malatesta. These instructions were obeyed, and Listmann in exchange sent remittances on London, accepted by 'Robert Morrison, Manchester,' and 'Jameson, Young & Co., Leith,' all payable at the end of May, 1886. These bills proved fictitious, and the total loss of the firm amounted to 1257 marks 48 pf. Ernest Schreck was also in this case the able correspondent.

---

10. In the case of S. & Co., manufacturers of dress materials, Listmann used again the name of the firm Malatesta, and succeeded to swindle the manufacturers of goods to the value of 9704 marks 34 pf.

---

11. Another manufacturer of dress materials, Fr. H., appointed also Listmann as his sole agent. Some small orders were paid promptly, and this made Fr. H. sufficiently confident to execute a large order, amounting to 13,479 marks, 60 pf., for which Listmann sent him London acceptances, payable, as the other bills were, with which he pacified his customers, at the end of May or beginning of June, 1886. It need not be mentioned that all these bills turned out fictitious, and that the manufacturer lost the whole of his claim.

---

12 & 13. The last two victims were a Bohemian manufacturer, who lost 28,000 francs, and a Bavarian firm, who were dropped in for 102,000 francs.

Of these 13 creditors only, the losses could be ascertained; but, no doubt, there were many other manufacturers who had been swindled and who, seeing that there was no chance of recovering anything, did not come forward, and kept their loss quiet.

But now the month of May, 1886, had dawned upon the world; the bills, distributed in such profusion, were soon due, and the volcanic ground of Naples became too hot for the beautiful

German trefoil, but especially for the two principals, Louis Listmann and Ernest Schreck. Arfest Schreck, who was 'travelling,' was recalled by wire, and after a serious consultation of war, Arfest undertook to 'face it,' for a time, in Naples still, to sell out what there was left, and to cash some bills. But 'Louis' and 'Ernesto' fled. *Vede Napoli è poi mori!* They had seen beautiful Naples, but they did not feel disposed to die for that. They bid the town good-bye for ever—it had seen too much of them—and escaped in time, duly warned by persons 'who knew' the fate that was waiting for them in Italy. Ernest Schreck went to London, and Listmann to Fernambuco; from thence he fled to Buenos Ayres, and fled again, his whereabouts remaining unknown for many years. But I strongly suspect that the gentleman could have been met in 1894 at the head-quarters of German sledge-drivers in London during a meteoric, short, and brilliant career, and that he gathered there new laurels and another small fortune in the guise of the *flying Dutchman*, adding new glory to his fame.

Towards the middle of May, 1886, the swindled manufacturers received the first intimation that 'something was wrong,' by a notification proceeding from a Hamburg solicitor, inviting them to attend a meeting of creditors of the firm of Louis Listmann of Naples, on Sunday, May 23rd, at Nuremberg, when propositions would be made with a view of arriving at an arrangement. The creditors appeared to a man, but who did not come was the debtor, the Schrecks, and the solicitor who had called the meeting together. By this means the swindlers had gained the time required, to bring themselves and their booty in safety. But to Arfest Schreck this did not prove of great avail, for he was soon afterwards captured, and leisure was given him in a German prison for two years, to reflect on his career in sunny Italy. Listmann and Ernest Schreck were indicted criminally by the public prosecutor of Naples and a warrant issued against them, unfortunately without avail.

The papers seized on Arfest Schreck proved clearly the conspiracy of the three criminals, and disproved Ernest Schreck's assertion, that he was no party to the frauds committed by the firm of Listmann, for an agreement, dated April the 24th, 1885, was found, in which the lion's share of the profits of the firm Listmann were secured to the leading spirit, Ernest Schreck.

At the 'dissolution of the partnership' he received in cash and cheques 67,407 francs 12c. and bills to the value of 46,597 francs 72c., Listmann, however, drew altogether 48,319 francs only of the disponible proceeds of the robbery. Although Listmann and Schreck had entered into an agreement, according to which Listmann had a loan of about 80,000 francs from E. Schreck, it must be understood that this could not be a *bona fide* transaction, because E. Schreck had been less than two years before a bankrupt. Besides, the letters passed between Messrs. Schreck showed the conspiracy between the lot.

Arfest Schreck acted finally as receiver of the stolen property. There were difficulties in the way of disposing of the acceptances in possession of the 'firm' at the time when it closed its career in Naples, and when the two principals had fled. Arfest soon followed their example and went to Germany. With the ultimate design in view to discount the cheques and acceptances, he repaired to Hamburg, and procured a place as clerk at a banking firm in Altona with the salary of 75/- a month. But the salary was of no consideration, the principle thing was the disposal of the bills, of which Listmann had handed to him 60,000 francs in Naples, and sent him other 36,000 francs in 39 acceptances from Rotterdam, at the eve of his departure to South America. Ernest Schreck forwarded to Arfest from London bills to the value of 37,000 lires, and later on other 16 bills of an unknown amount. It is stating but a well-known fact, that cash transactions are exceptions in the Italian trade; three and six-months' bills are the usual terms, and the firm of Listmann had to sell at the same conditions. This explains the great amount of bills in their possession when the crash came, the disposal of which became rather difficult and risky under the particular circumstances of the case. These difficulties were now removed to a great extent by Arfest's action, who managed in his position as a banking clerk, with the help of a third person, to get the bills successively discounted through a leading banking firm in Altona.

During this time Arfest kept up a brisk exchange of letters with his brother Ernest in London, and with his brother-in-law Listmann in America, the correspondence with the latter being conducted through some intermediaries and under assumed names. All the letters referred almost exclusively to the realization of the paper-property of the firm. The contents of this correspondence are most interesting, and significant abbreviations are used. So the defrauded creditors are simply called 'the dogs,' and very complimentary epithets are conferred to other hostile parties. Thus Ernest Schreck writes from London to Arfest on the 9th of July, 1886 :

'I hope you will take every precaution that they do not take you by surprise.. You may take it for granted that S. & Co. and their confederates (that means the creditors) will try to do you some harm. I know you are watched, and you are no match for such artful rogues as these detectives are. To Listmann, who is declared a bankrupt, do not make for the present any remittance, else proceedings could be taken against you, because you are initiated in the whole matter.'

In answer to this letter, Arfest Schreck wrote to Ernest Schreck :

'I do not think that the dogs have come across the scent. But it is not impossible, and an early change of air will do me good. I hope you will not object to my rather pressing terms with regard to the discounting of the bills, but you must not forget that I obeyed your call to come to Naples without delay, and travelled day and night to come there, knowing the whole time *what storm was brewing.*'

About the same time Arfest Schreck received a letter from Listmann, dated Fernambuco, July the 14th, asking for some remittances, and instructing Arfest to enquire whether there was any danger for him in Fernambuco, and if so, to cable to him—delightful humour, that does not leave the real sledge-driver even in critical moments !—the one word only, '*asino*' (donkey) ! Arfest made inquiries, and the information he received caused him to wire the 'donkey' over to Fernambuco and the '*asino*' put Listmann to immediate flight to Buenos Ayres, from whence he wrote to Arfest, asking him to forward to him the money for the discounted bills which had fallen to his share.

On the 4th of August Ernest Schreck sent from London a bill of 5,083 lires 70 c., accepted by G. Malatesta di Gennaro in Naples, to Arfest Schreck, with instructions, 'to let this bill pass through the same hands as the last one of 8,000 francs, case something went wrong, one person only could bring an a in which the name of Schreck would not appear, otherwise ' dogs' would make use of it.'

A few days later he writes to his dear brother again :

'Now with regard to the books, I have considered the matter. I do not want to mix Papa up with my matters, and I do not want to have anything more to do with Germany, and keeping my money there after you have left. It is not convenient to me, and besides too dangerous. As matters stand at present, I prefer to liquidate everything, and to deposit my money here with B. J. & Co., and the L. & C. Bkg. Co. Be therefore kind enough to withdraw the money at the savings-bank as soon as possible, and to send me cheques for it.'

Arfest gave at once notice of withdrawal, but he commenced now to claim his 'proper share ;' he refused repeatedly to transmit the money for bills he got discounted, and declared that if his claim was not considered, he would help himself to his share by a 'Turkish forced loan.' In answer Ernest Schreck wrote to him from London the following significant and interesting letter under the date of 19th of July :

'Represent Listmann the matter as I advise you, in a logical manner, and if he consents to let you have from the bills discounted up to December 30,000 marks, and if you will act towards me as a brother, I shall do my part and put this matter in order. The money, too, shall not be paid over to me until I furnish you with a legal, definite arrangement come to at Naples. Otherwise let Listmann keep his money, for things half done are not worth these sacrifices ; but a clean matter is worth anything, and he understands this, for he would keep then 35,000 marks in cash, after deduction of all expenses, and when he can move freely again, he can start anything and anywhere, and recover easy enough what he is sacrificing now.'

The Schrecks thought they had the cat in the bag already ; but 'man proposes and the Lord disposes,' and misfortune is often swift-footed. Ernest Schreck's suspicion was well-founded, 'the dogs' had found the scent of Arfest Schreck, and at the very moment when he thought of the 'change of air,' and had everything prepared to start for South America, he was arrested. In his possession were found nearly £700 in sovereigns, German gold coins and Bank of England notes, four saving-books representing a deposit of nearly £3,000; his pass-book at Messrs. Baurmeister & Jansen, in Ottensen, showing a balance to his credit of 19,585 marks, and a large number of acceptances from Italian firms. Besides 12 large boxes, filled with valuable goods of different kinds, were ready for shipping and destined to 'take a change of air' with Arfest Schreck, who intended to start business in the more congenial clime of the other hemisphere.

All the property was seized and transferred with the prisoner to the criminal court at Bautzen, where Arfest Schreck found free board and lodging in jail for two years.

Now a law-suit of a very peculiar character was instituted, and fought on both sides with great determination for the possession of the property seized. The creditors of Louis Listmann thought they were entitled to recover the seized proceeds from the robberies to which they had fallen victims, and concurrently with the pending criminal proceedings against Listmann and the two Schrecks, they joined in a civil action against the three swindlers. The criminal action failed, because the two principal offenders, Listmann and Ernest Schreck, kept successfully in hiding. Arfest Schreck became in prison mentally diseased, and was liberated after two years' detention. He left directly for England, and since that time (1888), nothing was done more in the matter, as the three criminals never set a foot on German soil again, and the German manufacturers were loth to prosecute. If thirteen English manufacturers had been defrauded in such a shameful manner, they certainly would have brought back the three brothers-in-law, and this could have been done easily enough, if the means required for this purpose had been forthcoming. Unfortunately, the Continental manufacturers are too cheese-sparing in such matters; they do not mind to overload the sledge-drivers with their goods, but if they are cheated, and the matter has to be fought out, their invariable principle is not to throw good money after bad, and to let the swindlers go out scot-free. And so it was in this case too. Nobody was willing to make a sacrifice and to risk anything to bring the scoundrels to justice. Worse still!

To save something at least, they came to an arrangement with the swindlers, and contented themselves with 7,000 marks of the seized moneys, leaving the lion's share to the two Schrecks, and withdrawing the action brought against the latter. How true did the Italian paper, 'Il Commercio' say in the article quoted:

'Where is the conscience of honest people? Where are the men who have an understanding for the important social and moral bearing of such matters? Who have the courage to speak the truth openly and plainly, who will unmask these swindlers, and call white white; and black black? In the cowardice of the just roots the courage of the wicked.

"ERNESTO" IN LONDON.

THE reader will ask: What became of these three gentlemen? Have these people reformed, after their lucky escape from the clutches of the law at the skin of their teeth? Have they turned over a new leaf in the new country? Well, if they had done so, these lines would have never been written. It would be wrong on my part to call up the ghosts of times passed. Besides, the people, as I must admit, are extremely clever, and I regret sincerely to have to proceed against them in this manner. But shall I, and can I have regard for them? Had they any regard for their victims? Must I not say to myself: what they have done yesterday to John, they will do to-morrow to Peter. Am I not morally bound to warn fellow-men against these dangerous and heartless people?

First of all I refer once more to the chapter 'More about the Sledge-drivers.' We find there Ernest Schreck a constant visitor at Lothar Lehnert's. This friendship certainly did not spring up till after the year 1889, for in that year Lehnert gave still about Schreck an information which was far from creditable and for which, in reproducing it, I decline to take the responsibility. Lehnert wrote under February 10th, 1889, about Henry Payne & Co., 17, Coleman-street, E.C., under which firm Schreck had established himself at the given address, as follows:

'This firm is established for about 8 months and deals wholesale in ladies' mantles, stuffs and hosiery. Thanks to the circumstances that German manufacturers are not subscribers to enquiry-offices, and obtain their reports from superficially informed English offices, the firm makes a satisfactory business. The name of the firm is: fictitious. The real name of the proprietor is Schreck, alias Stanley, alias Brown. A few years hence he bolted from here with a barmaid, and by mistake took some £5000 of other people's money with him. He was arrested, tried, and sentenced to two year's penal servitude. He is an arch-swindler, buys only carriage-paid on credit, and it cannot be warned against him with sufficient strength. Now the bandits have opened an office too at Aldersgate-street.'

I repeat once more, I do not take any responsibility for the correctness of Lehnert's information. Very likely he had heard something of Ernest Schreck's past, but did not know the real facts of the case, and made 'a stew' of it, which he sent out for a shilling. This information becomes, however, most significant if we compare it with another information given by the same Mr. Lehnert about the same Mr. Schreck, alias Henry Payne & Co., some twelve months later. On March 19th, 1891, Lehnert writes, in answer to an enquiry, about H. Payne & Co.:

'This firm is established since 1886, and trades as cloth merchants and commission agents at 17, Coleman-street, and mantle manufacturers at 17, Distaff-lane. Henry Payne is an old and experienced cloth-traveller, has excellent connections with the customers, and is travelling nearly the whole year round. The other proprietor, E. Schreck, is also an excellent man of business. The firm has a fine trade and is developing in a satisfactory manner. The people are respectable and diligent, have a working capital of £4000, are paying regularly, and are considered good for the credit of £400 they are asking for. They have their banking-account at the Central Bank.'

What was the cause of this remarkable change in the valuation of the firm H. Payne & Co. on the part of Mr. Lehnert? Very strange indeed! But an explanation may be found in the current account, delivered by Mr. Lehnert to the firm of H. Payne & Co. at the close of the second quarter 1891, where the latter is debited with the following items:

30/3/91	To agency S.W.		£7	10	0
Do.	do. Kl.		10	0	0
Do.	do. D.		10	0	0
Do.	do. R.		5	0	0
10/6/91	To goods *conto meta*		50	0	0
Do.	To commission D. G.—Sch. ...		20	0	0

I abstain purposely from giving the names, because that might be disagreeable to those who appointed at that time Schreck, respectively H. Payne & Co., their agent at the recommendation of Lehnert. I also abstain from publishing further accounts between the two 'firms.' But the account given discloses quite enough of the relations between the two honest men, and it is further illustrated by the 'confidential' correspondence exchanged between Lehnert and continental manufacturers. Thus, for example, Lehnert writes on October 15th to a German firm:

'I have succeeded already to secure for you an excellent agent in the person of the proprietor of the firm of H. Payne & Co., 17, Coleman-street, E.C. Should you come to London, please bring with you a complete sample-collection, that Payne may visit with you the customers and hear personally what they demand.'

This letter is written by Opitz and signed by him with L. Lehnert.

On the 3rd of January, 1894, Lehnert informed the same firm that he would arrive on the 7th of the same month in Hof in Bavaria, and that he should like to see there the recipient of his letter. As Opitz had to admit under cross-examination in the police-court at Clerkenwell, he travelled at this occasion under the name of Mr. Lehnert to Hof, where he sojourned at the hotel Prince Regent, personating this gentleman. He left London on the 4th, and arrived on the 6th of January in Hof. On the 8th already he called as 'Mr. Lehnert' at a manufacturer's in Asch in Bohemia, said he was on a business-tour and thought he would make use of the opportunity, and call personally to recommend the services of his office, if occasion should arise. Now, the fact is, that Lehnert and Opitz knew very well that *there was an occasion!* For this manufacturer had to proceed against a London agent of his, who did not pay over the moneys he had collected and had acted otherwise incorrectly, so that he stood in danger of criminal proceedings being taken against him. This matter was the real cause of 'Mr. Lehnert's' call, yea of his voyage, for this defaulting agent was no one else but H. Payne & Co., that is, his friend Ernest Schreck, and he had to be shielded, and the manufacturer cheated of as much of his money as possible. Exactly as the three confederates had conjectured, the manufacturer fell in the trap set to him. He considered it quite a happy chance that Mr. Lehnert called, and informed the latter confidentially of the matter against H. Payne & Co. It need not be said that 'Mr. Lehnert' at once offered his services. What followed further we shall read in the following pages. Let us hear what the defrauded and cheated manufacturer says himself:

'In Spring, 1891, my predecessor in business was persuaded by the pressing recommendations and representations of a small manufacturer of our town, Mr. X., to engage H. Payne & Co. in London as his agent. My predecessor had actually no mind to appoint there a representative, and to open connections with the English market, but he gave way to the constant pressure and even entreaties of Mr. X., who acted as mediator in this matter, and engaged H. Payne & Co. as his representatives. When I took over the business in 1891, I was also persuaded by Mr. X. to continue the newly created relations with Payne & Co., and far too late it came to my knowledge, that Payne was identical with Schreck, and that X. was an old friend of his. Payne & Co. gave me occasionally small orders which were always promptly regulated. Up to the end of 1892 the business kept within these small limits, and I did nothing to push it. Then came through Payne & Co. a large order for a well-known Huddersfield firm, which was executed and the goods were delivered in April. My invoice amounted to £380 10s. 8d., and the terms were cash within 30 days, with 5% discount. The account was not paid. I sent repeatedly manufacturer's statement directly to the Huddersfield firm, and to Payne for transmission to them, but without result, *i.e.*, no notice was taken of my demands.

'Finally I wrote on the 18th of December an energetic letter directly to the Huddersfield firm, and I was, of course, greatly surprised when they informed me that the amount had been paid already on the 11th September to Messrs. H. Payne & Co. I expressed to Payne my surprise at such irregularity, and he forwarded now to me a settling account, which I could not accept. This impudent and quite arbitrary account closed with a balance of £325 11s. 3d. in my favour, for which amount Payne enclosed cheque.

'I intended to draw a statement, and for this reason

did not acknowledge receipt of cheque, which I paid in at my bank, who informed me after a few days, that the cheque had not been paid.

'Now happened the most remarkable in the whole matter. Some months ago I had received repeatedly prospectus and circulars from the enquiry office of L. Lehnert. At the time when the cheque came back from London I received a visit from Mr. Lehnert, who came to recommend his office personally. Not being aware then of the organisation of the gang of swindlers, I thought the visit of Mr. Lehnert a lucky coincidence, and I did not hesitate to inform him of what had happened with Payne. Lehnert offered me his services in the matter, which I, however, did not accept for the moment, thinking that I could arrange the matter myself. I accordingly wrote to Payne & Co., and gave instructions to my bank to present the cheque once more; this was done with no other result than the first time, Payne & Co. did not pay.

'In the meantime I had made inquiries about Lehnert at the references given, and the answers being fairly satisfactory, I put the matter into his hands on the 10th of January, 1894. I had hardly done so, when I received an information about Lehnert, which very likely would have prompted me not to entrust him with the matter. I became suspicious and urged Lehnert to do something in the matter, and on the 22nd of February he informed me that he had succeeded to obtain from H. Payne & Co. a payment on account, which he transmitted to me after deducting a considerable part as his collecting-fee. From this time Lehnert wrote to me only when I reminded him of the matter in an energetic manner. When I found that he was not doing anything in the matter, I demanded the return of the cheque and the other documents. But he always knew how to evade this, and I became daily more and more convinced that he did not act honestly. In this conviction I was confirmed by his reluctance to bring an action against H. Payne and Co. All my demands in this direction were fruitless, and when I threatened to put the matter into the hands of a solicitor, he advised me to come to an arrangement with H. Payne & Co., and offered me in full settlement of my claim £100. I refused this offer, and demanded once more most energetically the return of the cheque, with which demand he finally complied in September, 1894. In the meantime, the articles about the 'Sledge-drivers' had appeared in the 'Cologne People's Gazette,' which made me conscious at once to what miserable and swindling devices I, with many others, had fallen a victim. I understood now the 'accidental' visit of Mr. Lehnert, and many other things which I could not explain to myself before.'

I may remark here at once that the manufacturer X., who induced the writer of the preceding letter and his predecessor in business to appoint 'H. Payne & Co.' as their agent, was an intimate friend of Schreck, and was one of his and Listmann's references at the time of their Neapolitan campaign.

From Lehnert's letters in this matter a few short extracts only. Directly at the return from his flying visit to Germany, Opitz wrote on the 11th January, 1894, to the manufacturer in the name of Lehnert: 'Referring to our conversation at my visit, I beg to inform you that I have just returned to London again. I find that your order for collecting your claim at H. Payne & Co.'s has not arrived yet. During my absence, however, some inquiries regarding H. P. & Co. have come to hand, and I have made careful inquiries into the position of the firm.' On the 20th of March Opitz-Lehnert writes again: 'Of course I could have brought an action against H. Payne & Co., but I thought it better for your interests to wait with it, because, under present circumstances, I do not think it would lead to any result, and believe that it is better for you to give the people a little more time, and try to get further payments on account, to such an extent and as often as possible.'

From this and other material referring to H. Payne & Co., it is clearly established, that Lehnert knew perfectly well the real character of Ernest Schreck. In spite of this, he did not hesitate to call, in the matter of B. Arnold & Co., the firm of H. Payne & Co. a most respectable one, and he did so during the time laying between Opitz's flying visit to Asch and the date of the last quoted letter. Lehnert was quite aware who had given 'B. Arnold & Co.' a reference, when he engaged the office at Guildhall-chambers, and he knew too who had introduced B. Arnold & Co. at the bank. He was perfectly informed that no one else but Ernest Schreck, as H. Payne & Co., had given these references, that Ernest Schreck was personally present, when this 'Arnold,' whom Lehnert later on 'identified' as de Groot, took the office; that Schreck had personally introduced this 'Arnold' at the bank, and that these two men were constantly in each other's company. What value is to be put on the references given by H. Payne & Co., may be safely left to the judgment of those concerned. A warning is needless.

Lehnert simply adjusted his informations to the requirements of his confederates. The reader is just asked to compare the last-quoted of Lehnert's information about H. Payne & Co. with the following about B. Arnold & Co., given under the 8th of February, 1894, to a customer who had become suspicious about this firm. Lehnert writes:

'Having reported to you about this firm once before, I have very little to add. What I ascertained since then about the firm is the following. About Arnold's own means very little is known in the City, excepted that he opened with *excellent introductions* an account at the City Bank. His account has been kept in perfect order, and the bank knows absolutely nothing to the disadvantage of the firm. In consequence of a great many enquiries which came to my hands lately, I took occasion to call personally at Arnold's, to convince myself with regard to his solvency, and to his ways of settling accounts, and I found that up to the present he has made considerable purchases, if also to smaller amounts only, and that he paid for them regularly within 30 days. B. Arnold says he is settling accounts for larger purchases in accordance with the customs of the Indian trade, and as long as he follows this rule, the execution of his orders amounting to some hundred pounds offers very little or no risk.'

This information is crammed with untrue statements like a tasty christmas-pudding with peel and raisins.

The excellent introductions at the bank reduced themselves to Messrs. H. Payne & Co., recte Ernest Schreck. The statement that the bank 'knows absolutely nothing to the disadvantage of the firm,' is false. Lehnert knew that the City Bank at that time had already closed the account of B. Arnold & Co. Lehnert's oft repeated statement, that he had made personally inquiries at the bank is equally false; he never inquired, as the manager of the bank is willing to confirm at any time. Lehnert's assertion, however, that he saw Arnold personally, is not to be doubted. But it was not his first visit, as he tries to make his customers believe; he was very often transacting business with 'B. Arnold & Co.,' and of what kind, he, Schreck, and 'Arnold,' know best. But if Lehnert asserts that he had convinced himself that 'all purchases were regularly paid within 30 days,' he speaks the untruth again, for at that time 'Arnold' had already defrauded a considerable number of German manufacturers, and many invoices had not been paid.

Having seen how Lehnert and Schreck had performed the sword-dance together from 1889 to 1895, it will be easier to understand the following conspiracy enacted by the two against a German enquiry-office, Messrs. Schmeisser & Co., and a Saxon manufacturer. But I am happy to state, gay 'Lothario' and earnest 'Ernesto' failed in this enterprise.

The conspiracy of the two was the following:

At Lehnert's instance the Saxon firm entrusted to H. Payne & Co. the sale of their goods for some districts of England, London included. Lehnert at this occasion had given the information about H. Payne & Co. which was quoted before, to the Berlin enquiry-office in whose employ he was, and this again had supplied it to the Saxon manufacturer. This occurred at the time when Lehnert debited in his books H. Payne & Co. with different amounts for procuration of agencies, and as among the latter the name of the Saxon firm is mentioned, and £5 put opposite it, I think I am not far wrong in saying that this £5 were the reward for giving the good report about H. Payne & Co. The Saxon manufacturer had at that time no connection with Lehnert's firm; he received the information through the inquiry office in Berlin, and had no idea that Lehnert was their correspondent, and that the information actually emanated from him. The reader, however, will see for himself through the artful conspiracy, when, later on, the swindlers are speaking for themselves in their letters.

First of all I shall reproduce a letter which the Saxon manufacturer addressed to Messrs. Schmeisser & Co. It is dated March the 7th, 1892, and reads as follows:

'In December last Payne wrote to me that the firm of Lang

Brothers in Manchester would buy a large parcel of goods, if I would agree to a certain price. If willing to do so, I should wire to that effect, and forward the goods on the same day, via Flushing. This left me no time to make enquiries; but I did not hesitate to execute the order, as cheque was promised on receipt of goods, and former transactions with or through Payne, about whom I had received first-class references, had gone in perfect order.

'I accordingly dispatched the goods without delay, but enquired at the same time about Lang Brothers at Manchester, and this information was so bad, that I gave immediately instructions to Payne & Co. not to deliver the goods to Lang Brothers, and I was confirmed in this decision as Payne had notified to me that the firm would not pay by cheque after receipt of goods, but by two and three months' bills. At the same time I asked Payne to return to me my sample-collection. Payne's answer from January 11th you will find enclosed. My answer was, that I did not feel disposed to enter into arguments, but that I would bring in an action, if my account was not settled within a fortnight. Since then Payne & Co., and later on their solicitors, have written to me, threatening first with an action, and proposing afterwards to have the matter settled by arbitration.

'It seems to me as if I had fallen in the hands of people whose character renders it not advisable to accept such a proposition. I hope, however, that your influence will prove sufficient to convince these people that it is advisable for them to satisfy my claim. Independent of the case of Lang Brothers, I had at a former occasion another case, regarding Samuel Brown at Manchester. You gave me a very unsatisfactory information about this firm. I refused accordingly to execute an order of Brown's that was sent to me by Payne, and I complied with his request to execute the order only after he had declared himself responsible for the amount. Later on Brown gave another, larger order, but I refused most energetically to execute it. Payne tried to force me by some brutal writing, but I remained firm in my refusal, and four weeks later Brown was a bankrupt.

'These two cases, and the circumstance that Payne & Co. always tried to palm off on me orders for their own account, have ripened my resolution to break off at once my connection with their firm. After what had happened, I think I was perfectly entitled to do so, and to my opinion, no Court of Justice and especially no English Court of Justice would order me to pay damages to Payne.'

Lehnert being at that time the confidential correspondent and agent of the Berlin enquiry-office, the latter sent to him the original letter of the manufacturer, and instructed him to collect the money due from Payne. Now happened an unheard of thing. Lehnert went with the letter of the Saxon manufacturer to Payne & Co., and this 'firm' snatched, as he declared to his employers, the letter from his hand, and used it for the purpose of trying to extort damages up to £5000 from the manufacturer, in threatening him with an action for libel. How it was worked will be seen by the following correspondence.

The first letter comes from Lehnert, and is addressed to the Berlin enquiry-office. He writes under the date of the 7th of April, 1892:

'In consequence of the remarks in your own handwriting, I have taken particular trouble with this matter and have made the most searching enquiries, to save myself all reproaches *à la* Lewin. On the strength of the communications contained in X.'s letter, which I regarded as correct, I 'gave it hot' to Payne & Co., and brought them into such a rage that they were quite beside themselves. I regret of having been misled by such a fine firm as X. are, who have quite misrepresented the facts, and if I had known the truth, I should have proceeded differently. Payne are now decided to bring the matter to a head, and will spare no expenses and troubles to prove to me, respectively to you, that they have the right on their side.

'To speak confidentially, the whole mischief originates from wrong information supplied to you from Manchester. To my regret, I find, for some time already, that you are not favouring me any more with enquiries from the provinces, and the correspondent you are employing has through his want of experience caused a very serious mischief, for Lang are far from being 'rotten', as he says, and I have learned myself from Payne's books, that he sold to them last year goods to the amount of £1670, which were promptly paid,* X. has decidedly placed himself in this matter in a false position. According to English law he has no right to dismiss an agent without notice, without arriving at an arrangement with him beforehand. The law is that, when no special agreement is made, notice must be given from season to season. Payne are accordingly entitled to bring here an action for damages. That X. is living in Germany does not interfere with the matter. In spite of this they can bring an action against him in London, and when the summons has been served on him in Germany, and he does not put in an appearance at the day of the trial, judgment by default for any amount can be obtained against him. It certainly cannot be executed in Germany, but it can be acted upon in England, and X., therefore, could not send any more goods to England, as he might expect to see them seized any moment on the strength of the judgment of the English court. I, therefore, advise him in his own interest not to take the matter too easy, and to come to a decent arrangement with Payne. P. have promised me not to take action until they have heard from me again. Payne are firmly convinced that they are in the right, and it is most advisable to act diplomatically. I for my part must confess, that I would not permit anyone to treat me as they were treated, and this the more, as Payne have always guarded his interests in every regard. When Mistrowski came into difficulties, and X. was engaged with £200—they fought like lions and finally saved him every farthing, when all the other creditors had to content themselves with 33⅓ per cent.

'At any rate, you will be well advised to forward to X. the enclosed newspaper-cutting from the 'Law Times' of March the 12th, 1892, by which he will see, that a foreign firm, in spite of all their objections, may be sued in an English court of justice.

'However, Payne has written directly to you and forwarded, too, all the papers and documents referring to the case, which he had printed for his impending law-suit already, and by looking through these papers, you will gain a clear insight into the matter. But I am anxious to hear soon what you think of the

* It is significant, that this firm a few weeks after this letter had been written, was declared bankrupt.

matter, and whether you are still of the opinion expressed in your letter of the 10th. At any rate, P. have convinced me by documentary evidence, that X. has misrepresented the facts to you. He declares that the order he received in December, '91, was so pressing that he could not make enquiries regarding Lang Brothers, but this firm was very well known to him already since April, '91, and Payne themselves had given him in May, '91, a report about this firm which was far from very satisfactory!!!

'I return you too the original letter of X., dated 7/3/92, that you may compare the assertions contained therein with the printed letters. (In red ink).

'My expenses for nearly a whole day's loss of time to investigate the matter thoroughly, writing reports, postage, etc., amount already to 25 marks.'

Very likely Lehnert would have thought twice before writing this letter, if he had known that Schreck, (H. Payne & Co.) had addressed on the 2nd of April already the following letter to the Berlin enquiry-office:

'Your correspondent, Mr. Lehnert, has handed over to us a letter addressed to you by Mr. X., under the date of the 7th m.p.,* under the condition, and with the request, to furnish him with documentary evidence to disprove the calumnies contained therein, or else, if X. was right and we were wrong, to give him cheque for the amount claimed.

'We have complied with this demand, as you will find by enclosed papers, and we have returned him too the letter of X. after we had taken from it 50 *fac-similes*, of which we had verified four by a public notary.

'Mr. Lehnert, who is employed by us in particular cases, and who, accordingly, is connected with us in a similar manner as he is with you, has shown us in confidence, *as this was his well-understood duty*, your letter, and we must confess to you that the contents of the same have surprised us in so far, as we would have expected from the chief of an institute of such a repute and such an importance as your's, that he would *think before he writes*.

Amongst experienced and respectable people it is, as you may

* It is the letter which in Lehnert's version was snatched from his hand by the 'firm' of H. Payne & Co.

know, a rule, first to inquire into a matter, and then to judge. You have done the latter, but you have omitted to do the former, and your remark, of which we have taken careful notice, 'that these people do not pay over the money they collect,' is really simply revolting. We have very often received cheques for Mr. X., and he will confirm, that we always transmitted them promptly. Regarding the £19 now in question, we have informed the man already on the 30th of January, that in consequence of his action we would hold and not pay over that amount, and we have also promptly informed the man that this amount had been paid to us on the 19th of February, and that we intended to keep it. If you can name to us another London firm, who would have acted differently under similar circumstances, the cheque is at your service. But you will face with this and other rash conclusions like the notorious ox on the mountain.

'Having taken the liberty to pass derogatory remarks about us in your letter to your London correspondent, you will have to put up with hearing our opinion, and this is, that we should really pity the firms who are relying on your informations, if you are always acting in such a hasty manner, and dispatching your business in such a way.

'The report of Mr. Lehnert about yourself is a guarantee to us that you will read now the papers without prejudice against us and then judge impartially, and also that you will be honest enough to admit openly your error.

'This letter is written with no animosity at all.

'We know that you are not personally responsible, and that you acted *bona fide* in giving the information about Lange, which caused the whole mischief.

'The firm X. ought to have given you an opportunity to inquire into the truth of our reclamation and the details given at the same time, and the whole conflict with all its consequences for X. would have been avoided.

'But your hasty remarks *with such people* are not justifiable, even if written under the influence of X.'s epistle and in a momentary passion, and this especially on the part of a gentleman of your experience in such matters, and of so great a moral responsibility.

'In thinking calmly, you will find so much, and to prevent a further correspondence and other steps, we expect from you a clear and concise direct answer to our letter.

'Yours, etc., Henry Payne & Co.

'P.S. We regard this letter as private, and neither Lehnert nor X. have received a copy of it, but we have left it to the discretion of the former to peruse it in our copy-book.'

The following letter was addressed by H. Payne & Co. to the Saxon firm at about the same time:

'We wrote to you for the last time on the 5th of March, and in answer we received through Mr. Lehnert, the London representative of the Berlin enquiry-office of W. Schmeisser & Co., the letter which you addressed to the latter on the 7th inst., with the request to furnish either refuting documents or forward cheque for £42 7s. 2d.

'We regret sincerely that a firm of apparent respectability as your's, can go astray so far, and we consider it our duty towards ourselves and our fellow-men, you included, not to foster the further development of such evident moral aberations and their consequences, by writing out the cheque demanded, but to make you take, through our solicitor, an *English Pill*, the three-fold ingredients of which, to use figurative language, shall have, for good or bad digestion, a disinfecting, cooling, and finally tonic effect.

'We comply now with the demand of your representative, and refute logically and by documentary evidence the distortions and grave untruths contained in your letter of the 7th p.m.

'You are mentioning three causes why you take the agency from us, and you allege they are a justification for your action.

'These three causes are according to your statement:

I. '*The case Lang Brothers*, as mentioned in your letter.

'To this we have to remark:

1. 'That you knew Lang Brothers a long time before you sent the goods.
2. 'We are not responsible that Lang Brothers demanded, contrary to our first arrangement (cash on delivery), 3 or 4 months' time, and we gave them 2 and 3 months' acceptance. Such things happen every day, and are of no consequence in your branch of business. We have,

accordingly, acted quite correctly, or have you still to find fault with something?

'The enquiries you made, and the information you received about Lang Brothers were worthless. It may be expected that you have at least so much sense as to understand, that we must be better informed, doing business with the people, than an enquiry-agent who hears the name of the firm for the first time and supplies a shillingsworth of trash to the Berlin enquiry-office. Your action in this matter was accordingly simply provoking and '*extra stupid*', as we also said in our letter of the 11th January, which you will find printed on page 17 of the enclosed papers.*

'There is no excuse or evasion.

II. '*Case of Samuel Brown, Manchester.*

'In this matter you show your real character, for it requires a great deal of depravity to write such a thing and especially to an enquiry-office. Brown's large order amounted to £20. You do not mention this, and also not that we required Brown at your instance to pay cash, and that we took the responsibility for this amount. You are also suppressing the fact that Brown fell a victim with other large firms to a crisis in the waterproof trade.†

III. '*The third case* you plead in justification of taking from us your agency is, that, as you say, *Payne always try to press on me orders for their own account.*

'You show yourself in this case in the same miserable light. We gave three orders only for our mantle manufactory. The first and second we returned to you, because of delayed delivery, the third we cancelled for the same reason. Will you tell us now, how we pressed our orders on you? If you had suspected that your

* It will be remembered that the firm of Lang Brothers, in spite of the 'better information' of Messrs. H. Payne & Co., became bankrupt and was dissolved a few weeks later.

† Mr. X.'s information regarding Brown was correct too, and disproved all what Schreck (H. Payne & Co. had to say about this firm to induce Mr. X. to execute Brown's orders.

letter will come into our hands, you certainly would have given more plausible and less ridiculous causes for your malice.*

'We do not believe that you really are the stupid German Michael who you pretend to be in your letter to the Berlin enquiry-office, but we truly believe to know your motives, aims and ends of your malice, and we shall prove this in an English court of justice.

'Now to the consequences:

1. 'The miserable way how you acted render it a necessity to disinfect your dirty linen, which our solicitor will have to wash in a short time; this has cost already a lot of time, trouble, work and expenses, for which you alone are responsible, and for this, we mean for the disinfection (1st edition), we debit you in our current account with £50.
2. 'According to English law we demand one season's notice, and we claim on this count £300.
3. 'For loss of commission on orders which you are now executing, we claim £100.
4. 'In spite of our conciliatory and just attitude you have written your letter of the 7th p. m. to the Berlin enquiry-office. This letter contains serious misrepresentations, direct untruths and vile slanders; it is addressed to a first-class Berlin enquiry-office, that is to an institute where, as you must have been aware, and as you were too, such a communication was bound to do us serious harm, the consequences of which in this case could not be gauged and measured.

   'The seriousness of your action is further increased by your suppression of the fact that we have rendered you in the matter of Mistrowski a real service, and you will have difficulties to explain how, after having received, at your own admission, first-class references only about our firm, you can say now, that you had fallen into the hands of people with whom it is dangerous to agree even to arbitration.

* Mr. X.'s assertion that Payne were pressing on him orders for their own account, does not refer to the orders for the mantle factory at all, but to Payne giving orders in their own name and selling the goods at higher prices to Mr. X.'s customers in England. This he stated distinctly in his letter of January 9th, 1892, to Payne & Co., as the principal cause why he dissolved his connection with them as his agents.

'The malice is a little clumsy, but we shall take care to have the motives brought out properly.

'Your letter, accepted by the Berlin enquiry-office, as if your claim had been as correct as a manufacturer's statement, was sent in the ordinary course of business to their London correspondent, and this brings you civilly and criminally in the clutches of the English law of libel, and you will feel something of a cold shudder after you have informed yourself what this law of libel means for you, with regard to money, and may be criminally.

'It is no business of ours to give you the information you require; we leave this to you, and you will hear that nobody can save you.

'To collect the amount of damages, you may trust to us; it will give us exceptional pleasure to prove to you in this regard our capabilities.

'Our claim *ad* 4 is £1,000 for this special libel; if we should find out some more libels, we shall increase our claim in adequate proportion.

'We shall give you time to consider the matter and to make enquiries, up to April the 15th; if we do not receive then a cheque for £1450 in addition to the £42 you are claiming through the Berlin enquiry-office, and for which we have a counter-claim, and if you have not surrendered until then at discretion and declared your unconditional acceptance of all other conditions we may impose, we shall serve you with a *writ*, and then the matter will cost you about £3000, and we shall look to it that the money is paid.'

When the 15th of April passed and the cheque for £1450 did not arrive, and when the 'friendly advice' of Mr. Lehnert was not heeded, H. Payne & Co. increased their claim to £5000, and put the matter in the hands of their solicitor, who threatened to take immediate action. But the Berlin enquiry-office and the Saxon manufacturer were not to be frightened into submission. They had seen clearly through the devices of Mr. Schreck and Mr. Lehnert, and had recognised that these two gentlemen tried their hands at a game of extortion. Mr. X. accepted service of writ, and the rest was silence. The two noble confederates buried their battle-axe, and nothing was heard more of H. Payne & Co.'s

'English pill,' of their claim, and of their action. As soon as Mr. X. shew fight, they considered discretion the better part of valour, and withdrew. The infamous part, however, which Lehnert had played from the moment when the confidential letter confided to him by his employer was 'snatched from his hand,' caused the Berlin enquiry-office to dismiss him, and this decision was the easier arrived at, as a short time ago Lehnert had played them a perfidious trick with his other confederate, G. Opitz, of whom we shall hear later on.

THE ENQUIRY-OFFICE L. LEHNERT, alias 'LIMAN & CO.'

IN the two articles of the 'Cologne People's Gazette' devoted to the enquiry-office of L. Lehnert and Liman & Co., I observed a certain reserve, because I could not believe that a man in the responsible position of an enquiry-agent, to whose hands actually the fate of many young and striving firms is entrusted, should become a party to such abominable swindles.

I had, certainly, for years past received complaints from German manufacturers regarding Lehnert, but no really serious case came to my knowledge, and I, accordingly, felt disposed to regard these complaints as petty denunciations, of which, unfortunately, German manufacturers become often guilty by their neglect of inquiring thoroughly into matters. However, I took careful notes of all, and kept my own counsel. Lehnert I had not seen in my life before I confronted him at the occasion of my trial. With the same feeling of incredulity and reserve I received the accusations that were made against Lehnert in September, 1894, by the London agent of a German manufacturer, an Englishman, who called on me after he had tried for a fortnight in vain to find my address. The manufacturer had, before that, already put heaven and earth in motion; he had applied to the German Consulate General in London, with many other victims of the long-firm swindler B. Arnold & Co.; he had also sought the assistance of 'Scotland Yard,' but everywhere he received the poor consolation that nothing was to be done, because the proofs were wanting. The fact was, that nobody took the trouble to procure these proofs. In Germany, the public prosecutor would have taken up the matter at the expense of the public exchequer; but in England such

LOTHAIR LEHNERT

(after a Photograph).

'I hope you know me when we meet again.'

Shakespeare.

a prosecution is left to the private individual, and that surpasses the comprehension of the German manufacturer, because it is against the German custom, and puts the prosecutor to such expenses, as are equally foreign to German notions. The German manufacturer had read many of my articles, and there the idea struck him, that I would be the right man to take up the matter.

The agent submitted to me some letters which really amounted to a most serious indictment. But the proofs were wanting, and I declared, I could and would not believe in Lehnert's guilt until substantial proofs were given. The agent then took me to the solicitors Messrs. Osborn & Osborn, Exchange-chambers, Copthall-avenue, E.C., who were perfect strangers to me. These gentlemen, the agent told me, were in possession of documents implicating Lehnert in a most serious manner. Mr. Albert Osborn then actually produced some documents, of which I commenced to extract notes, but he stopped me from doing so, explaining that he could not let me do so without the permission of the owner of these documents. I asked who the owner was, and Mr. Albert Osborn mentioned a Mr. Hesse, who formerly had been an intimate friend of Mr. Lehnert.

I went now with the agent to Mr. Hesse, to obtain from him in the first instance the permission to take copies from the documents deposited with Messrs. Osborn & Osborn, and secondly to ask him for some explanations. Mr. Hesse told me, he would first consult his solicitors Messrs. Osborn & Osborn, but he complied with my other request, and informed me how he had obtained possession of the documents. He said: 'I was formerly in partnership with my brother as M. & E. Hesse, and we had a flourishing business which brought us every year some thousand pounds of clear profit. In 1885 we had transactions with M. Sugar & Co., and the heavy loss we sustained through this firm, combined with other losses, led to the ruin of our business. The principal proprietor of the firm of Sugar & Co. fled the country, and we did not save a single penny. At present the fugitive of former days is the partner in an enquiry-office. But you know how cautious one must be in making such assertions, and I must leave it to you to take your informations from the documents at Messrs. Osborn & Osborn, if those gentlemen advise me that I may permit you to do so. These documents came in a very strange manner into my possession. A friend of mine, a Mr. Berliner, took care of some papers for a Mr. Zucker. Mr. Berliner died, and at the request of his sister, I looked through the papers he left behind, and at this occasion I found the papers now at Messrs. Osborn & Osborn, the perusal of which is certain to greatly amuse you. The matters are, in fact, so interesting that they ought to be published. I intended to do so already, but one of the concerned parties threatened with an action. Not to be taken by surprise, I brought the whole of the papers to the solicitors. If I could find only this 'Rollo,' the correspondent of the 'Cologne People's Gazette,' I would hand all the papers to him, that he might bring a little more light into the matter. I have here a few numbers of the 'Cologne People's Gazette,' where similar things are disclosed.'

I asked Mr. Hesse whether he would let me have the papers for a consideration, but he replied, 'London did not contain money enough to induce him to do so.' 'But,' he inquired suspiciously, 'what do you want with these papers, and why are you taking notes? Has a Mr. Lehnert or a Mr. Opitz sent you?'

I appeased Mr. Hesse by assuring him that I did not know either Lehnert or Opitz, and that I had only heard very much of these two gentlemen. I told him further, I had an interest to obtain detailed information about these two, because I had heard of Opitz having done much harm in company with a certain Sugar, a man named Schütz and other swindlers, by very extensive long-firm swindling. Mr. Hesse remarked my information was quite correct, but he would have to see first his solicitors before giving me the permission to take copies of the documents. I would understand this precaution, he said, because he did not know who I was, and for what purpose I required the copies.

I had to leave without having obtained my object, because Mr. Hesse, as he told me afterwards, entertained a suspicion that I had come as a spy sent by Lehnert, who had become his enemy since he knew of the documents being in Mr. Hesse's possession.

After I had taken copies of the documents, of which I am now publishing a part, I instituted the most searching and extensive inquiries with the result, that I gained the conviction of having discovered two most dangerous swindlers. Lehnert I felt disposed to consider the less guilty party, in fact, a misled man, and this explains and excuses the moderate language I used with regard to him in my two articles containing the disclosures. But after having made personally, and by correspondence, further researches in England and Germany, in which undertaking the 'Cologne People's Gazette' rendered the greatest service, I must confess that the case of the enquiry-office, Lehnert-Liman, and of the two proprietors, Lehnert and Opitz, assumed far more serious features than I had anticipated. For this reason I do not hesitate to disclose the part of the two heroes 'from the cradle to the grave.'

Lothar Anton Lehnert was born on December 13th, 1850. His mother was Hortensia Lehnert, and who his father was is not known. His mother married later on, became divorced, and married for a second time. In 1870 Lehnert left Berlin, where he had lived at a Mr. Wichmann's, 13, Karlstrasse. He gave notice to the police that he was going to London, from whence, according to his statement, he returned on the 6th of January, 1875, to Berlin, taking lodgings at 13, Markgrafenstrasse. During these five years of his absence from Berlin he was, however, in Vienna too, and the information he gave about himself to the police is incorrect, for he did not return to Berlin from London, but from Vienna. About his sojourn in Vienna strange stories have reached me, but my informants not being able to prove their queer assertions by documentary evidence, I prefer to pass the matter over in silence. Lehnert remained then in the German capital up to 1882, excepted a few months he spent in 1880 in Stettin, and notified in 1882 to the police his departure to Vienna. During his stay in Berlin he married a young lady who was engaged as singer, Miss Lambert with name, at the Reichshallen Theatre, and he lived with her for two months in apartments at the tailor Genske, 7, Kochstrasse. Lehnert was at that time without occupation and was kept by the earnings of his young wife. His visits to Vienna, and later on to Amsterdam, were apparently connected with the profession of his wife, who appeared in both towns on the stage. On the 2nd of May, 1884, Lehnert and his wife notified to the Berlin police their departure for Liverpool, and this must be considered the date of his emigration to England. This agrees too with the statement Lehnert made under oath when examined at my trial in the Central

Criminal Court, and in which he asserted, he had immigrated to England in 1884, and had established his enquiry-office in 1886. His wife performed in 1884 in Liverpool, and later on in London, where Lehnert obtained a situation as clerk at the firm of Brasch & Rothenstein. In 1885 he was suddenly dismissed for reasons which, in my opinion, were not well founded, at least, the statements made to me, are so confused and contradictory that I would commit an injustice in repeating them and parading them as true. In the same year, and shortly after his dismissal from Brasch & Rothenstein, he was appointed by Messrs. Jahnke & Fölsch, forwarding-agents in Hamburg, their London agent, with a yearly salary of £200. After the first year already this salary, however, was reduced to £100, because his activity did not come up to the expectations of his employers. He asked then Messrs. Jahnke & Fölsch for the permission to establish an enquiry-office, and to use the address of their office. But long ago Lehnert had actually started this business already, without asking their permission, as 'Liman & Co.' at his private address, 1, Millbrook-road, Brixton, S.W., an address that hardly can be called an appropriate one for an enquiry-office. It is, therefore, very significant that Mr. Lehnert, after having received the permission of his employers to establish an enquiry-office, did not transfer his already established office to the City, but left 'Liman & Co.' at Brixton, and opened another office under his name L. Lehnert, at 14, Trinity-square, E.C., where, besides of Jahnke & Fölsch, known to the latter, also a third firm had their abode. I may state here that at that time Mrs. Lehnert acted as clerk to her husband. I have a great many informations in my possession which are written in her handwriting, and this enables me to say that also a part of the letters of the notorious swindling firm Hart & Co., were written by Mrs. Lehnert. Since 1885 Lehnert was closely connected with a great number of such long-firm swindlers, and if I do not say he was their partner, then I simply omit to state a fact for which internal evidence is in my possession. I could go even farther, for proofs are not wanting, that he also caused some 'long-firms' to be started by his friends, really celebrated members of the fraternity. He was on most intimate terms with 'Bernard & Co.,' and passed daily hours in their office; he also visited Holm at the time this unfortunate man, who was convicted of fraud and died in prison, was still established in Sun-street. Holm was also connected with Opitz, Schütz and Zucker, as partner in the firm of Bernard & Co. After the dissolution of this firm and the flight of Schütz, Lehnert was a daily and most regular visitor at Zucker's office, who had opened a new 'firm' under the style of 'Morris Brandt & Co.,' at 20 Coleman-street, and the house-keeper says, Lehnert was in his daily visits as punctual as clockwork. What business had he at this swindling firm? The cheques of Morris Brandt & Co. furnish the answer.

'Morris Brandt & Co.' departed in peace, and like a 'jack-in-the-box' Mr. Zucker, alias Sugar, reappeared 'round the corner' as Messrs. 'Hart & Co.,' of which event in the career of this gentleman with many aliases we spoke already in a preceding chapter.

Before this strange transformation scene was enacted, Lehnert, however, took the precaution to discourage the creditors of Morris Brandt & Co. from troubling themselves about the vanished firm, and from going to the expense of taking proceedings. To this purpose he gave to the enquiry-offices who employed him as their London agent, the following report:

'24/9/86, Morris Brandt & Co., London, E.C., 20, Coleman-street. I have very little to add to my telegram 'Ceres Mars dubious agents without means.' The firm was established a few months ago, apparently they are representing a house at Plauen, but they do not get any orders, and are not anxious to do business. The firm is a fictitious one, and is breathing their last, because they will be turned out in the course of the next days for arrears of rent.'

'Private: If the customer who addressed this inquiry to you is not a banker, then he is rotten. Morris Brandt & Co. are offering by advertising paper-credit against 1 % commission, and your customer, very likely, has obtained such an acceptance for a consideration of 60 marks. These bills are marked with rubber stamps as payable at the London Continental Bank.'

This report was written by Lehnert himself. It served his purpose in every regard. He showed himself well informed by the postscript to his letter; he knew events would prove his information true with regard to the firm enquired after; he let the people know that Morris Brandt & Co. had absolutely nothing, and that it was useless to proceed against them, and to throw 'good money after bad.' It was a correct information, perfectly true, and yet how untrue and deceitful! Why did not Lehnert say who 'Morris Brandt & Co.' was? Why did he not say: 'It is the notorious swindler Zucker, who has cheated you already as Martin Sugar & Co., as Bernard & Co., and under other aliases.' Mr. Lehnert was very careful not to betray this little secret, for what would become of the new firm, which was being hatched at this time already? Should he tell the truth and cut in his own flesh by ruining his dear friend Zucker, who was presenting him with cheque after cheque! On the 10th of June, 1887, he received still from Morris Brandt & Co. a cheque under his, Lehnert's, name (of which will be found a facsimile on the following leaf). But how many cheques were given to him under other names? I have quite a collection of these cheques, all drawn by Morris Brandt & Co., and payable to a number of different persons at the London & North Western Bank, and all these different persons were Mr. Lehnert, and all the different signatures were his, according to the opinion of ***Mr. Thomas Henry Gurrin***, the well-known expert, to whom I had these cheques submitted through my solicitors, Messrs. Osborn & Osborn. The same opinion was expressed by Mr. Gurrin with regard to the cheques of Hart & Co. When this new firm had blossomed forth in the place of 'Morris Brandt & Co.,' and had transferred their quarters from Coleman-street to Lime-street, as described in the 'Cologne People's Gazette,' Lehnert was again the faithful friend and adviser of Mr. Zucker in his new guise. The two 'gentlemen' met every morning in a small coffee-shop near Lehnert's office in Trinity-square, and witnesses are prepared to affirm that Zucker always brought with him the letters Hart & Co. had received from the continent, that he handed them over dutifully to his partner, who read them, and returned some letters to Zucker with instructions what to answer, and took others, very likely the most important ones, with him, to have them answered to his diction through his 'clerk,' Mrs. Lehnert, who signed 'for Hart & Co.' as a Mr. Hassfeld!

'Messrs. M. Hart & Co.' had an account at the Royal Exchange Bank and the cheques were signed in the name of that firm by Zucker. Lehnert received under his name from Hart & Co.

ESTABLISHED 1868.

No. B37499 London 10 June 188-

The London & North Western District B

53, NEW BROAD STREET, E.C.

Pay Mr L. Lehmert or

the sum of [redacted]

£ [redacted]

Morris Porquede

BANKING HOURS 10 TO 4, SATURDAYS 10 TO 2.

This Cheque must be signed at the Back by the person to whom it is payable.

was useless to proceed against them, and to throw 'good money after bad.' It was a correct information, perfectly true, and yet how untrue and deceitful! Why did not Lehnert say who 'Morris Brandt & Co.' was? Why did he not say: 'It is the notorious swindler Zucker, who has cheated you already as Martin Sugar & Co., as Bernard & Co., and under other aliases.' Mr. Lehnert was very careful not to

wh
tru
wh
of
un
the
un
all
di
the
sig
H.
ch
Th
ch
in
qu
'C
an
me
Tr
alv
the

who read them, and returned some letters to Zucker with instructions what to answer, and took others, very likely the most important ones, with him, to have them answered to his diction through his 'clerk,' Mrs. Lehnert, who signed 'for Hart & Co.' as a Mr. Hassfeld!

'Messrs. M. Hart & Co.' had an account at the Royal Exchange Bank and the cheques were signed in the name of that firm by Zucker. Lehnert received under his name from Hart & Co.

cheques for £10, £15, £2 and £7 8s. But under other names he received and receipted in his own hand, as Mr. Gurrin declares, cheques for £5 3s, £2, £5, £20, £1, £3, £15 16s., £1, £1, £60, £1, £15, £1, £71 19s. 7d., 10s., £1 5s., £67 17s., £1, £110, 6s. and £125. All together Mr. Lehnert drew in cheques from 'Hart & Co.' £543 4s. 7d. And how much did he receive in cash? A nice little income for the short space of hardly ten months that this firm existed! It certainly spelled trouble, anxiety, even ruin and death to some German and Austrian manufacturers! But what matters! Every one for himself!

Why did Zucker part with so much money? What for was Lehnert so richly paid? For 'professional services'! We need just read the report about the swindler Zucker, now Hart & Co., and we shall understand. The new firm, of course, sent letters out broad-cast to come into connection with continental manufacturers, and these, of course, again, made enquiries at their enquiry-agents. Now, Lehnert was acting at that time as confidential agent and London correspondent for 23 of these offices distributed all over Germany and Austria. Thus most of the enquiries made were sure to come to his hands. But Lehnert knew too the firms who were the customers of these 23 agencies, and he supplied their addresses to Zucker or any other swindler with whom he was working. In this way he made double sure of the victims who were to be trapped by the information destined for them. Thus runs his report, written in his own hand and in my possession, about 'M. Hart & Co., 8, Lime-street, London, E.C.

'This firm is established for some time, and is exporting goods of all kinds to Australia, where they are said to have a brother in Melbourne. It is thought they are doing a satisfactory business. The proprietor of the firm is considered a respectable man of means, he comes from a good family, and is said to have rich relations.'

How could an honest man give such a report about a notorious swindling firm? The same Zucker, whom Lehnert knew *so* well, and who had only just stopped swindling and defrauding as 'Morris Brandt & Co.,' had become now within a few weeks 'a respectable man of means.'

M

A few months later the same enquiry-office asked Lehnert to give them now 'a detailed, absolutely correct and prompt information regarding Hart & Co., and as if to confirm his former report, he writes again with his own hand :

'This firm is established for some time as exporters of fringes, buttons, nails, hard-ware, clocks, paper, etc., to Australia, where a relative is conducting the business of the firm.

'During the last months they have also commenced to cultivate the Indian market. The business is moderate in its extent, but seems to prosper. The proprietor is considered a respectable man with some means ; he pays regularly and a credit of £150 could be given.'

The audacity and baseness to give such an information, really surpasses all limits. Lehnert knew that the 'respectable proprietor' of the firm had committed endless frauds and swindles, that he had a small attic for his office, with a rickety chair and an equally dilapidated table as office furniture, that his balance at the bank at that time amounted to 10/6, and that he possessed no stock whatever, and this fellow he recommends to 23 continental enquiry-offices in his capacity as confidential agent, who, acting on this information, recommended the fellow to numberless manufacturers. One's blood boils in reading such a perfidious report! Can there be anything more dangerous to the commercial community as such a conspiracy between a well accredited enquiry-office, influencing others, and long-firm swindlers ?

But the fraud does not stop there. Amongst the papers, which I call now my property, is also the copy-book of the firm of Hart & Co. It is in itself a most remarkable reading. I must, of course, resist my temptation to reprint it, but I cannot omit to give some extracts from this most interesting book.

First of all I must state once more that a great part of the correspondence is in the handwriting of Mr. Lehnert's 'clerk.' To these particular letters are belonging, too, those written to the unfortunate Mr. Wolf, whom the losses he sustained at Hart & Co., drove to self-destruction. The one letter I mentioned in the article published in the 'Cologne People's Gazette,' runs as follows (page 50 of the copy-book, in Mrs. Lehnert's handwriting) :

'Mr. Josef Wolf, Vienna.—In answer to your esteemed letter of the 22nd inst., we comply without delay to your request and give you the following firms as our references :

'Messrs. Jahnke & Fölsch, 14, Trinity-square, London, E.C., Mr. F. C. W. Wagner, Water-lane, London, E.C., Mr. Ch. A. Owitch & Co., 21, Nicolai-strasse, Zwickau, i/ Saxony.

'If you should desire it, we shall supply you with more references, but our firm is also well-known to the following enquiry-offices in your town :

'Lesser & Liman, Franz Josef's-quai; Creditschutz, Maria Theresiengasse; Providenz, Gonzagagasse.

'But do not keep us waiting too long for the goods, because the matter has been protracted already. Most respectfully,

(Signed) per M. Hart & Co., M. Hassfeld.

[On the following pages will be found the facsimile of this letter. On a third page will be found a facsimile of a congratulation card, signed by Mrs. Lehnert. By comparing the handwriting of this card, the letter addressed to Joseph Wolf by Hart & Co., and the letter addressed to Philipp Wagner on another page, the reader will find that the three documents are written by the same hand.]

What swindle! All the references given were given directly or indirectly by Lehnert. Jahnke & Fölsch he was himself, Owitch was the confederate of the long-firm swindlers sent to Germany to give references, the three Vienna enquiry-offices knew of Hart & Co. through Lehnert only, and relied upon what their 'confidential London agent' told them. Poor Wolf was well served! This sad case having been mentioned before, with that of Messrs. Kuhrt & Schilling, we need not dwell longer on it, and shall have a peep into this copy-book. What extensive correspondence! No country of the continent where Messrs. Hart & Co.'s letters had not been directed to. In Germany we find at random the following towns benighted with Messrs. Hart & Co.'s correspondence: Stuttgart, Berlin, Erlbach, Nuremberg, Schmiedeberg, Gedendorf, Allersberg, Offenbach, Braunschweig; Austria is favoured to a still greater degree; there are many letters addressed to Vienna, Prague, Brunn and the industrial districts of Bohemia, but also smaller towns are not forgotten; as: Kuttenberg, Leitomischl, Schmiedeberg, Karlsbad, Neuhaus,

29. Mai 8

Herrn

Josef Wolf

Wien

Im Besitze Ihres Geehrten vom 22. ct. beeile ich mich Ihrem Wunsche zu entsprechen und Ihnen als Referenzen folgende Firmen aufzugeben:

Herren Jahncke & Pollack, 14 Trinity Square, Tower Hill.
London E. C.

Herren J. C. W. Wagner & Co., Water Lane, Lower Thames Str.
London E. C.

Herren W. A. Preibisch & Co. Nicolai Str. 31, Zwickau i/S.

Auf Wunsch stehen noch mehr Referenzen zu Diensten

auch dürften unsere Firma genügend tüchtige Aus-
kunfts-Bureaux, die

Lasser & Linnen, Franz-Josefs-Quai
Creditschutz, Maria-Theresiengasse
Providenz, Gonzagagasse

kennen.

Lassen Sie uns mit der Waare aber ge-
wiss länger warten, da wir so [illegible]
[illegible] sind.

Hochachtend
M. Karl & Co.
pp. H. Hasfeld

May your Christmas be Happy and Joyous

Frohliche Weihnachten
wünscht

Familie Lehnert

Mühlhaus, Meseritsch. Hungary, Croatia, Transylvania, Bosnia, Servia, Russia, France, Italy, Holland had not to complain of being neglected by the London City-firm in Lime-street; that Hart & Co. ordered pianos from half-a-dozen firms, watches, clocks, violin-strings, cloth, embroideries, boots, shoes, haberdashery, sticks, gold and silver paper, we can well understand; but it is rather difficult to understand what these exporters to Australia wanted with such articles as broad-beans, eggs, sausages, hams, poultry, wines from Sicily, butter, olive-oil, ptarmigans, tons of onions. The business of this firm was, however, not confined to the sale of merchandise; they were also financial agents, and their advertisements in German papers to the purport that 'a London firm' is prepared to give paper-credit, and to exchange acceptances for a small commission, brought them within three days some dozen customers, and Hart & Co., with 10/6 at their banker's and no banker's credit whatever, entered into 'discounting' bills (that is by exchange of acceptances) of 10,000 marks, 2,500, 1,500 5,000, 3,000 and up to 20,000 florins, and making a nice, tidy amount by commission. Hart & Co., of course, never thought of taking up their own acceptances, and there they expected to make their haul; for if they succeeded to put bills into circulation, which they had received for their and their confederates' worthless acceptances, they pocketed the money and left it to the poor drawer to pay for it. Unfortunately for Messrs. Hart & Co. one of those wicked papers who spoil the honest trade of these good people, got wind who the discounters were, and what game they were playing, and the warning published by this and reprinted by other papers, brought Messrs. Hart & Co. in one day quite a shoal of far from pleasant letters. They had to disgorge the acceptances they were holding, and had to content themselves with the 'commission' they had drawn.

Could anything give a better proof of the swindling character of this city-firm, than this glimpse in their copy-book? To this general survey, I shall just add a few details. Hart & Co. wrote to Mr. W. H. Moore at Rennes, to supply them with eggs. Mr. Moore seemed greatly pleased and flattered by receiving an inquiry from a London house, and he was quite in a hurry to secure such good customers. He wrote:

'St. Malo, October 1st, 1888.

'Gentlemen,—I received your letter this morning, when I was just starting for this place to superintend the shipping of my goods, and I have shipped directly from the market to your address.

10–1200 chests eggs, middle size, selected.
10–1200 „ „ large, Normandy.
1–1200 „ „ extra qual., Normandy, as sample

I charge you the lowest prices.

10 chests 7/-	£42	0	0
10 „ 8/3	£49	10	0
1 chest 8/6	£ 5	2	0
	£96	12	0

'I have no invoice formulas with me, and ask you to excuse this. My conditions are net cash, f.o.b. St. Malo. As I try to work up a great trade by contenting myself with a small profit, I shall be only too glad to supply you with any kind of goods you may require. I am sending you too one sample-chest of my extra quality. Should the quality meet with your approval, I should be pleased to receive from you weekly orders. This being our first transaction, I shall be obliged by cheque per return. If you are also dealing in butter, I can supply you.'

'Yours most faithfully, (Signed) W. H. Moore.

115, Route de Nantes, Rennes.

Telegraphic address: 'Moore, Rennes.'

Hart & Co. received the eggs and sold them forthwith at Leadenhall Market, without even taking the trouble to advise the kind sender of the receipt of the goods. Mr. Moore waited until the 10th of October, and then he wrote:

'Messrs. M. Hart & Co., London. Gentlemen,—I am without news from you. I am anxious to hear from you how you like the goods. Paris spoils the whole trade, because the prices are much higher there than in London. But your orders shall have my best attention. Faithfully yours, (Signed) W. H. Moore.'

Hart & Co. found time now to answer, which drew under the date of 13th October, the following letter from Mr. Moore:

'Your letter of the 11th inst. has really surprised me. The eggs were sent directly from the market, and they were quite fresh at the time. Your customer tries very likely to secure a reduction. Competition is very great, and if people cannot make money by fair means, they try to do so by foul means. At this time of the year there are always a few bad eggs amongst the lot, but I cannot accept any reclamation, and particularly as the goods were sent on the 1st of October, and now we are writing the 13th. I shall delegate somebody to inspect the goods, and have to ask you for cheque by return. All reclamations regarding eggs must be made within three days after arrival.'

Hart & Co. did not lose their equanimity. The pan-cakes prepared from the sample-chest had certainly convinced them that no objection could be taken to the quality of the eggs. It was useless to maintain a claim on this account. Mr. Moore's agent had also to be kept from paying Messrs. Hart & Co. a visit in their imposing offices under the roof of a four-storied dingy house, and Messrs. Hart & Co. decided, therefore, on paying Mr. Moore in full—with their own three months' bill. Glorious! In three months' time many things may happen. Life is short, especially that of long-firms. Mr. Moore was accordingly favoured by return, as he had asked for, with the remittance. But, somehow, he did not appreciate this promptness on the part of Messrs. Hart & Co. He smelled 'rotten eggs,' and indignant as he felt, the following epistle flowed from his pen :

'I received your registered letter, but I do not understand its contents. You seem to think that I do not know the business. Three months' time for eggs! What next? You must be mad! The great loss you are trying to make out, is bosh and nonsense. The goods were shipped directly from the market. I am for many years in business in a large way, but never before a similar complaint has reached me. Your customer is rotten and not the eggs. He demands credit for three months. Really! how ever can you sell to such a fellow. I must have your cheque by return, and should also like to know which mark was bad. You received three different marks from three different markets. I am astonished at the result of this first transaction, it makes an end to our connection.'

There were great rejoicings at this letter in the 'sledge-driver' office of Messrs. Hart & Co. A respectable firm could answer such a boorish letter in one way only—by contemptuous silence.

And this Messrs. Hart & Co. did to their hearts' content. Mr. Moore was not worth even a stamp to them. Nothing more was to be got out of him, and Messrs. Hart & Co. did not want his eggs, fresh or rotten. They could feed on pancakes without him. A Moscow firm had sent them a fresh supply of 100 chests Russian eggs, and even the Russian Consul General, whom the defrauded merchant had called to his assistance, could not prevail on the City-firm of Hart & Co. to settle the account. Their principle was not to pay, and some egg-merchants in Hamburg, Berlin and Maros-Varsarhely (Hungary), were taught the same lesson.

Mr. Moore waited until the 5th of December, and not hearing from Messrs. Hart & Co., he wrote to them:

'I am astonished at your silence. That is not the way to do business! (Happy Mr. Moore! How little he knew of the ways of sledge-drivers!) And how about your doubts that I would not be able to supply your great demands? And how about the increasing inquiry, and the brisk sale round Leadenhall-market? I should have thought you would buy more. Write by to-morrow.'

The morrow came, and many morrows more; but to Mr. Moore's sorrow, the day never dawned that brought him the money, or even a letter only from Messrs. Hart & Co., the rotten egg-merchants, as he called them.

Messrs. Hart & Co.'s 'clerk,' Mrs. Lehnert, was kept busy. There was a great deal of correspondence. The firm was dealing in everything and anything, as Australian shippers do. Thus we find Mrs. Lehnert writing on the 27th of April, 1888, quite a string of letters. Here a few of them. A manufacturer in Lodsz (Russia), is honoured with the following missile: 'We heard the name of your esteemed firm mentioned as capable of executing large orders,' etc. To a dealer in raw sticks in Carlstadt, Croatia, she writes: 'Your esteemed firm was recommended to us for the supply of sticks.' A firm in Czernowitz, Bukovina, is informed: 'We have seen samples of broad and horse-beans, which, to all appearance, came from your firm.' I wonder whether each bean was stamped with the firm's address, to inform Messrs. Hart & Co. of their provenience? A firm in Brunswick is asked for price-list and samples of German sausage and Westphalian ham. Ham and eggs are going beautifully together, and Mrs. Lehnert writes therefore to an export company in Hungary: 'We are dealers in French eggs, but having often enquiries after Hungarian eggs, we should like to know whether you can promptly execute large orders.' Who eats, wants to drink too; accordingly an Italian firm in Riporto is informed that 'their esteemed name' was mentioned to Messrs. Hart & Co. 'as exporters of Sicilian wines, and as we are doing business in Italian produce, we should like to have a trial with your wines.' In way of precaution against too great an acidity of the Sicilian wines, Mrs. Lehnert enquired at the same time at a firm in Navachio about the supply of salad-oil. But 'man lives not on bread alone,' he requires refinements too, and to a firm in Erlbach is written: 'We have an export order for catguts, and your firm having been recommended to us,' etc. Yes, 'music gladdens the heart of man.' How mistaken Schiller was when he wrote:

'You make your home where music you do hear,
For good men only have for music love and ear.'

Who would contradict Lehnert when he called Hart & Co., in his information, 'clever and experienced people, who knew their business?'

This sledge-driving concern lasted up to March, 1889. Towards the close of the preceding year, Hart & Co. had received still the bicycle bells from K. & Sch., and they paid with an acceptance which, when falling due, came, after an excursion to its native place, duly back to Germany protested. Messrs. K. & Sch. had an agent in London, and through him they made now inquiries what had become of Hart & Co., who did not answer their letters. The agent found the office of Messrs. Hart & Co. closed, and heard they did not attend any more there. He went now to Lehnert and asked whether he did not know something about these people. Lehnert, as well-informed enquiry-agent, knew something, of course, and he told the agent that poor Mr. Hart was suffering with galloping consumption, that he had gone to the South of France, from whence he very likely would never return, as his case was a hopeless one. The agent duly reported to his firm what he had heard from 'a most reliable source,' and in consequence the German manufacturers abstained from bringing an action for the recovery of their claim. It is needless to say that 'poor Mr. Hart' was 'not dying;' if his case was a case of consumption, it was one of consumption of food and drink, and instead of galloping, he was walking quietly in the streets of the city. But in shielding his friends and staving off actions, it was a favourite idea of Mr. Lehnert, to remit them pitiless to the sick- if not the death-bed. In another swindling-office, of which we shall hear more later on, he reported his friend Opitz ill, and stricken with fever in Burmah, and during all the time he met every day with Opitz in a restaurant at Coleman-street.

The facts were, that Zucker at the time when he was still 'playing at 'Hart & Co.' with Mr. and Mrs. Lehnert, had opened another sledge-driver office at 11, Leadenhall-street, as 'Freeman & Co.' A Mr. C. Lewin had allowed him to put a table in his office, and to adorn the door with a small plate bearing the inviting name of Freeman & Co. Zucker succeeded, as I know by evidence in my possession, to swindle, under this new name, some of his former victims for the second, and even third time.

Mr. Lehnert received, of course, inquiries regarding this new firm. Having proclaimed 'Mr. Hart' dying with galloping consumption in the South of France, he could not proclaim him now living, strong and healthy in London, and thus the incognito of Mr. Freeman remained guarded in this case too. But the information was a remarkable one, if we consider the relations between the two. Lehnert wrote:

'29/8/89. G. Freeman & Co., London, E.C., 11, Leadenhall-street. This firm exists since the beginning of the present year, and is reported to export cloth, hardware, pianos, etc., to Australia, and to work hand-in-hand with a relation living there.—That sounds very nice indeed, but I do not believe it. I can never see this Mr. 'G. Freeman,' only a certain C. Lewin (a great friend of your firm), who has his office next to that of Freeman, and looking at the intimate relations between these two, it seems as if they were working together, and as if Freeman was played out in the place of Lewin, who has lost all credit. At any rate I advise caution.'

Why did Mr. Lehnert not say what he knew: this Freeman is no one else but the well-known long-firm swindler Martin Zucker, alias Hart & Co., alias Morris Brandt & Co., alias Bernhard, alias M. Sugar & Co. Why? because he dared not say so. Even if Zucker had not turned against him, the enquiry-offices would have found out, by comparing his former informations, that their 'confidential agent,' Mr. Lehnert, is a swindler too. In the information just quoted, Lehnert gave also a kick to another intimate friend of his, to Mr. C. Lewin, whose pretended friend he remained up to the day of his flight of London, when under remand for conspiracy to defraud. At the time when Lehnert gave his information about Freeman-Zucker, he knew quite well that Mr. Lewin was trading on his own account, and that he had only permitted Zucker the use of his office, for which Zucker had to pay a small weekly rent, with which he remained in arrears not settled to this day. At any rate Mr. Lewin was able to prove to my solicitors that he was no partner of 'Freeman & Co.,' and that he holds an I.O.U. from Zucker for arrears of rent, which the latter signed: 'Mr. Sugar, trading as Freeman & Co.'

The reason why Lehnert gave an unfavourable report about 'Freeman & Co.' was the following: Lehnert had kept the money for the bicycle-bells for himself, and had refused to pay Zucker his share. This annoyed Zucker, and he established 'a firm' for himself. This again was contrary to the intentions of Lehnert, and a tension arose, with the result, that Lehnert used his influence against 'Freeman & Co.' Zucker found this out, and after the fall of the last-named firm, the two became friends again. Zucker opened then a new long-firm as Mr. Sugar in Hatton-garden, and Lehnert's office supplied again the necessary favourable informations to Continental customers and enquiry-offices. Mr. Opitz, the so-called manager, but in fact, partner in Lehnert's business, when cross-examined in the preliminary stage of my trial, had to admit that Zucker, alias Sugar, was a swindler, but he declared him now to be 'an honest and respectable man.' Knowing who Opitz was, I doubted the veracity of this testimony, and wrote to the creditors of Mr. M. Sugar, the now honest and respectable firm of Hatton-garden, and they were singularly unanimous in their judgment, that Zucker was as Sugar what he had been under all his other aliases: a swindler, who had cheated them. Thus a firm of Hanau wrote to me:

'Zucker was introduced to me at the occasion of my last visit to London through a Mr. Sch. He traded at that time with a certain D. under the firm of Mr. Sugar, in antique silverware, and just then a great demand existed for this kind of goods, and rendered it a profitable business. I was told that D. did not advance sufficient capital. To my opinion, Sugar was not the only swindler, but a whole nest of them existed, and they put him forward and used him for their purposes. I entrusted him stock to the value of 12,000 marks and appointed him my agent, making it the conditions of our arrangement, that he was to manage the matter, that the stock remained my absolute property, that he had to conduct the sales, that all sales had to be made in my name, and all the moneys received, paid over to me at the close of each month. I did so under the impression that the English law corresponds with the German law with regard to agencies, and the stock entrusted to an agent can be disposed of and removed by the owner at any time, and the agent dismissed without notice, and prosecuted criminally, in case of irregularities. Acting on this supposition, I entertained the business. Unfortunately I was deceived, and learned to my loss, that the English law is a different one, and this experience cost me in the case of Sugar over £1,000.'

When Lehnert and Opitz decided to prosecute me for libel, they were not slow to recognise, that Zucker would be called on my part as a witness, and that this could turn out very dangerous for all of them. As soon as I had heard that an action was to be brought against me, I really thought too of Zucker, as my prosecutors had surmised I would. But I came too late to prevent him from escaping. When I sent a confidential person to make enquiries, Sugar's office was closed; the house-keeper said 'everything' had been removed; a 'Mr. Hassfeld' called only every morning for letters, and Mr. Sugar had gone to the sea-side, and would not return for some months. Very much to the seaside indeed! Mr. Sugar had fled to New York, where he reappeared as Mr. Harris; but he did not like the new world, and went to Antwerp, where he disappeared. It is quite within the range of possibilities that Mr. Zucker opens somewhere an enquiry-office, and, after having Mr. Lehnert for his teacher, it is not to be doubted that he will know how to conduct it.

Very characteristic is also another case, in which Lehnert committed a grave breach of confidence. I mentioned already his relations to Mr. Hesse. The latter had to stop payments in consequence of the heavy losses he sustained at the hands of

Opitz. In spite of Mr. Hesse's knowledge of the intimate relations existing between Opitz and Lehnert, he remained on friendly terms with the latter. Mr. Hesse established later on a business under the name of his wife, who was supplied with the capital required by her brother. The business certainly bore no comparison with that he had before his bankruptcy, but nevertheless, he made a living. He called himself the manager of his wife's business, and before the law he certainly was entitled to do so. (I give this as my opinion without having investigated the matter.) Lehnert had become aware of it, that Mr. Hesse had obtained possession of Berliner's papers, so seriously implicating Lehnert, and when Mr. Hesse declined to part with them, the honest enquiry-agent resolved to have his revenge, and to render him harmless. Hesse heard of this scheme, and he induced a friend in Germany to make an enquiry at Lehnert's about the firm of his, Mr. Hesse's, wife. The information given and written by Mrs. Lehnert was a very unfavourable one, and reached Mr. Hesse in due course. He was justly indignant at this 'friendly service' Lehnert had rendered him, and invited this gentleman to give him a call. Lehnert not suspecting what had happened, did so, and was surprised when Mr. Hesse did not recognise his greeting but addressed him abruptly and roughly in asking: 'Lehnert, will you tell me what kind of information you have given about me? Lehnert denied of having given any information at all, but when Mr. Hesse held the original paper before his face, he declared it with a forced smile, as a little joke. He said, he knew a trick was to be played on him, and so he thought to answer with a tit for tat, amounting to nothing more or less than a joke. Mr. Hesse would not hear of such jokes and declared, he would have a joke in his turn, and send copies of the documents in his possession to all the continental enquiry-offices who employed Lehnert as their confidental agent and correspondent.

When Lehnert saw that Mr. Hesse meant what he said, he became greatly frightened, and implored 'his old friend' to forget and forgive the little matter, which really had not been done in a spiteful spirit. But Mr. Hesse told Lehnert that he knew him well enough to come to his own conclusion what to think about the matter. Finding Mr. Hesse inexorable, Lehnert threw himself on his knees before Mr. Hesse and implored him not to execute his threat. 'Do not make me unfortunate!' he cried. 'Do not ruin me and my family! Have pity on me! Take a stick and give me a good thrashing! only do not let my firms know! I shall put everything right again. Enquiries are sure to come again, and you shall see how I answer them.'

Well, Mr. Hesse gave ear to Lehnert's implorations, and promised not to act as he had threatened, if Lehnert would act honestly. 'I have also to keep a family,' he said 'and I do not want to be wantonly ruined by you.'

A short time after this occurrence, Mr. Hesse, who was manufacturing buttons in a small way, thought to open a connection for his firm with a large German button-manufacturer, and he wrote the following letter to Lehnert (the original in my possession and published with Mr. Hesse's permission).

'London 20/2/1890. Dear Lehnert, would you write out for me from your directory the addresses of manufacturers of bone-buttons in Germany and elsewhere, also manufacturers of studs and slings in Berlin? I mean such firms as Mathias Achsler, Ansbach, who is represented here by Benthner Kühn. Yours Hesse.'

At the back of this letter Lehnert wrote out a list of the desired addresses and returned it to the sender.

Soon afterwards Lehnert received an enquiry from a button manufacturer in Ober-Bieber about the character and position of the firm L. Hesse, and whether £150 to £200 could be safely credited. Lehnert answered immediately:

'In answer to your esteemed letter of the 16th inst., you will find the information you desire on the next page. I beg to offer you my services for enquiries regarding England at the same charge, and remain, yours most respectfully, L. Lehnert.'

This letter is signed by Lehnert himself, the information on the back, however, is written in Mrs. Lehnert's handwriting, and runs as follows:

'L. Hesse & Co., London, E.C., 52, Fore-street, E.C.

'This firm is established for some years and is doing a good and satisfactory wholesale business in all kinds of buttons. Proprietors are respectable and experienced people, who know their branch, and are well introduced in the trade. They keep a well assorted stock. It is thought they are possessed of sufficient working capital. They are paying regularly, and the people are considered good for a credit of £150 to £200 in goods.'

[On the following pages will be found a facsimile of the above-mentioned letters as well as the report.]

With regard to this matter, Mr. Hesse told me soon after the publication of my two 'incriminated' articles in the presence of his son, that Lehnert brought this letter to him. 'This is for your kindness that you did not interfere with my employers,' he said in handing the letter to Mr. Hesse, asking him to read it, and then to close it and post it, what Mr. Hesse did. Soon afterwards the German firm gave Mr. Hesse the credit he had demanded, and this in spite of an unfavourable report of another enquiry-office, which was incorrect in being too much to the disadvantage of Mr. Hesse.

To verify the facts, I wrote to the manufacturer in Oberbjeber, who was kind enough to forward to me in the most obliging manner all the correspondence referring to this matter. I saw from it in the first instance, that Mr. Hesse had told me the absolute truth, as he in general does not make a secret of his misfortune. But I saw, too, what danger, yes, public danger, enquiry offices as a whole are constituting, because they are under no authoritative control, but to the contrary, shielded in many regards by the existing laws.

What I am objecting to principally is: The enquiry-offices undertake to supply reliable informations about any firm in any place of the world for a ridiculous fee. It is evident the enquiry-offices cannot keep agents everywhere, and therefore they should not try to make people believe that they are represented in all parts of the world by their agents. I know one particular case in which a German enquiry-office addressed the post-master of a village, in sending him a small fee, to give information about a manufacturer established in the place, whether he was good for a credit of 16,000 marks. The post-master gave an excellent report about the firm, on the strength of which the credit was given. Two months afterwards the manufacturer had stopped payments. The best of the matter is, however, that the post-master who gave the information and the manufacturer were one and the same

L. LEHNERT.
SPEDITION—AUSKUNFT—INCASSO.

14, TRINITY SQUARE, TOWER HILL,
LONDON, E.C. 18. October 1890

Herrn
Philipp Wagner
Oberbieber:

Die mit Ihrem Geschr. vom 16. crt. gewünschte Auskunft finden Sie beistehend.

Ich halte mich für Ihre weiteren Aufträge auf ganz England zu den gleichen Preissätzen, bestens empfohlen und zeichne

Hochachtungsvoll
L. Lehnert

9486 18/10/90

L. Hesse & Co., London E.C.

82 Fore Street

Diese Firma besteht seit mehreren
Jahren und macht in allen Sorten
Knöpfen en gros ein ganz hübsches
Geschäft das befriedigend geht.
Inhaber sind achtbare und tüchtige
Leute die die Branche verstehen und
bei der Kundschaft eingeführt sind.
Sie verfügen über ein wohl assortir-
tes Lager. Man glaubt daß genü-
gende Betriebsmittel vorhanden sind,
Zahlweise war bisher eine ordentliche
und für einen Waaren Credit von
£ 150-200 - hält man die Leute
gut

person, and thus he had reported, for a small consideration, about himself! The enquiry-office certainly acted *bona fide*, but it acted carelessly, and took for granted what a perfect stranger reported—about himself.

I say the enquiry-offices ought to charge four times as much as they are charging now, but they ought to make then conscientious enquiries regarding the solvency of the firms or persons enquired after, and they ought to be made legally responsible for their informations. Enquiry-offices ought also to be licensed, as the pawn-brokers are, and such persons ought only to be granted a license, who are able to give security to a large amount and prove their irreproachable respectability. If an enquiry-agent commits an error and gives an untrue information, he ought to be cautioned, after three warnings he ought to be fined, and if he then still proves himself unreliable, his license ought to be cancelled and his office closed. The employees of enquiry-offices ought to be sworn in that they will act conscientiously, and their salaries ought to be fixed by the government in such a manner, that they are not depending on bribes paid to them by swindling-firms.

How are matters standing at present? Everybody can open an enquiry-office. No capital is required, there is no risk, cash is paid for every report, and there are 'extra profits' of which the enquirer has no suspicion. Let us make an end to this crying evil! In the first instance the manufacturers ought not to give their trust to the first best loafer, and be blinded by the name of 'enquiry-agent.' As long as the government does not regulate this important branch of business, old-established and well-reported enquiry-agencies only ought to be consulted, for they only offer a certain guarantee for the correctness and genuineness of their informations, and these great offices ought to combine and form a ring, agreeing not to give informations under a certain lowest fee.

The merchants and manufacturers could help themselves too to a considerable degree by reorganising and improving the existing, and framing new societies for trade-protection. How easy would it be, for example, if the exporters would found a society for their own protection with a salaried confidential agent in every important centre of commerce, who would control the reports given by other enquiry-offices, to whom all incoming orders would be submitted, and who eventually would also act in legal matters. I tried such a plan on a small scale with some gentlemen residing in London, and in conjunction with some manufacturers. The venture answered very well, but to these good people, who stumble over trifles, our charges, which were treble as high as the customary low fees of enquiry-offices, appeared in the light of an unwarrantable overcharge; they did not consider that we made careful enquiries in each case and were not contented with simply copying from the registers. Many people also thought that our society was a benevolent institution, and ought to make all the enquiries at its own expense out of pure brotherly love, and we were thanked in advance and 'referred to Heaven, who would reward us for our services.'

If enquiries of a mysterious nature were addressed to me personally, I always made all the researches required for my pleasure and my own instruction, without charging anything. In one case, a small German manufacturer had already given up the hope to recover the money due to him from a notorious 'sledge-driver.' The matter was placed into my hands by the 'Cologne People's Gazette,' and I succeeded to make the fellow disgorge his evil gain, and to pay in full what he owed. Not to disclose my address, I sent the money without deducting anything for collecting-expenses, postage, etc., to the paper, and they transmitted it, also in full, to the poor manufacturer, who seemed highly delighted, and in acknowledging with many thanks the receipt, expressed the hope 'that I had been rewarded.' By whom? I wonder what the good man was thinking. But he need not have troubled himself on this account, for it was and is my principle and my sport to rescue from the 'sledge-drivers' their booty free of charge, and the 'Rhenish Westphalian Gazette,' when defending again their friends, the noble guild of London 'Sledge-drivers,' will be well advised to take note of this, and not to father upon me again some mean and ludicrous motives.

But to return to Mr. Lehnert, I must remark that the button-manufacturer from Oberbieber, had made enquiries regarding Mr. Hesse at a good many enquiry offices, and that the reports he received were, with one exception, all equally favourable. How did this happen? Simply, because they received their information through Lehnert. What humbug! The manufacturer, being a cautious man, and trying to be on the safe side, goes to the expense to enquire at different offices, and receives from them a report emanating from the same source. He has, of course, no idea of it, and acts on the strength of this unanimous opinion. The most suspicious and cautious man must fall a victim to such doings.

To one of the enquiry-offices who received this information, Lehnert prefixed the following lines:

'*Caution!* You will greatly oblige me if you pass on this information in as few words as possible. Hesse is an old friend of mine, is thoroughly conversant with the button-trade, which he knows better than anyone else, and nearly all informations regarding this branch I obtain from him.'

That is really an elevating admission. An enquiry-office relies on the informations of a man engaged in a particular trade, and gives him thus an opportunity to destroy the credit of his competitors. I have not the slightest intention to imply that it was done in this particular case, and that Mr. Hesse abused the confidence put into him. But I want to show what is done in the enquiry line, and to attack the system as followed by Mr. Lehnert.

I mentioned already, that one of the informations given about Mr. Hesse was unfavourable. It said:

'Emil Hesse opened a few years ago a business in partnership with his brother under the style of M. & E. Hesse, in 14½, Adel-street. This firm became bankrupt. Hesse became then a dealer in antiquities and failed again in 1887 for the second time. He went then into partnership with a Mendelsohn, trading under the latter's name, and this business was bought in 1888 for Mrs. Leah Hesse by her brother Mr. Falke, for, as report has it, £1000. The cause of this change in the proprietorship and the style of the firm is, that Emil Hesse with his antecedents would hardly have obtained credit under his own name, for his reputation is not the best one.'

When the manufacturer obtained these contradictory reports, he, to be quite sure, enquired once more from Lehnert, whether he had not made a mistake, and Lehnert answered:

'In receipt of your favour, I think I am better able than any one else to give you reliable information about the firm of L. Hesse & Co. As you are aware, I am a forwarding agent, and in this capacity many deliveries of goods to L. Hesse are passing through my hands. Knowing by this chance that L. H. & Co. are buying much from the button-manufacturers F. & L. in S., I asked their local agent for information. He showed me that he supplied L. H. & Co. during the last few years with buttons to the value of nearly £3000 and that all was paid for regularly. The proprietress of the firm, Mrs. Leah Hesse is besides possessed of considerable means, and was left, it is said, a great legacy at the death of her father a short time ago. I think that the contradicting reports are based on confounding the firm with Mr. E. Hesse, who is now employed in the business of L. Hesse & Co., and who is judged unfavourably from former times. But he is not the responsible proprietor. I, for my part, would not hesitate to credit him £100 to £200.'

In justification of Mr. Hesse I feel bound to add, that the manufacturer lost nothing, and that his goods were returned to him without any objections, when he, growing suspicious again, asked Mr. Hesse for the return.

The difference in these reports shows the different moods of Lehnert towards Mr. Hesse. First they were great friends; then Mr. Hesse got hold of some incriminating material against Lehnert, and in consequence of this Lehnert's rancour and his subsequent bad report. Then follows his humiliating apology, a renewal of his friendship and excellent reports, and finally hatred again, which attains such a pitch, that Mr. Lehnert throws aside all former favourable reports about Mr. Hesse, and publishes through his literary scavanger Stein-Semansky in the 'Rhenish Westphalian Gazette' the following information:

'Under this ficticious name a man is hiding, who started last year at this address a small ink-powder and smelling-bottle manufactory. He is over and over in debts and cannot pay anybody. To distrain is absolutely useless. In 1887 he made a scandalous bankruptcy and has not paid a single farthing to his creditors.'

Beautiful, is it not?

OPITZ, THE TRAVELLER TO THE EAST.

AFTER having looked at the history of Mr. Lehnert, we shall now occupy ourselves with the past of his old friend and confederate, Mr. Opitz, and with him we reach the third degree of comparison. Mr. Ernesto Schreck's history was interesting, that of Lothario Lehnert more so, but the 'curriculum vitæ Gustavi Opitzii,' on whom somebody conferred the degree of F.D. (it does not read *Fidei Defensor*, but *Fraudis Doctor*), is certainly the most interesting of all.

Gustave Bernard Opitz was born on the 11th of April, 1848, at Zittau in Saxony, and he lived in his paternal town up to 1867. His last address there, or to speak correctly, that of his father, was No. 450, Frauenstrasse. On the 8th of May, 1867, Opitz appeared voluntarily before the military authorities at Annaberg, to be enrolled, in accordance with the German military laws, as soldier; but he was declared unfit for military service, and therefore had not to join the army. From that time Opitz became a globe-trotter, and his native town did not see anything of him until 1872, when he reappeared there 'a grand toff' with an American, a 'Mr. Farrington.' He took out a new passport, and returned on the 2nd of November to the new world, of which excursion we shall have more to say by and by. At present we have still to mention what is known to the German authorities and private persons in his native place about Opitz when 'young and innocent.' His parents were highly respected people, and his father occupied an influential position as officer of the government. The boy Gustav, however, seems to have caused some anxiety to his worthy parents, for he is described in the official registers as a 'frivolous and artful child.' The parents were spared the sorrow to witness the last phases of his career, but they saw enough of his adventurous life, the father having died only in 1884, and the mother as late as 1893, and since 1872 their son visited them only once or twice, and then stealthily, at night-time; for he had good cause not to show himself publicly in his native town again. His visit with Mr. Farrington to wit, was a very expensive affair to some good people in Saxony, as will be seen by the following letters of a highly esteemed gentleman, who lost over it 150,000 marks. He writes:

'About the antecedents of Opitz, I am not able to tell you much. I know him only since 1872, when he appeared here quite unexpectedly with a Mr. Farrington from S. Francisco, (California). He stayed for a few months, and tried to dispose of a territory in Nevada, in which he succeeded. I can but say that I consider Opitz a very dangerous man, for he is slippery like an eel. I personally was engaged in the matter with 150,000 marks, which I lost. Opitz came once more here to visit his father, and at the instance of the public prosecutor a warrant was issued against him. This was brought to his knowledge, and he disappeared during the night. I must mention, too, that a few days ago our police asked me for some information, which I gave to my best knowledge. I advise everybody to beware of this man.'

In another letter the same gentleman writes:

'As I informed you already, Opitz came here in 1872. He submitted to me a project to acquire a territory in Nevada, containing, according to his statement, an inexhaustible wealth of boratic limestone, and he produced samples, which were really marvellous. Opitz had very likely heard from his father that I had been interested in the successful floating of some companies. However, I declined, and he addressed himself then to my friend the councillor of commerce X., from L., knowing that I was in close relations with this gentleman. My friend evinced a greater interest for the matter, and his son studying chemistry at Leipsic, he found an opportunity to show the samples to professor K., and to inform him of their origin. Mr. X. was in constant communication with the firm B. L. & Co. at Leipsic, and mentioned the matter to the proprietors.

Soon there was a great enthusiasm for the project, and this was increased, when the privy councillor of commerce, Mr. Z., asked to be permitted to take a share in the concern. The resolution was now come to, of sending over two experts as our confidential men, that they may investigate the matter. Opitz and Farrington deposited an amount covering the expenses of our confidential men, in case they would report unfavourably. Mr. L. made it a condition that a nephew of his, a Mr. V. be chosen as mining expert, a demand that, of course, was willingly granted, and as chemical expert, professor K. recommended a Dr. S. Both gentlemen were engaged by us, and having received detailed instructions, started on their voyage in company with Opitz and Farrington. Five weeks had passed, when we received a cablegram from our representatives reporting in general terms favourably on the matter. A written report followed, confirming this opinion in an exhaustive manner, and describing the concern as a lucrative undertaking. I think they valued it at one-and-a-half million. The bargain was concluded, and the Saxo-American Borax Company formed. As Opitz had great local experiences, and left a small part of the purchase-money in the company, he and another German were appointed managers. Following their advice, a factory was erected, a chemist engaged, and the manufacture of borax started. The reports were addressed to me in accordance with a resolution of the company. I received also samples of our borax, which were pronounced of excellent quality by Messrs. B. & L. But the demands for money did not cease. Our experts had fulfilled their mission. Dr. S. returned, but Mr. V. we were told, had gone to Japan. *We have never seen him again.*

'We were at work for a whole year, and had not received a single dollar, for all the moneys from the sales were expended again by the management, and one day a letter reached me with the information, that a new borax-field had been discovered, much richer than ours and besides much cheaper, and if we did not want to be ruined by this competition, no choice was left to us but to acquire it. In Nevada we had paid 100,000 dollars, the new territory was to be had for 20,000 dollars.

'I called a meeting together, and reported to the gentlemen

about the matter. They were unanimous that we were obliged to buy, and I was the only one who declared, he would not part with any more money, excepted one of our number would inspect personally the old and the new territory.

'This was approved of, and I was elected for this purpose. I started on the 4th of October in the company of a young man, whom I intended to appoint as manager on the new territory. After a fearful passage, lasting nearly twenty days, we reached New York and started at once for 'Hotspring,' as our territory was called. After another tedious journey we arrived there one evening in the darkness, and the next morning I knew already how we had been cheated.

'Our factory was quite isolated, and 25 Chinamen and 4 horses did the work required. On the whole of the territory was not a drop of water. What was required had to be brought by rail, a distance of 20 miles. Our borax was sold at 25 dollars, and the production cost us 90 dollars.

'I, of course, dissolved at once the whole concern, and went to San Francisco to get the advice of the German Consul General. I was told by him that Opitz had bribed V. with a large sum to report favourably, and that V. had gone with this money to Japan. That the raw material on the territory was not of the quality as represented to us, for this our chemical expert has to answer. That I have no regard to take towards Opitz, you will comprehend.' Yes, I do comprehend it!

Thus ended the mysterious Borax-affair at the close of 1873, and the gentleman who wrote the above letter very likely will be pleased to hear a little more what *fraudis doctor* Opitz was doing since then.

As mentioned before, Opitz was in 1867 in Zittau, and appeared before the military authorities. But according to his depositions during the last trial, he declared under oath, that he was living in 1866, 1867 and 1868 in London, and in 1869 in Paris, 'on his income.' In 1870, he says, he was in the employment of Messrs. Fabre & Co., in Yokohama, and he maintains that he remained in this situation for seven years. Soon after the Franco-German war, however, he declares the firm dismissed him. That these statements are not to be reconciled is evident. Then he swears again, that he was travelling for this firm in Japan up to 1873. But we know on the strength of official documents and the letter quoted, that he arrived in 1872 in Zittau from America, and that he returned there a few months later and remained in Hot-spring until the close of 1873. As it is impossible for a man to be bodily at the same time in two different places, it is evident, that Opitz cannot have been in Japan in 1872 and 1873, as he maintains. In 1874 and 1875 he sojourned, according to his statement, in San Francisco, and I cannot disprove this assertion. I accept also as true his statement that he came in 1875 to London and established himself in St. Mark's-square, Dalston, as commission agent. I believe him too when he further says, that he does not remember more the number of the house where he was living; that he transferred his 'business' to Cheapside; that also in this case he does not remember more the address; that he was representing German and French firms, that the business did not pay, and that he transferred it for this reason to his friend 'Riley.'

In 1876 he lived again in the gay French capital 'on his income,' and from 1879 until 1883 he was, he says, in the employ of the firm of Messrs. Volkart Brothers in Bombay, who have also a branch office in London, the chief seat of the firm being Winterthur in Switzerland. Opitz swore that he left in consequence of a disagreement with the chief of the firm. After this he formed in 1884 a limited company for the manufacture of bricks and tiles in Bombay, and then we are confronted again by the duplicity of his being, for on a later occasion he states he made the acquaintance of Lehnert in 1883 at London, and Lehnert himself again maintains he came to London in 1884. I, of course, believe both gentlemen, and content myself, to repeat Mr. Opitz's confession that the company he founded *stopped* making bricks and tiles, and very likely something else too. Not to lay idle, he established directly afterwards in the same year, with a Mr. Martin Cohen, a firm styled Martin Cohen & Co., exporters and importers in Bombay. Asked why he did not open this business under his name, Opitz explained that Cohen's name was not known in India, and his was. He admitted, too, that the firm was started without any capital whatever; but, in spite of this, he went in 1885 to London to open there a branch of the firm, and this he did at

9, Great St. Helens. However, for particular reasons, not as Martin Cohen & Co., but as McEntee & Co. The business of these firms left him time to establish with our old friends M. Zucker and Schütz another firm under the style of Martin Sugar and Co. Opitz denied in his cross-examination under oath that he was a partner in this firm, which he admitted was a swindling concern, but he did not deny that he was a visitor in their office and had transactions with them. But, if he had gone on with his action against me, I would have proved by many witnesses that Opitz acted as partner, and represented himself to many firms, in giving orders for goods, as co-proprietor, personating one of the partners. Of these witnesses I mention only a few. Mr. Edward William Seward, who was in 1885 a co-proprietor of the 'Somerset Manufacturing Company,' says, he received at that time from Martin Sugar & Co., an order for goods to the value of £175, of which about three-fourths were delivered. 'This being our first transaction with the firm, I gave them a call for the purpose of seeing Mr. Martin Sugar or one of the partners. I was received by a member of the firm, but he did not understand English, and I spoke accordingly to the clerk, who asked me whether I was particular about seeing one of the proprietors of the firm. I answered in the affirmative, and the clerk, whose name was Drewry, said he would call Mr. Opitz. He did so, and Mr. Opitz came, and was introduced to me as the principal of the firm. I inquired whether he was satisfied with the quality of the goods, and he said he was greatly satisfied, indeed. I asked after this for cheque, but Opitz said the firm paid punctually at the proper time, and not before, and I would have first to deliver the remainder of the order. This would have been done, if Sugar and Opitz had not bolted in the meantime. The clerk Drewry told me they had left without paying him his salary. The creditors instituted criminal proceedings against the swindlers, but a promise of payment was made through a third party, and this promise was accepted. But up to this day not a penny has been paid.'

A similar deposition was made by Mr. B., who supplied goods for £60, and lost the whole amount.

Mr. James Culverwell declares he received in 1885 an order from Martin Sugar & Co., Guildhall-chambers, which he executed.

He never received payment for it. Mr. Culverwell says he had only to do with Opitz, who represented himself as the proprietor of the firm Martin Sugar & Co. He saw also Lehnert very often in the office of the firm, and some people more, who could not speak English. 'I lost,' the witness proceeds in his depositions, '£90 with Martin Sugar & Co., and I have not the slightest doubt that Opitz was a partner of the firm, and that Sugar & Co. were long-firm swindlers. If a third party had not intervened and promised payment, we would have proceeded criminally.'

Mr. H. says with regard to Martin Sugar & Co.: 'I knew Martin Sugar personally, and I had transactions with him when he was trading as Martin Sugar & Co., at Guildhall-chambers, the same address from whence the swindling firm of B. Arnold & Co. did their mischief.

'It was in August, 1885, when I came into business-relations with the firm. I knew that Opitz, Zucker and Schütz were trading together under the name of Martin Sugar & Co. The result was, that I and my brother, with whom I was in partnership at that time, lost £800.

'I was nearly every day in the office of Martin Sugar & Co., and I met there always the three partners, Opitz, Zucker & Schütz, and they together bought from me goods and arranged the terms. The firm lasted only a few months, and in Oct. already the fellows had bolted.'

In view of the depositions of these and other witnesses, it cannot be doubted that Opitz was the principal in this swindling concern, and yet he had the audacity to declare under oath, that he had credited the firm of Martin Sugar & Co. with 40,000 marks, which he finally lost. The worth of this assertion is evident, for Opitz had to admit, that he and Cohen started their business without any capital, and the different banking accounts he kept at this time for his different firms, show clearly that he was without means. He had to admit under cross-examination that he was trading at about the same time and had banking accounts as G. Opitz, Walter Arnold & Co., and L. L. Clarke, and that these accounts were closed with a balance in his favour of 3d., 2/-, and 3/5. How he, under such circumstances, could credit to a firm that was in existence a few months only, an amount of nearly £2,000, even the most perverse friends of the 'sledge-driving' fraternity will be hardly able to explain. The whole affair appears in a stronger light still, when we find that Opitz in his bankruptcy, puts down the firm of Morris Brandt & Co. as debitors with £2,000. We know already that the proprietors of this firm were Lehnert and Zucker, and we know too that Lehnert offered to buy this debt of £2,000—for £10, adding that this claim is not worth a penny to anybody else. What shuffling and shifting! Who could unveil it to its whole extent!

At the time when Opitz was driving the sledge of 'Martin Cohen & Co.,' he was also the lucky proprietor of the 'wealthy firm McEntee & Co.,' 9, Great St. Helen's, E.C. But this Mr. 'McEntee' shared the fate of all the strange friends of Mr. Opitz; he disappeared, if he ever existed, by going to Australia, and Mr. Opitz never saw or heard anything more of him; at least, so he declared under oath. In consequence of this very sad occurrence, Opitz transferred his office to 17, Great St. Helen's, and he traded there under his name for a few months as 'export and import merchant,' until he found a partner in the person of John Mouat, Esq., with whom he opened the firm of 'John Mouat & Co.,' permitting the firm of G. Opitz to disappear.

John Mouat, Esq. was a gentleman in rags and tatters, with hardly any boots to his feet, whom Opitz had picked up in the street. In spite of being raised quite unexpectedly to the dignity of a City merchant, poor John Mouat had to pass still many a night with no other blanket over his head than the canopy of heaven. For giving his name to and bearing the responsibility of the firm, and for signing the bills given in payment for goods obtained from the continental manufacturers, John Mouat drew the magnificent daily allowance of eighteen pence, and being extremely fond of 'a little drop' of 'Scotch hot,' there was hardly anything left for a dinner in a fried fish shop, and poor John died too very soon where he had lived—in the street.

October, 1885, had broken in—a dismal month, especially for the 'great traveller in the East,' to whom the firms of 'Martin Cohen & Co.' in Bombay, 'Martin Sugar & Co.,' 'John Mouat & Co.,' and G. Opitz, in London, gave a bad head-ache. The creditors of these highly respectable city-firms grew impatient, and judgment-summonses and bankruptcy-notices came down on the great traveller like a hailstorm. Is it to be wondered at that he recalled his vocation and went travelling again to the far East? The 15th of October, 1885, was the day when Mr. Opitz embarked in Cardiff on board a coal ship bound for Bombay. Did he so to escape his creditors? Did he so from fear? Nothing of the kind! At least Opitz declared under oath, 'that all what I had written in the 'Cologne People's Gazette', about his flight in a coal-ship was utter nonsense.' The ship he sailed in was, he said, the *Monk Seaton;* she was laden with coals, it was true, 'but it was ridiculous to call her for that a coal-ship.' This assertion is very amusing, for the owners of the steamer write, that the *Monk Seaton* neither before nor after 1885 served another purpose than carrying coals. That Opitz fled the country he denies with great tenacity. He says, he received a telegram from his partner Cohen, to come as quickly as possible to Bombay, and for this reason he embarked on board the ship carrying coals, but which was no coal-ship, to get as quickly as possible to India. That a passenger steamer would have served this purpose better, the experienced traveller would not see. When the creditors discovered that nothing was to be done with Martin Sugar & Co., John Mouat & & Co., and G. Opitz, they let the matter drop, and Opitz returned to London again in the following year. There he found 'a nice mess.' His firms had disappeared to be sure, but 'these fools,' Zucker and Schütz, as if to help the creditors on the track, had installed themselves in the old offices at 17, Great St. Helens. Opitz cleared them out forthwith and settled down in 22, St. Mary-axe, E.C. 'Just round the corner you know.' Here Opitz remained until 'he had the misfortune to become bankrupt,' as he puts it. Through an advertisement Opitz came into connection with a Manchester firm, of which incident he makes a great deal. It is a highly respected firm. But the connection did not last long, because it did not answer the expectations of the Manchester people; but they did not lose anything through Opitz, and this is certainly something of which he may be proud, even if the merit lays with the cautiousness of the firm. The German firms, who had to do with Opitz, were not equally fortunate. By the kind assistance of the well-known enquiry-office of Messrs. Schmeisser & Co. in Berlin, and from the official documents in the bankruptcy proceedings, I was enabled to convince myself that the business carried on from 17, Great St. Helens and 22, St. Mary-axe was one of the most artful and successful in the history of London 'sledge-driving.' The 'fortune' of Mr. Opitz at that time consisted of £35.—With this amount he secured the first requirements of successful 'sledge-driving', a banking account, and the honour fell in this case to the 'London and North-Western Bank.' Why should Opitz have opened a larger account? Had he not Lehnert to his friend, who at that period held an influential position as enquiry-agent? Against the 'heavy artillery' of Mr. Lehnert, the London enquiry-offices, even such renowned ones as 'The Credit Index Company Limited,' 13/14, Abchurch-lane, and Messrs. Stubbs, Limited, Gresham-street, could not make a stand, because they would speak the truth only and report in a quiet concise manner, whilst Lehnert wrote fiction in a blustering, flourishing style. His informations were always five times the length of the reports of other enquiry-offices, who contented themselves with stating facts. Lehnert's principle, to the contrary, was: words, words, words, as German manufacturers like it, losing thus unconsciously much of their time. Lehnert knew that lengthy epistles were in demand in Germany, and he supplied them without having even approximately the source of information at his disposal, as they are possessed by such firms of high standing as mentioned before.

Let us look at the reports given at that time about Mr. Opitz. First of all I shall reprint a memorandum of Mr. Gustav Opitz addressed *ad usum delphini* to Messrs. Louis Loewy & Co. Now this firm was again Mr. Opitz himself. Accordingly Opitz wrote to himself, and gave his references as follows:

MEMORANDUM.

From Gustav Opitz. To Messrs. Louis Loewy & Co.,
17, Great St. Helens,
London, E.C., 22/2/86.

Regarding your request to supply you with references in connection with my order No. 484, your manufacturer can inquire at the following firms: Messrs. M. Bernard & Co., 4 Bury-street, E.C., Messrs. M. & E. Hesse, 17½ Addle-street, E.C., Messrs. Liman & Co., enquiry-office, Berlin.

That is really touching. M. Bernard & Co.! Who were they? Opitz, Schütz, Zucker, Holm, Lehnert. Consequently Opitz, therefore, after having written to himself as Loewy, gave himself as Bernard as reference! No wonder that under such complications he finally got so mixed up that he did not know who he was. How Messrs. M. & E. Hesse came to the honour of being given as references, they, maybe, could not explain themselves. But who Messrs. Liman & Co. are, we know again. 'They' were Mr. Lehnert, and he gave about Opitz, as he had to admit in the witness-box, the following report:

'Information from Liman & Co.,

1, Millbrook-road, Brixton, London, S.W.,

'About Gustav Opitz,

17, Great St. Helens, London, E.C.,

March 1st, 1886.

'The person inquired after is the London buyer for some Indian firms, for whom he is buying all kinds of goods for the Indian market, and forwards to their destination. He is considered an experienced man of business, who is possessed of some means of his own and financially strongly supported by his Indian firms, and it is thought that credit to a fair amount may be given.'

It is to be seen how 'traps and sliding-doors' are used in this case already. First a favourable report, followed by a sentence which permits a retreat when things went wrong. In this case, however, matters did not go quite smooth, as Lehnert's report was supplied to Messrs. Wilhelm Schmeisser & Co., in Berlin, who, with their customary cautiousness, inquired at the same time at the renowned office of Messrs. Stubbs, Limited, whether G. Opitz was good for 3,000 marks, and their answer was:

'G. O. rotten, Hands off.'

These three words broke Mr. Opitz the neck, and he found it in consequence advisable to change his address from Great St. Helens to 22, St. Mary-axe. Soon afterwards Messrs. Schmeisser and Co. addressed another inquiry to Lehnert, whether Gustav Opitz was good for 10,000 marks, eventually more, and Lehnert answered on the 26th of July, 1886:

'*Re* Gustav Opitz, 22, St. Mary-axe, London, E.C.

'G.O. is established since 1883, and is exporting goods of all kinds, especially cloth and woollens to the East-Indies. According to the official shipping-list he exported last year considerable quantities; and there is no doubt that his business is a prosperous one. He is born in Saxony, held for many years first-class positions in Indian and Chinese houses, and seems to have used this opportunity to secure for himself good connections for whom he is acting now as buyer. He is considered an experienced man of business, who is fond of screwing down the prices and to buy as cheaply as possible. It is not doubted that he is possessed of means, and a short time ago, it is said, he came in for a considerable amount of money at the death of his wealthy father. Besides he is representing in London one of the largest Manchester firms. It is thought the mentioned amount of £500 can be credited to him.'

From the very first line it is to be seen that Lehnert gave this information against his better knowledge, and wrote a pack of untruths. He knew perfectly well that Opitz had been swindling a few months ago with 'Sugar & Co.,' that actions without end were brought against him, and that only his boundless 'cheek,' one of the most prominent characteristics of the 'great Orient-traveller,' kept him afloat.

But Messrs. Schmeisser & Co., who at that time did not distrust Lehnert yet, wanted to see clear in the matter, and they enquired therefore once more at Lehnert's and at Stubbs'.

To the former they wrote on the 28/7/86:

'In March a.c. we received from another enquiry-office in London a report about Gustav Opitz, saying laconically: 'Rotton, Hands off.' You report the man good for 10,000 marks. We do not know now which of these two informations is to be relied upon, and ask you to let us know whether you can maintain your report in its entirety; otherwise please rectify.'

Lehnert answered by return:

'31/7/86. I know the man for a considerable time in my capacity as forwarding-agent, and being aware at which bank he keeps his account, I enquired there first of all, and received a very good report. The firm of whom he has rented his offices, and who is a large Japanese exporting firm of excellent repute, gave me likewise a good report. Besides the man is representing one of the leading Manchester firms, Messrs. Louis Behrens & Sons, and they certainly would not entrust their representation to a rotten firm. Further, he is the European buyer for an important firm in Bombay, to whom, as the official shipping-lists are showing, he is sending every week large consignments of goods, amounting often to £2,000—and for this reason already he cannot be 'rotten,' because no English firm would give him credit. I hear from another side, that he had some time ago a dispute with two of our inquiry offices; this arose over a collecting matter; there were some differences, and it is said that Opitz sent away the agents of the enquiry-offices, in a far from polite manner, and forbade them to interfere again.'

In this letter Lehnert's craftiness is plainly visible again. He says he became aware at which bank Opitz kept his account. It could hardly have been otherwise, for Lehnert introduced Opitz at the bank, the London & North Western Bank. Lehnert says further, he made enquiries there. This is simply an untruth. Banks will not give informations about their customers to private persons, and if they had made an exception in Lehnert's case, the report hardly would have been a good one, considering that Opitz opened his account with £35 only, and never kept more than a few pounds at the bank.

At the same time when Messrs. Schmeisser & Co. wrote to Lehnert, they addressed also the following 'further inquiry' to Messrs. Stubbs, Limtd.:

'Your information regarding Gustav Opitz runs verbally: 'Rotten. Hands off.' From another office we received to-day about the same person a report to exactly the contrary effect, and recommending O. for a credit of 10,000 m. To whom are we to believe? Please let us know whether you can maintain your report in its entirety, or rectify eventually.'

Messrs. Stubbs answered:

'We cannot understand who can recommend that man for £500—or any credit at all. He was connected with M. Sugar & Co., and is established for some time, but lately only he took an office for himself at 17, Great St. Helen's. Opitz pretends to represent Messrs. Louis Behrens & Sons of Manchester, but at our inquiry these gentlemen (a great firm) inform us they know O. only from answering an advertisement of theirs for an agent. O. gave satisfactory references, but did not fulfil the expectations of the firm. It is said, he was formerly in Bombay, dealing principally in German fancy goods, and is reported as having small, if any means at all. He has also no stock, and only a few samples. Some of his connections are considered far from satisfactory. Until a short time ago he was alone, but now he seems to keep a clerk. If you do not object, we should be glad to know the source from whence you received your information. With regard to O.'s credit, we confirm our former report, and would do business only for cash in advance.'

Messrs. Schmeisser & Co. addressed now an energetic reclamation to Lehnert, which he answered as follows, on the 18th of August, 1886:

'I am greatly obliged to you for your communication of the 11th inst. regarding Gustav Opitz, 22, St. Mary-axe, E.C. I have since then spared no endeavours to make new enquiries in every direction, and I succeeded the better in it, as I meet the man nearly every day at dinner at the same table, know him for many years, and act as his forwarding agent, which offers to me a better insight into his affairs, as anyone else can boast of. Stubbs's informations are quite worthless in my eyes, and this the more, as I happen to know some of his inquiry-agents, and accordingly know, too, in what easy-going manner Stubbs's reports are manufactured. I could mention to you more than ten cases in proof of it, which came to my personal knowledge. With reference to this particular report about G. Opitz, I declare there is no question, but it was dictated by motives of malice. He had last year a quarrel with Stubbs about a collecting-matter, and he made head against these people in a very unceremonious manner—to speak candidly, I would have done exactly the same. It is not true that Opitz was connected with Martin Sugar & Co. This firm simply consigned goods through his agency to his Indian house,* amounting in all to some £5,000. Opitz made to these people against the bills of lading considerable advances, and through an

* This 'Indian house' was Martin Cohen & Co. in Bombay, Opitz's firm, who sold the goods which he obtained by fraud as Martin Sugar & Co.

error of judgment on Opitz's, and false representations on Sugar's part, the goods fetched finally £1803 12s. 10d. less than the advances were. When Opitz, to recover this amount, had finally to sue Martin Sugar & Co., the people bolted and left him in the lurch. Proof: enclosed judgment.* '*He pretends to represent Messrs. Louis Behrens & Co.*' That is rather strong. That he is actually representing the people is proved by the enclosed market report and the enclosed private letter of the chief of the firm, Mr. Oscar Behrens, to Mr. Opitz. '*He has very small if any means at all.* Enclosed Seyd's report, which is not coloured, and recommends Opitz for a credit of £100. I think very much of Seyd. With regard to small firms he is always cautious and reserved, and his reports are ten times more reliable than those of Stubbs, because Seyd has excellent sources at his disposal, which are closed to the proletarian institute of Stubbs. Opitz's turn-over amounts in one year to £10,000. This is not much for a shipping firm according to English ideas, for here things are measured with a different measure to that of Germany; to be great here, one must have a million. '*He keeps no stock.*' Well, why should he as a shipping firm? I know hundreds of firms, who are shipping goods to all parts of the world, turn over millions, never see a box in their place of business, have a small office of two rooms only, often in the third or fourth floor, and one or two clerks. The London buyer or commission-agent of trans-oceanic firms, and that is Opitz's position, sends the samples out, receives from his firms the order, and gives this in his turn to the manufacturer. The latter sends the goods through a forwarding agent to London, and he advises in due time the commission-agent of the arrival of the goods, and receives immediate orders to ship them on board of this or that trans-oceanic steamer.

'To-day only I had 480 chests China. If my customers would have kept this in stock before shipment, they would require warehousing-room with a rental of £3000. Stubbs send their nonsense into the world without assuring themselves properly in what

* This judgment was a fraud. Actually Opitz brought the action against himself (for he was also Martin Sugar & Co.), and he did so in the first instance to hide his connection with this long-firm, against whom criminal proceedings were pending, and for the second he prepared thus his unavoidable bankruptcy. He knew that nobody would appear to defend the action, and it was thus easy to him, to sue and to obtain judgment.

kind of business a man is engaged. They certainly take Opitz for a simple agent, who is representing a few German firms, and like many others, goes begging for orders to the wholesale houses. In such a capacity he certainly would not require any credit. But if Stubbs had put their noses to page 340 of the official shipping-list for the year 1885 he would have read :

Gustav Opitz, 17, Great St. Helens, East India, China. Woollen goods, Manchester goods, clothing, piece goods, pencils, glass, machines. Value £7882.*

'The lists are unfortunately bound and so voluminous, that I cannot transmit them to you, but you will take my word for the correctness of my quotation. There is no question about it that Gustav Opitz is possessed of some capital, for with nothing one cannot buy anything in London.† His Indian house‡ must be supporting him, or how could he buy goods for £7882? He must get credit, for the transport of goods to India takes 4 or 6 weeks, another 4 weeks are required for the sale, and 3 to 4 weeks before remittances reach him. Who has no means, or very little only, shall just show me the trick to buy goods for £7882 and to pay for them.§ That were the views that induced me after consideration of all the facts to recommend the man for a credit of £500. At any rate, I may claim to be well-informed in this case, and I think you will have found yourself by a comparison of reports with those of the competition, that I am able to bring ten times more to light in special cases, than all the other enquiry-offices in London. And this is quite natural, because my social position is a different one to that of the drunken lot of fellows who are making the enquiries for Stubbs. After having explained these facts, I can but maintain fully my informations of the 24th and 31st July, and I hope that you will agree with me. I should not like to underbind the credit to a man, who is

* Very nice and true. But the fact is that Opitz paid VERY little, if anything at all, for these goods. I have got a number of bills which he gave for goods from German manufacturers, but which he never paid, and in fact he did not even mention the names of these manufacturers in his bankruptcy in 1887.

† Not buy, but obtain by long-firm swindling.

‡ Martin Cohen & Co., who had no capital, as Opitz had to admit under oath as partner of the firm.

§ I think Mr. Lehnert and his friends knew the trick how to buy goods and NOT to pay for them.

esteemed by all who know him as honest, experienced, and diligent, and I feel convinced that you share in this my opinion, in spite of contradictory reports. Most respectfully,

(Signed) L. Lehnert.'

'*Postscript.*

'*Some of his connections are not considered satisfactory?* Well, who are they? Such general phrases are easily uttered, but they ought to be substantiated.'

Audacity, thy name is Lehnert! But for such a dear friend as Opitz was, Lehnert could well write such a tissue of lies and falsehoods, and even run the risk to give to himself a *testimonium paupertatis*. For Lehnert knew at that time already what was unavoidable in the nearest future, and that Messrs. Stubbs's report with its classical brevity: 'Rotton, Hands off!' would be justified to the hilt. And how would Mr. Lehnert then compare with the 'drunken lot of fellows who are making enquiries for Stubbs'? How would he shine in his superior social position? Would also Messrs. Schmeisser consider Messrs. Stubbs's informations worthless? For, a few months later Opitz was bankrupt and travelling to the East as passenger in a coal-ship, glad to have escaped his creditors and to the police, who had 'an eye on him.' Lehnert had now only to prepare for this event and to cover his retreat in regard to Messrs. Schmeisser as well as he could. A few months later when Opitz had obtained what he wanted, we find him therefore writing the following supplementary information:

'G. Opitz, 22, St. Mary-axe. This firm has suffered great losses, and will be hardly able to overcome the crisis, I should advise not to give any further credit.'

This was certainly very conscientious; but at the very same time when Mr. Lehnert issued this warning to Messrs. Schmeisser, Lehnert became the reference for Opitz under two new aliases, which the latter chose, at two banking institutes. Opitz, to wit, opened, when the account in his own name had ebbed down to 3/5, under the name of Walter Arnold & Co., another account closed soon afterwards with 2/1, and a third account as L. L. Clark, which was closed when the bank held still the magnificent balance of 3d. for this firm in their coffers. The proprietor of L. L. Clark was, according to Mr. Opitz, a 'Mr. Summers,' for whom the account was opened with £50 in the maiden name of Mrs. Lulu Opitz.

When Opitz had to admit under cross-examination that he opened these accounts in these names, it was really distressing to find, that Mr. Arnold and Mr. Summer shared the sad fate of poor Mr. McEntee. Poor Arnold had gone a-travelling to Australia, and was never heard of again, and poor Summer met the same fate in Russia. One consolation remains, and that is that Arnold and Summer were never seen before their disappearance, and that their fate was not a reality like that of poor V., who was never seen again and heard of after he had reported on the celebrated borax-fields in Nevada. His disappearance, and how he came to write this fatal report, were and are a real mystery to his friends and relatives.

Looking at these remarkable disappearances, it seems as if Mr. Opitz, with his admirable dexterity in letting vanish the actors in his original plays, would succeed exceptionally well as manager of a Punch and Judy show.

His predilection for the East Indian trade is easily explained, for his 'affiliated' firms were all exporting to India. We have already seen that Opitz was 'driving' at the same time, so many firms, as to render it impossible to him to find the leisure to drive still another one; to an ordinary being, at least, this would have been an impossibility. But Opitz is an extraordinary man, and so we need not be surprised to find him engaged in another concern too. Before I tore the veil from his face, I thought he had been in business relations only with Messrs. Bernard & Co. (or Barnard & Co. as the swindlers spelled the name on some letter-headings). Since then, however, I found in looking at the City-solicitors through the papers seized by the Police, when they cleared out the office of this long-firm after the arrest of Holm, alias Holland, that Opitz had actually found time to conduct a part of the correspondence of Messrs. Bernard & Co. It was of special interest to me, that the letters addressed to the Italian hat-manufacturer, whose address Mr. Lehnert had supplied to Messrs. Bernard & Co., were all written by Opitz. But a little mishap happened nevertheless to our fine gentleman. Going under so many names, it is not surprising to find that he got mixed up a little, and did not know 'where we are.' He signed inadvertedly a letter instead with Barnard & Co. as G. Opitz, and this had rather unpleasant consequences for him. For after the conviction of Holm, and the dispersion of the Bernard gang, the Italian manufacturer, (whom I had called as a witness at my trial), sued Opitz. I, of course, need not mention that this did not help the manufacturer to anything, who lost to his £400 another nice round sum for lawyer's costs. When things came to the worst, Opitz, to wit, declared himself bankrupt, and having done so, he went for a change of air to Bombay, never heeding the summonses of the court of bankruptcy, escaping thus his public examination, and preventing the proceedings to be closed. I, having the good fortune of having become a creditor of Opitz, who has to pay to me the heavy costs of his abortive libel action, certainly could force him now to appear, as his trace is no longer lost. But I would have to open the proceedings at my own expense. The English law permits thus to any bankrupt to bring a libel action, to put the defendant to a great deal of expenses, which to recover from the bankrupt is as likely as to draw blood from a stone. The English law prescribes that a foreigner, living in foreign parts, when bringing an action in England, has to give security of costs; but a foreign bankrupt living in this country may prosecute a subject of Her Majesty the Queen for libel, without giving any security for costs whatever. This is my case. I, a naturalized British subject, was wilfully prosecuted by the foreign bankrupt Opitz, and lose my costs, because he as a bankrupt is supposed not to possess anything.

But let us return to the year 1887, when Opitz escaped English justice in flying to Bombay, where he remained until 1889. The wind had blown over, and he returned to England, and became, according to his statement, in 1890 secretary to the 'Eastern Exchange,' which position he held, as he says, up to 1892. According to his depositions he did not do business on his own account since he became a bankrupt in 1887, and he did not ask for credit. But I have before me a really beautiful matter, which, however, appeared to Lehnert a real sour apple, when he had to bite into it at the Central Criminal Court.

A Crefeld firm intended to go amongst the exporters, and not knowing how to start the business, they inquired at Messrs. Schmeisser & Co. for information, and asked them whether they could procure for them a competent agent, who had a thorough knowledge of the Indian market. Messrs. Schmeisser & Co. thought quite correctly that London was the proper place for obtaining the agent and the information required, and they entrusted accordingly the matter to their confidential agent, Mr. Lehnert. In answer to their inquiry, they received from him under the date of the 21st of January the following epistle, which is far too interesting to be withheld from the reader. Lehnert writes:

'Informations regarding firms of some standing, in such places as Bombay, Calcutta, Rangoon, Madras–Dehli-*(sic)*, Colombo, etc., can be obtained here within two or three days, and they are equally reliable as the enquiries made in those places, because the London Banks and exporters who are trading with the East, are in closest touch with all these firms. The charge for enquiries made in this manner amount from 2/6 to 3/–.

'In the following pages you will find an excellent report how the business is transacted. My reporter has spent the last 20 years in the East, and is now with his family on a recreation tour in England. I can but advise your client to communicate directly with that gentleman. Should letters be sent to him, please to forward them to me, as his address is at present very unsettled. In the Indian trade I am one of the most competent, as nearly all my best friends here are engaged in this business.'

(*The following pages are written by G. Opitz to Lehnert, who forwarded them in continuation to his introductory lines to Mr. Schmeisser.*)

'With your enquiry regarding velvet and silks for India, you have found in me the right man, for nobody has made in these articles such a gigantic business, and, therefore, nobody can give you more detailed information regarding this matter than your most obedient servant.

'In one season, it is not very long ago, I sold in Bombay, Delhi, Lucknow, and Cawnpore for only three firms, N. Edela Flechere, Perunegel in Lyons, and Heckel in Elberfeld, silks for one and a quarter million francs.

'Business is done in the following manner: The agent of

the manufacturer takes on the sample-collection firm orders (indents), and at delivery of the goods the manufacturer draws 30 days after date on the customer, with documents attached, that is, he affixes to his bill or draft the invoice, bill of lading, and insurance policy, and sends it travelling with these attached. This draft with documents he transfers then either to a local banker, or directly to one of the London Exchange Banks, who have their branch establishments in India (the 'Chartered Bank of India, Australia, and China' is the best), and this bank holds then the draft, in the place where the customer is domiciled, until he takes it up, and for cash only he receives the documents which enable him to receive the goods. Credit, accordingly, is never given, and in case where the bank knows the customer well enough to deliver him the goods without previous payment in cash, the bank does so at their own responsibility, and not at the risk of the manufacturer. This way of dealing restricts the risks so far, that the manufacturer can suffer a loss only if a customer refuses to take over the goods against payment of the draft, and if he cannot be forced to do so by judicial proceedings, because he is not worth the costs. But in such a case he does not get the goods. The manufacturer or his agent must then dispose of them otherwise, that is, they must sell them to some one else, and if this cannot be done to the full original price, a small loss may occur, and this difference between the price at which the goods were ordered and the price at which they were sold, constitutes the only risk which the manufacturer has to bear in this trade; but even this only happens, if manufacturers are sending out travellers who have no knowledge of business matters in India, and who do not know the customers, and think it is not worth the trouble to take detailed informations regarding the customers, because they do not get the goods without payment. In this manner a lot of goods are thrown finally at their hands. We in Bombay know quite exactly with which of the native firms we can transact business without any risk. I, for example, know intimately every customer in the different branches. I am personally on friendly terms with most of them as I transact all my business affairs personally, thanks to my knowledge of Oriental languages, and thus never require an interpreter. But for a man who is a stranger in India, it is very often a difficult task to know the black ones from the white ones. I hope this observations will fulfill their purpose, otherwise I am with great pleasure at your services with further informations.

'I am now as well as decided to start in March on my fourth voyage round the world, but this time it shall be confined to the East, that is, India, Burmah, the Straits, Japan and China. I have come to an arrangement already with six English firms of the first rank, on the following basis: Duration of the voyage, one year; contribution for expenses by each firm, £100, which includes salary, travelling, and all other expenses, and 3 % commission on all orders after drafts have been taken up. Should you hear of someone among the wide circle of your acquaintances who should like to participate under these conditions, please let me know and recommend me, but I care only for manufacturers who are really able to deliver, for I cannot work and lose my time with insignificant firms who lose their head when orders are pouring in.

'I intend to take altogether ten agencies, at £100 each, my travelling expenses being thus about covered. I think I am certain to sell goods this time for £100,000, and even with 3 % I should be left at the end with some £3,000. But if I get in Japan my railway-plant contract, which according to the letters of my broker, Matzagdios, is but waiting for me, then I shall earn at least twice that sum.

'But more when I see you, and this very likely will happen in the course of next week.

'In the meantime friendliest greetings, also from my wife to yours; and always with pleasure at your services,

Faithfully yours, (Signed) G. Opitz.'

The letter had its effect, as Mr. Lehnert could see by the following:

Enquiry from Wilh. Schmeisser & Co., Berlin, to Mr. L. Lehnert, London, regarding

'*Bernard Opitz*,' 34 Ayton-road,
Stockwell, London, S.W.

Agent and Commercial traveller for the East.

'He tries to get the agency for a small-arms manufactory for travelling in the East. Can he be trusted, and can samples worth

1500 francs be confided to him? Is he experienced and clever? How is his past, and his way of conducting business?

No. 29612. Berlin 2nd April, 1890.

'Please write an answer on other side of this leaf.'

It will be remarked that Opitz applied in the name of *Bernard* and not *Gustav*. This was done as a precaution to cover his identity with *that Opitz*, about whom Messrs. Stubbs had reported: 'Rotten! Hands off!' and to prevent Messrs. Schmeisser to detect this in looking through their registers. Lehnert's answer to this enquiry was:

'The person enquired after held formerly for some years a position in Japan, and visited repeatedly the sea-ports of Japan and China. He is now for some time in London, and makes preparations to start in a short time on a rather important travelling tour in the East for a number of first-class English firms. He represents houses as Lions, Lions & Son; Barkley & Son, Limited; Welsch, Margetson & Co.; Parker, Son & Rayment, and some other manufacturers.

'He receives from each of the firms he is representing £100 travelling expenses and a commission. According to the information given me by the named firms, the man is clever, experienced in business, and enjoys their fullest confidence. I believe, therefore that your subscriber can participate without misgivings at this collective travelling tour and trust him (Opitz) with samples to the value of 1500 francs.'

Lehnert gives here the names of some leading English firms who, as he declared, had already engaged Opitz for this travelling tour. The facts, however, were, that Lehnert had not enquired at these firms, but that he was given by Opitz as a reference, and then he gave the names of the firms to Messrs. Schmeisser, supposing correctly, that his word would be taken and no enquiries made.

The enquiries of Messrs. Schmeisser were caused by the following letter which Opitz had addressed from his own abode at 84, Ayton-road Stockwell, London, S. W., to the Belgian firm. He wrote:

'I beg to inform you that I am arranging with some first-class English houses, to make, as their commercial agent, a tour to the

Straits-settlement, China and Japan. Being convinced that I could at the same time do good business in your article, I take the liberty to offer you my services, and this at the same terms which are agreed upon between myself and the other houses I have the honour to represent, that is: duration of the voyage 12 months, during which I shall visit the ports of Singapore, Batavia, Hong Kong, Canton, Shanghai, Nangasaki, Kobe, Tokio, Yokohama, and such other places as I shall choose during the voyage, with a sojourn of at least 4 months in Japan.

'I engage myself not to represent more than ten houses, not wo of them dealing in the same article.

'Each of these houses will pay me £50 before my departure, and £50 more six months later, and it is understood that this sum of £100 has to pay me for all my travelling expenses, salary, and all other claims, excepting a commission of 5 per cent. of the amount of all transactions made, or introduced through my intervention, and payable after settlement of the said amount.

'I should like to remark that my commercial experiences in Asia are dating back for 20 years, during which time I was engaged in business in Japan and China, also that I know very well the countries which I intend to visit, also the people, their languages and their requirements. The trade, especially with Japan, but also with China, being at present on the point to expand into more important dimensions than in the past, a more advantageous moment could not be chosen for the acquisition of customers, and of gaining a good footing in this most important commerce.

'In the expectation to have a favourable reply from you, I have the honour to present you my most respectful compliments.

'Bernard Opitz.

'I have come to arrangements already with the following firms:

'Barclay & Sons, Ltd., London, medicine and drugs; Welch and Margetson & Co., woollens; Jacobson and Hamilton, Manchester, hats and caps; Lion, Lions and Son, London, boots and shoes; Perkin, Son and Rayment, optical instruments; Broots and Hawkes, Birmingham, small ware.'

Actually, however, Opitz had not come to arrangements with all these firms, but only with two of them, who later on sued him for the return of the advance made, and the samples entrusted to him. On the strength of Lehnert's report, his statement, however, was accepted, and the Belgian firm answered his letter as follows:

'We have received your esteemed letter of the 29th March last, and waited a little before replying, so as to have your proposals examined by our Committee of Administration.

'We would be disposed to accept them, only our Committee desires that at the same time you should represent the 'L'Union des Papeteries, Societé Anonime,' rue d'Arenberg, at Brussels, as our Administrators are also those of this Company.

'We observe the same course in different representations of our two houses, given amongst others for America. It would be worth mentioning that the representation of the 'Union des Papeteries' would give you but little trouble on account of the smallness of the samples, and besides this you will earn more commission. We would have to allow you for all costs, £50 for each house.

'Please examine the above, so that we may have time to make up for you a good and handsome collection. We would then pay you for the Society 'Union des Papéteries,' and also for our house £50 on your departure, £50 six months later, and 5 % commission on all orders sent to us, as well as those sent by you to the 'Union des Papeteries.' The whole to be paid after settlement of the accounts. Immediate reply will oblige,

'Yours, etc.'

Now ensued a lively correspondence between Opitz and the Belgian firm, and I give first the following letter, which was addressed to Bernard Opitz under the date of the 12th of May, 1890:

'We received your esteemed letter of the 5th inst. Our negociations with the 'Union des Papéteries' are not yet terminated, but until now we are not able to come to an understanding, as this company is already represented in Japan, and as for China, they have not yet decided to have it visited.

'Our managing director is going to Brussels shortly, and will try to persuade the company to pay part of the costs for the journey.

'In the event that the 'Union des Papéteries' should decide not to participate, we shall try to replace this house by another, and with an advantageous article.

'We will soon let you know.

'The samples of weapons will be ready for the 26th inst. Please let us know if you absolutely want a price list in English.

'Tell us the approximate date of your departure and of the day you would come to see us.

We remain etc.'

Opitz answered on the 16th of May:

'I have the honour to acknowledge the receipt of your esteemed letter of the 12th inst., and to thank you for the information which you were kind enough to give me.

'As I am certain to secure good orders for the 'Union des Papéteries,' I should regret very much if you could not prevail upon them to accept your propositions. But even in that case you will certainly find another firm dealing in an advantageous article.

'I do not require absolutely a price-list in English, and if this should cause you difficulties, it will be sufficient for us to have more French ones, and I shall translate them when occasion requires it.'

On the 26th of May he wrote again:

'I regret to have to inform you, that I shall not have the time left to pay you a visit before my departure for the East.

'I hope that you were able to come to an arrangement with the 'Union des Papéteries' or with another firm, and that all the samples are ready. For all the arrangements for my immediate departure are nearly complete, and I would ask you to send to my address all that I have to take with me before the 1st of June, that is, not later than Saturday. Otherwise I shall be obliged to postpone my departure.

'Expecting to have the pleasure to receive your answer by return. Yours, etc.,

(Signed) Bernard Opitz.

Now the gun factory answered on the 27th May, 1890:

'We received yours of the 16th and 26th instant.

'We could not succeed in persuading the 'Union des Papéteries' to entrust you with their representation for your voyage, but we have been able to get over the difficulties by asking them to give you a complete collection of their papers, and their lowest prices, to which they have consented. We shall have this collection during this week, when we will have it forwarded direct from Brussels, at all events you will have it in good time. You will have to transmit to us any orders you may take on the samples of this company, to have them manufactured by the 'Union des Papéteries,' and we trust, as you say in your letter of the 16th, that you will succeed in doing good business in paper.

'As to arms, we shall send you the collection to-morrow and send you invoice at the same time.

'We are sending by same post as this some of our illustrated catalogues.

We are etc.'

This letter was followed by another, dated May 30th, 1890.

'We have the honour to hand you herewith invoice of our samples of arms a/c., amounting to 391fcs. 15c., which we shall place to your debit of sample-deposit. We shall send a parcel containing the samples of paper of the 'Union des Papéteries' and illustrated price-list of our arms. It is leaving to-day by mail via Ostend. We think you will have them by the time mentioned. The prices given you in our invoice, are the lowest at which we could sell these articles; our other arms in our illustrated catalogue are to be sold at the prices mentioned therein, and the conditions are given on the first page. Please acknowledge the receipt of this, and wishing you that you may do good business on your journey.

We remain etc.'

Opitz answered:

'I have the honour to acknowledge the safe receipt of your esteemed letter of the 30th p.m., and the documents mentioned therein, and also the two parcels of samples.

'But you have omitted to remit to me the first payment of £50 in accordance with our agreement, and I ask you therefore to send it to me by return of post, because I must depart on Friday, the 6th instant, the latest.

'I thank you most sincerely for your good wishes and I assure you that I will do all I can to succeed in doing good business and to justify your confidence.

'Awaiting your reply, please accept etc.

(Signed) Bernard Opitz.'

The £50 were the real matter of importance. He very likely waited with anxiety, but the 4th of June brought him relief in the form of cheques and notes, and Opitz acknowledged the receipt in the following letter of the 7th of June:

'I have the honour to acknowledge safe receipt of your esteemed letter of the 4th inst., with your remittance of £50, in accordance with our agreement, for which I thank you and enclose receipt. I shall depart on Tuesday, the 10th inst.'

From this date Opitz gave no sign of life, and on the 4th of April, 1891, the Belgian firm wrote to him as follows:

'A year ago we gave you a collection of samples for your journey to Japan.

'Being deprived since then of your agreeable news, we address to you this, to let us know your results.

'Awaiting your reply,

We are, etc.'

No answer came, and the Belgian house inquired again at Messrs. Schmeisser, who wrote to Lehnert on the 9th of April, 1891:

'Under the date of the 5th of April of last year, you gave us under the number 8,000 an information referring to Bernard Opitz, London, S.W. You told us that this honourable man would travel for some first-class houses to China and Japan, and that he received from each firm a collection of samples and £100 travelling expenses.

'In consequence of this information, a Liège gun manufacturing firm sent to him a valuable collection of sample-guns, worth 1,200 francs, and they enquire to-day whether we are not in a position to inform them how the gentleman is doing, especially whether he has spent their money in comfort in London, and whether he has flung away their guns, for they never heard a word

P 2

more from him. You can certainly hear from the first-class houses, whom he was to represent, to what end this man has come.

'Sincerely,

(Signed) W. Schmeisser.'

Lehnert answered on the 14th of April:

'I obtained information that B. Opitz has gone in July, 1890, by steamer from London to Colombo. It is said he resigned the representations which he had accepted, in order to be enabled to devote himself exclusively to the representation of a Manchester firm, for whom he had to conclude contracts for the fittings of spinning mills in the Colonies, and who guaranteed the whole of his travelling expenses of £1,000. In Burmah, it is said, he was seized with fever. According to reports from there he left directly for Australia. His samples, it is pretended, are deposited with a firm at Colombo, whose name I am not able to ascertain, and O. intends, as it is said, to bring them with him at his return from Australia. His relations are not possessed of more detailed news. Judging from his last letter, which arrived here a few months ago, it is thought that the samples possibly are already on their way back from Colombo. At any rate, I ask you to procure for me a Power of Attorney that I may take possession of the samples as soon as they become recoverable.

'I entertain, however, very little hope with regard to the recovery of his travelling expenses, as the man in fact has really travelled. But I shall be very glad if I get back the sample-collection, and in this I shall succeed may be, as the relations make the impression of respectable people.

The local firms who made payments in advance to O. have not heard from him since he visited Colombo.

(Signed) L. Lehnert.'

'P.S. That is really a cheap way to make a tour round the world. What clever ideas some people have.'

The contents of this letter were communicated by Messrs. Schmeisser & Co. to the Belgian firm, who sent the power of attorney to Messrs. Schmeisser & Co., who on their part forwarded it again to Lehnert.

The Liège gun-factory addressed after this a further letter to

Messrs. Schmeisser on the 28th of April, 1891, informing them of having received a communication of one of the firms whom Opitz had mentioned when offering his services, to the purport, that the great Orient-traveller was now Secretary to the Eastern Exchange in London, and asking Messrs. Schmeisser to press now the matter to the best of their ability.

This letter was also forwarded to Lehnert, who answered a few days afterwards :

LIÈGEOISE *v.* OPITZ.

'In answer to your esteemed letters of the 23rd and 26th inst., I have succeeded in arranging the matters in a satisfactory manner, and the samples are already in my possession. What shall I do with them? I further received a payment of £5 on a/c of the advanced travelling expenses of £50. The repayment of the remainder I agreed to accept in monthly instalments of £5. What you communicated to me on the 26th, I could have told you yesterday already, but I thought to wait until I heard the cheque was paid. The matter appeared strange to me from the very beginning, but I could not make out the people at 4, Spenham-road ; one sees every time a new face. The gentleman with whom I was conferring yesterday is a sea-captain, who had just returned from Australia. According to the tax-collector's book, the house is rented by L. L. Opitz, and the cheque I received was also signed by L. L. Opitz. With one word, I was very energetic and succeeded very well. But whether Mr. Bernard Opitz had started on his voyage or not, whether he was living in the house or not, I was unable to ascertain.'

On the 27th of May, Lehnert wrote again to Messrs. Schmeisser. The letter is apparently written in Opitz's hand-writing, slightly disguised, but I do not want to pass an opinion, and content myself to give the letter :

'In accordance with your instructions, I have handed over to-day the 7 guns and 16 revolvers to Mr. Argles. The number is correct, but the goods look rather dirty. Enclosed you will find my account for expenses, with which I ask you to credit me. With regard to O., nothing is to be done more, as I have made an arrangement with him. If he does not keep up his payments regularly, then we can proceed against him at the best with a civil action. In accepting the first instalment of £5 you have waived the right to take a criminal action, if such an action could have been taken at all. Enclosed I return copy of invoice. Yours faithfully,

(Signed) pro. L. Lehnert, Albert Lange.'

We see Mr. Opitz was shielded against a criminal action, as he and his friend and protector thought. Of a civil action the two gentlemen were not afraid, and they did not trouble about paying another instalment. Messrs. Schmeisser, accordingly, reminded their confidential agent of the matter, and he answered on the 6th of August, 1891:

'The chances to get now anything from Opitz are very bad, for, as far as I can judge, he has nothing. In an action brought against him, he agreed this week before the registrar to pay £2 a month. But I shall watch the matter.'

To another reminder on the part of Messrs. Schmeisser, Lehnert answered on the 5th of September:

'LIÈGEOISE *v.* OPITZ.'

'I have watched the matter but cannot obtain any further payment, for the simple reason that the man has nothing. If you want to sue him you will have to pay £5 10s., and may be more, according to the line of defence the man takes. I do not think it advisable to throw good money after bad, and I am confirmed in this opinion by having heard yesterday, that he is for some weeks already out of a situation. But I will do as you instruct me.'

Nothing was paid, of course, and a further letter from Messrs. Schmeisser drew on the 17th of November the following consoling answer—'short and sweet'—from Lehnert:

'The case is hopeless. The debtor is proceeded against from all sides, and I recommend not to throw good money after bad. I have very little hope.'

As Lehnert admitted in the witness-box, Opitz was helping him in his business already at the beginning of 1891, and Opitz himself declared under oath that he became Lehnert's manager at the beginning of 1892. Was it not Lehnert's duty to tell simply to Messrs. Schmeisser, that Opitz was his employee? Instead of this, he pretended not to be able to find Opitz, and to ascertain, whether he had gone on his voyage or not. From beginning to end Lehnert acted dishonestly towards his employers, and it was unavoidable that he was finally found out and dismissed, as mentioned already.

Mr. W. Schmeisser writes in this matter:

'You will have received the papers referring to the matter Henry Payne & Co. and Lehnert. Lehnert has cheated me too shamefully with Opitz. If he had acted *bona fide*, it would have been his duty to act in the interests of the Liège firm and our own. Instead of this, he kept silence, because he was evidently going hand in hand with O. At that time I trusted Lehnert still implicitely. He was always extremely well-informed about swindling firms and knew artfully how to strengthen the confidence I bore him. To-day I see clearly what then was to me unexplicable and often puzzled me. Thus for example Lehnert warned in his report against a swindling firm and added: 'The enquiry came to you from N. N. in B.' How did he know it, as we did not give him the slightest hint where it came from? He simply played the trick to give to his accomplices the addresses of German manufacturers, the former gave their orders, and if we made an enquiry at Lehnert's, he knew the firm who enquired, because he had furnished the address to his confederates, and sometimes he did not mind to turn round and warn. But as Lehnert was named an official enquiry-agent in Regenhart's Almanac,* which enjoys a very large circulation, many enquiries were addressed to him directly. Lehnert had too great an income through his connection with our firm, as to deceive us frivolously and to open our eyes to his doings. Payne and Co. very likely thought to make a great deal of money out of the matter of K., and they betrayed Lehnert, and that broke him the neck with us.'

Two years had passed since the 'Voyage to the Orient' had come to grief, when the Belgian firm instructed their London agent to take proceedings against Opitz. The agent did his best, but he could not find the great traveller, and thus the matter remained in abeyance, until the articles in the 'Cologne People's Gazette' were

* His name was removed after the appearance of my articles.

published. The Belgian firm became by this means aware that Opitz was living still, and they addressed themselves in consequence to the paper, and at the same time instructed their agent to communicate with me. Thus I became enabled, with the kind assistance of Messrs. Schmeisser & Co., to disclose the whole swindle. The Belgian firm decided now to proceed against Lehnert and Opitz. As soon as they heard of this intention, Lehnert wrote to them on the 25th of February, 1895, the following letter:

'During the six years I had the misfortune to represent the enquiry-office of Schmeisser & Co., in Berlin, I was also entrusted to collect some moneys for your company. Amongst these debts was also an amount of £50, and some samples from G. B. Opitz, 4, Spenham-road, London. After a great deal of trouble I succeeded to arrange the matter in the manner that Opitz made on the 27th of April, 1891, a payment of £5, and gave acceptances for £45, and returned the samples, I giving him in exchange a receipt in full for your claim. I must remark that I gave the receipt on the back of your power of attorney, that was sent to me by Schmeisser to arrange the matter as well as I could. I was consequently greatly surprised to hear that a solicitor here brought an action against Mr. Opitz for having cheated you of £50, and stolen your samples. My books are proving that I remitted to Schmeisser on the 29th of April, 1891, those £5—and one year later, when I resigned the agency, £45—in acceptances (not taken up). The box with samples I handed over on the 22nd of May, 1891, to Mr. Argles, in conformity with Schmeisser's instructions. As Mr. G. B. Opitz is now one of my employees, it is tried to show that I helped him to cheat you, which is quite devoid of foundation. Quite to the contrary. I arranged the matter at the time to the best of your interest, and when Opitz has not paid the remainder, then the only cause for it is that the intended travelling-tour has unfortunately turned out a great loss to him, which he could not repair yet in his present situation. He is an honest man, and I feel convinced that he will repay you as soon as he can, and in the same manner as he has paid the houses who had engaged him for that tour. If, accordingly, the mentioned steps were taken with your consent, please enquire as soon as possible about the facts at Schmeisser's, and withdraw your consent.

Regarding Opitz, I promise you that he will pay your claim as soon as he is in a position to do so. Yours, etc.,

(Signed) L. Lehnert.'

I am of opinion that Mr. Opitz would have acted far wiser and more honestly if he had repaid this debt in good time, instead of bringing a costly libel-action against me. Thus ended the great 'tour to the Orient,' where it was generated, in London. There was, too, the 'fever' bred, which sent Mr. Opitz from Burmah to Australia, just as the galloping consumption, which sent Mr. Zucker to the South of France.

THE SLEDGE-DRIVING TRIALS.

IT is repugnant to my feelings to write about matters concerning myself. But the pressure brought on me on the part of my friends, and the interest of the cause I have taken up are inducing me to overcome my scruples, and to say a few words about my trials and what led to them.

I said just now 'my trials ;' but they would much better be called the 'trials of the Cologne People's Gazette.' When staying in Essen to consult and to instruct the solicitor Mr. George Heinen, who is representing myself and the 'Cologne People's Gazette' in the libel-action we brought against the 'Rhenish Westphalian Gazette,' this gentleman, in perusing the voluminous material submitted to him, and in hearing my answers to his questions, was struck that I had actually played a far more important rôle in these sensational trials, than it would appear from the reports of the German press, the 'Cologne People's Gazette' included. Mr. Heinen actually seemed to arrive at the conclusion that something was withheld from the public, and he declared openly that the public at large would share his fate, and be struck like by a thunderbolt from a cloudless sky, if they knew all the details brought to his knowledge. To prevent the 'thunderbolt' doing any harm, I shall construct here with due care a 'lightning conductor,' feeling at the same time, however, that nothing has been withheld from the public.

The editor and the publishers of the 'Cologne People's Gazette' have for years blindly trusted to my reports, because they knew, by their thorough knowledge of the case, that they were right in doing so. To put it plainly: they knew that I did not write these dangerous matters for gain, and they knew further, that I went in my researches regarding the modern knight-robbers to such expenses, that rendered it quite impossible to make my work materially profitable to myself, as no newspaper would have paid a honorary sufficient to refund my expenses.

Mean insinuations made in the vindictive spirit of party-hatred were directed against the paper I represented, and every means was tried to delude the public into the belief that the publishers of the 'Cologne People's Gazette' in their craving for sensational news, were paying me to fabricate, at the expense of truth, those incredible and fictitious 'stories,' which created such a sensation amongst the German manufacturers. I, personally, was quite pushed in the background. 'Rollo' was to them nothing more nor less than one of those starving wretches, who are earning with pen and ink a few pence to buy bread for their hungry offspring, and of whom many a one is not very particular about the truth, if it helps him to sell the wares of his brains to editorial sensation-mongers. It never occurred to these friends of the 'Knights of Industry' to see any noble motives underlying our action. And more, there were not many who believed that what I wrote was true, line for line, and word for word. Even our solicitor Mr. Heinen was sceptical, and he was converted only, after he had sifted with me the material. But from day to day he understood better the impregnability of my position, until we reached after ten days hard work, and sometimes night-work into the bargain, the last page of the documentary evidence in my possession.

It is true, I was paid for my work by the 'Cologne People's Gazette,' but the question of honorary was always treated as a formal matter only. I declared repeatedly that I did not require any honorary, but the publishers insisted on my accepting it. The relations between the proprietors of the 'Cologne People's Gazette' and myself were simply different to those as may exist in the 'Rhenish and Westphalian' Provinces between newspaper-publishers and their correspondents, and this fact certain people would not understand.

One newspaper accused us of making sport of the war against the 'sledge-drivers.' If it gives pleasure to our enemies, we shall admit it. Yes, the fight is a sport to me, but I consider this sport a duty. I was in a position to cultivate the sport, and this made the sport a duty to me. These are things which are above the comprehension of the journalists with down-trodden heels and torn trousers, of whom a paper in Essen has secured a specimen. From my point of view, also the editor and the publishers of the 'Cologne People's Gazette' regarded the sledge-driving fraternity, and I am thankful to them that they opened their columns to me, and rendered it possible to lead such a merciless war against the 'Knights of Industry.' The 'sledge-driver' journalists really paid me a compliment in an Essen paper, in declaring me a powerful antagonist. They were right. The 'powerful antagonist' has pressed them so hard in the corner that they squeaked.

When I commenced 'the war' against the swindling enquiry-office of Lehnert, I did not hesitate a moment to tell the publishers of the 'Cologne People's Gazette' that I might expect a libel-action. Quite to the contrary, I said, I hoped it would come to it, and in my second article against Lehnert-Liman & Co., I even declared in the 'Cologne People's Gazette' that all 'explanations' on the part of Lehnert would be of no avail, and that a prosecution alone could satisfy us. We even went so far as to say, it was a necessity to bring the matter to a head, that it might be proved in a court of justice with what cunning and to what a pitch the art of sledge-driving had been brought in London, to the detriment of German and English trade. I was quite aware how dangerous it was in England to be involved in an action with such cunning liars, for such fellows will lie themselves, so to say, out of the nook from the gallows. Their really fiendish proceedings were a proof to me that I had judged the matter correctly, but I did not rely on witnesses, but only on the documentary evidence in my possession, by which the sledge-drivers were bound to fall, because they could not well deny their own hand-writing. I was of the opinion that it was but my duty to fight out the action, and when Lehnert wrote to me through his solicitor, I should disclaim my accusations and apologize, I had him informed at once that my solicitors were Messrs. Osborn and Osborn, who would accept service on my behalf, and that I hoped they would have an opportunity to do so as soon as possible. The proprietors and publishers of the 'Cologne People's Gazette,' however, proved their magnanimity also on this occasion, in declaring their solidarity with myself. I was just at that time for a longer stay in Germany, and we resolved to regard ourselves as one person, and to carry on the war against the sledge-drivers in the name of the 'Cologne People's Gazette' to the bitter end, and to defeat them, cost what may, in which we succeeded with the help of excellent counsels in a glorious manner.

After the battle had been won so splendidly, the publisher, who had come over from Cologne to be present at the trial, wished to state publicly in the report, that someone else wrote for the occasion on my behalf, how I shared in the expenses. I was against this, because we had declared ourselves solidary, and could not well part now as victors. The merit of having done such signal service to commerce, said I, belongs to the 'Cologne People's Gazette,' and not to the publishers or to myself; we were but single individuals, belonging to the personal of the 'Cologne People's Gazette,' but not the 'Cologne People's Gazette.' In the first place the merit belongs to the chief-editor, Dr. Cardauns, who had turned grey over the matter. But I am not responsible for his sleepless nights. The guilty party are the 'sledge-drivers.' Without the chief-editor we could have done nothing, if he had not put at our disposal 'a piece of blank paper' in the columns of the 'Cologne People's Gazette.'

That 'Messrs.' Opitz and Lehnert committed a foolish act in bringing these libel-actions, everybody will admit to-day. They were bound to know, in reading my articles, that I had much more material in my possession than I made use of in my writings. But from the manner in which I wrote, they must have seen, too, that they were quite in my hands. Generally, it is accepted as a rule, that it is not safe to throw with stones in glass houses. Why Lehnert and Opitz threw stones, nevertheless, is explained by the circumstance that I had gone at that time to Germany. The two 'gentlemen' thought I had fled in fear of their threatened libel-action, and that I would not return again. It was evident to them I had heard whispers, and on the strength or weakness of these, I had written my articles. Unable to justify what I had said, I escaped the consequences in leaving the country. There was a chance to pose cheaply as injured innocents, to prop up the fading lustre of this unique enquiry-office in 46, Queen Victoria-street, to gain a victory, and to demolish 'Rollo.' And so the stone was set rolling with a light heart. A libel-action was brought against me as publisher of the 'Cologne People's Gazette' in England, with a claim of £1000 damages. At the same time, to have their revenge and something to boast of, they took criminal proceedings against Mr. E. Hesse, of whom we had much to say, as author of the incriminated articles, knowing all the time that he had nothing whatever to do with the writing or publication of the incriminated articles. But the 'gentlemen' had made a gross mistake in their calculation, and great was their dismay when they heard that I had returned. It was very inconvenient to me, because I had still to transact important business in Germany, but when I heard that Mr. Hesse had been summoned, I hurried back to England to explain before the magistrate who the real author was.

On the 23rd November, 1894, Hesse had to appear for the second time at Guildhall Police-court. His prosecutors had secured as witness a Mr. Rewman, about whom I do not want to say anything, as he has died a short time after his appearance in the witness-box against Mr. Hesse. Rewman declared under oath that he called at Hesse's, and that the latter read to him the articles in the 'Cologne People's Gazette,' and added that he had written them. Rewman said, he had said in answer to this declaration: 'Whoever wrote this article was well-read in Goethe and Shakespeare; if he spoke the untruth, he ought to be punished for telling lies; but if, what he says was true, he ought to be punished still harder, Hesse, he declared, told him then, that he was willing to part with the incriminating material in his possession for a consideration of £1000. Hesse and his son declared to the contrary, as mentioned in my article, that Rewman came as an emissary of Lehnert's and offered the £1000 for the documents.

At this junction I stepped in the witness-box and declared, that I was the author of the articles, that I took the full responsibility on myself, and that I would justify my assertions. Accordingly the summons against Mr. Hesse was dismissed, and through his solicitor, Lehnert now applied for a summons against me, an application which was made into a 'warrant' against me by the German official organ of the long-firm swindlers.

The action against me was, however, dismissed, I being the 'publisher' and correspondent of the paper in London, and the *fiat* not having been obtained in the High Court of Justice.

Before this Lehnert's solicitors had tried already to obtain an injunction in the High Court to prevent me from publishing any more articles against their client. But this application was not granted, and the judge remarked, that I could write what I liked, as Lehnert had the remedy in his hands in suing me. This decision was reported in the said German paper to the effect, that the publication of the weekly edition of the 'Cologne People's Gazette' had been prohibited. One lie more or less did not matter much.

The next application that I might be prosecuted for libel was granted by the High Court, and a few days later I had the pleasure of being served with the writ.

The scene of the preliminaries to the trial was Clerkenwell Police-court, and with adjournments for eight and fourteen days, the matter was dragging on there for an almost unbearable length. The cross-examination of Mr. Opitz, however, fully compensated for this loss of time and expense, and forced him to admissions which rendered it advisable to him not to appear again in the witness-box at the Central Criminal Court, and to let the verdict be entered for me. The magistrate, Mr. Horace Smith, was quite willing to hear the matter out in the Police-court, but he declared the case was so important, that he was distinctly of opinion that it ought to go before a jury, and he would not take the responsibility on himself to decide the matter, even if every word what I had written was the truth. After a short consultation with my solicitor, Mr. Albert Osborne, who had conducted the case in an admirable manner, I decided in not going on any further in the Police-court, but have myself committed for trial at the Central Criminal Court.

This gave the swindlers and their literary friends an opportunity to publish in their organs in Germany the news that 'Rollo had been sent to the Central Criminal Court to receive sentence for his libels against Messrs. Lehnert and Opitz,' and Lehnert wrote triumphantly the same lie to a merchant in Cologne, hoping by this strategem and by the intervention of the gentleman whom he addressed, to gain over the publishers of the 'Cologne People's Gazette.' After another adjournment at the C. C. C., the trial came on on the 25th March, and the curiosity was great how the matter would end. It had to be decided whether I had wilfully disturbed the trade, undermined the credit of London firms, and injured the true interests of German exporters, or whether what I had written was true, and done in the best interests of commerce.

Up to the opening of the case, Lehnert and Opitz could be seen walking together in the precincts of the court, smiling and confident, as if victory coud not fail them. They did not know that we knew so much! Finally the hour came, and they gloried to see me in the famous dock at the Old Bailey. Judge and jury, counsels and solicitors, and everyone else engaged in the case, were convinced that the trial, with its 'hundred-weights' of documentary evidence and the score of witnesses from the continent, would last at least a week. But I could not help having a presentiment, that the trial would come to an abrupt end. I could not imagine, that it would take eight days to find out who and what the prosecutors were, and that the valuable time of the court would be taken up for days with washing the dirty linen of a swindling enquiry-office.

My solicitors were Messrs. Osborn & Osborn, Exchange chambers, Copthall-buildings. Mr. Albert Osborne, a young but extremely clever solicitor, had taken for months the greatest trouble to study every detail of the case, and to prepare it in a manner that was convincing where the right was laying. Mr. Osborn secured for me as counsels Mr. Charles Mathews, Mr. Gill and Mr. Avory, who also took the greatest pains to master the matter in all its intricacies. Mr. Commissioner Kerr presided at the trial, and after the jury had been sworn in, the clerk of the court put the usual question to me, and I pleaded 'not guilty' and justification. It was not surprising to find that the prosecution had altered their tactics, and put now Lehnert's action in the foreground. Opitz had left the Police-court morally demolished by the clever cross-examination of Mr. Albert Osborn, and it seemed therefore better to keep him in the background and to put forward 'honest' Lehnert, against whom nobody knew anything—*we* excepted. His counsel, Mr. Kemp, opened the case for the prosecution in a very clever speech. He said, quite correctly, the 'libel' I published amounted simply to this, *that his client, Mr. Lehnert, had abused his confidential position to introduce notorious swindlers as respectable firms to German manufacturers, to defraud the latter, and then to divide the profits of the robbery with the swindlers, whom he had recommended.* These malicious libels, Mr. Kemp proceeded, had been really disastrous for his poor client, whose business was in consequence of my undefensible action nearly ruined. The worst, however, Mr. Kemp maintained, on the strength of the instructions he had received and believed to be true, was the motive for my action, and this he said, was to ruin Lehnert, that I may get his customers for my own business, which was of a similar character to that of his client.

Mr. Kemp made this unfounded statement on the strength, that I had called into existence the 'German Trade Protection Society;' but he did not know that I never was the *sole* proprietor of this institution, as people tried to make believe, and he also did not know, that at the time of the trial, and actually a long time before the trial, I had absolutely nothing whatever more to do with the 'German Trade Protection Society,' and had also no share in the concern.

The 'German Trade Protection Society' was besides not intended to act as a regular enquiry-office, but to take up only special cases, and to protect the exporters against the 'sledge-drivers,' and sham-enquiry-agents. I, unfortunately, was not in a position to let it be known already in 1890, that the suspicious dealings of Lehnert were at that time the cause, that I with some gentlemen founded the 'German Trade Protection Society. The cause that induced us to act, exists to-day as it existed then, and the disappearance of Lehnert has not altered anything in the matter; there is simply a dangerous swindler less, but as long as the small enquiry-offices are permitted to exist, as long will there be Lehnerts, more or less worthy of the original. These swindling enquiry-offices are actually growing up like mushrooms, and their founders and conductors are for the most part dubious persons, whose past would not bear investigation. These offices remain the mouse-traps for manufacturers, and it is impossible

Q

to warn too often and too strongly against them. I do not want to recommend here any enquiry-office in particular, but it ought to be a strict rule, to take informations only from long established offices, whose reputation is above suspicion.

Let us return to the trial. After Mr. Kemp had finished his opening address, the translation of the incriminated articles in No. 596 and No. 670 of the 'Cologne People's Gazette,' 1894, were read, and then was called as first witness a Mr. Müller, who was the head-clerk in Lehnert's office, and who made occasional enquiries for his employer. Mr. Kemp proved by this witness 'publication' of the incriminated articles in England, as required by the law of libel, and had done with him. But not so Mr. Mathews, who made the witness confirm the strange arrangement of the offices of the double-firm Lehnert-Liman, with its different street-entrances and the different office-entrances, and the different names on the different doors, as described by myself in the incriminated articles.

I hope Mr. Müller will take a warning from the fate of his former employer and master; for he has established himself since then as enquiry-agent in Newgate-street, and if his office has two different entrances, this certainly will not induce him to use a double firm, a practice which may be advantageous to the user, but misleading and dangerous to the public.

Another of Lehnert's clerks proved also having bought one copy of the incriminated paper at Mr. Siegle's Library in Lime-street, and Mr. Mathews did not take the trouble to cross-examine, as I admitted publication and authorship, having taken the responsibility for both upon myself.

And now came the 'prosecutor' himself, Mr. Lehnert, who entered the witness-box with a regular 'city bag' in his hand. His long, thin figure, his drooping lower jaw, his sallow complexion, and the small dark eyes, who seemed always on the watch, did not make quite an agreeable impression, and this effect increased steadily during the time that Mr. Lehnert had to stand the fire of Mr. Mathews's cross-examination.

How different Lehnert must have felt now to his other appearance in the witness-box in Dresden, when he came there to give evidence against Hammerstein. Here Lehnert declared under oath that he came to London in 1884, and opened business as enquiry-agent in 1886. In Dresden he swore again, according to a printed report on Hammerstein's trial, published by G. Rossberg in Dresden, 1892, that he had left Berlin 35 years ago, and was an enquiry-agent in London for ten years (that is since 1882). In 1883 he swore, he gave already from London unfavourable reports about Hammerstein, which is in direct contradiction to the deposition in my trial. The fact is, Lehnert was not in London, and was not an enquiry-agent at the time when he declared in Dresden that he had reported about Hammerstein, *and Hammerstein was convicted on Lehnert's evidence.* To my view it becomes thus a duty to the German authorities to re-open the case of Hammerstein, to have a new trial, if possible, and if not, to do something for him by way of grace. There is no doubt, Hammerstein was a dubious character, but this is not sufficient to sentence him to 12 years' penal servitude. The judge certainly had to go by the evidence brought before him, but why were no enquiries made regarding the principal witness, Lehnert?

Lehnert received for the 'services he rendered' a special reward of 1,500 marks. When he returned to London, a friend said to him: 'But, Lehnert, how could you depose like this against Hammerstein? You knew it was not true, and you have yourself quite enough to answer for!'

'Well,' Lehnert answered, 'I received £75. Business is business. If Hammerstein had paid more, I would have sworn to the contrary to what I deposited now.' 'But, suppose the matter would leak out!' the friend remarked. 'Well, then I would go travelling for some time!' 'And suppose you were caught?' 'Then I suppose I would get for some time board and lodging for nothing! Worse things may happen!' Lehnert said with a laugh.

I say, if a man is convicted on the strength of the evidence of such a witness, then the case ought to be re-opened as soon as possible, and there is every reason to surmise that this is the case of Hammerstein. For in his printed 'letters of thanks,' Lehnert quotes the following one from the Chief-judge of the Criminal-court at Dresden, Dr. Eberhardt.—The letter is dated June the 10th, 1892, and reads as follows:

'My dear Mr. Lehnert,—I am very sorry to hear that you had

to suffer some persecution in consequence of the part you took in the case of Hammerstein. But the consciousness of having done a good action will comfort you. Without the great exertions you made in clearing up the matter, and without your well-founded informations, a conviction of this dangerous swindler *would have been well-nigh impossible.* And it is a great public duty to counteract the doings of these international swindlers.'

Should the authorities think it right to clear up the matter now, with a view to shorten the term of penal servitude to which Hammerstein was sentenced, I am willing to put my services at their disposal. I can produce witnesses who are prepared to swear that Lehnert committed wilful perjury. It needs but to read carefully the cross-examination to which Lehnert was subjected at my trial, and to remember that not one of the 53 witnesses I had summoned at a great deal of expense from England, Scotland, Ireland, Italy, Belgium, and Germany was called, and it will be seen that Lehnert convicted himself of gross perjury by his own confessions.

His own counsel asked him: 'Have you read the libels against you in the 'Cologne People's Gazette,' and is it true what is said there?' Lehnert's answer (under oath) was that he had read the libels, and that there was not a word of truth in them.

Mr. Mathews made these last words the beginning of his masterly cross-examination. 'Not one word of truth, Mr. Lehnert?' he asked with a tinge of well-played sympathy. 'Not one word!' Lehnert answered with great decision, and full of righteous indignation.

'Are you quite sure?' the counsel asked again.

'Quite sure.'

To a string of questions, which were put rapidly, and answered often rather hesitatingly, Lehnert made the admissions that his office consisted of three small attics on the top-floor of 46, Queen Victoria-street, that two different entrances were leading to this house, that at each entrance to the house and also at the two doors to his office he had painted a different name, and that one of these two names, Liman & Co., was that of a Berlin firm, established since 1879 or 1880, for whom he was acting as agent since 1886.

Mr. Mathews: Are you still acting as agent for this firm?

Lehnert: No. The Berlin firm has sold the business to someone else, but I made before that an agreement with the firm that I could use their name in future.

Mr. Mathews was very curious, and wanted to see the agreement, but Lehnert, after furraging about in his handbag for a long time, was not able to produce more than a few circulars, which proved that there was a firm of Liman & Co. The agreement, however, he was unable to produce, and so he declared finally that the name of Liman & Co. was always painted at his door, in 14, Trinity-square, as well as in 46, Queen Victoria-street, and the name of Jahnke and Foelsch, too. This firm, Lehnert declared, he had represented for many years, but they had dismissed him as their agent on the 23rd of October, 1894, in consequence of the libels published in the 'Cologne People's Gazette.'

Mr. Mathews sympathised again, but was a little anxious to know whether the firm of Lehnert was still in existence. Highly offended the witness burst out: 'My name is Lehnert.' Mr. Mathews did not doubt this, but he insisted to have his question answered, and then Lehnert had to disclose the fact that his firm had been turned into a 'limited company' on the 6th of March, 1895 (during the postponement, and a fortnight before the trial), under the style of 'Lehnert Limited,' that he had been appointed director and Mr. Opitz secretary. Why was this change made? 'To get money to go on with these *wanton* actions,' Lehnert answered, quite forgetting that he and his friend Opitz had brought the actions. About the number and the persons of the shareholders, the subscribed capital, and other trifles, Lehnert was not able to satisfy the curiosity of counsel, and he referred Mr. Mathews to the secretary. But Mr. Mathews would have none of him; he preferred Mr. Lehnert, and asked his opinion about Mr. Opitz in his new secretarial dignity. Lehnert declared, he had always found him an honest man, and Opitz was enjoying his unlimited confidence as secretary of 'Lehnert Limited,' as he had been enjoying it when manager of Lehnert (unlimited).

Mr. Mathews's curiosity was not to be satisfied. He asked now about the arrangements of the office, and elicited that it was 'in the good olden times' as counsel suggested, as described in the incriminating articles, but that since then some alterations had been made. The number of clerks was formerly nine, Lehnert declared, and Mr. Mathews seemed greatly surprised. 'Nine?' he exclaimed, 'Mr. Müller told us there were never more than five,' and I may remark that Müller spoke the truth. Mr. Mathews became again quite sympathising and enquired: 'Has your business gone back?' and Lehnert was not slow to answer in the affirmative, and to mention the cause: it was the appearance of those wicked articles in the 'Cologne People's Gazette.'

Now Lehnert had to give an explanation why Opitz signed 'L. Lehnert,' and why he personated Lehnert in receiving callers and new customers. Lehnert explained that it was of no consequence whether he or Opitz received visitors, and whether the latter took one for the other, and with regard to letters, there were so many, that he could not sign them all, and he had given authority to Opitz to sign his name. 'But surely he could have found time to put before your name the two letters p.p. (*per procura*) that people may not be misled to take the signature as yours,' Mr. Mathews remarked, to which remark Lehnert had not to offer any explanation.

Mr. Mathews went now on to ask Lehnert whether he had been present at the cross-examination of Opitz in the Police-court, and this being admitted, whether, what he had heard there, had not shaken his confidence to his former manager and now secretary to the new company, 'Lehnert Limited.' Lehnert said there was no cause whatever for it. Mr. Mathews said he was surprised at this assertion, and he took now the witness through the damaging admissions Opitz had been forced to make. Lehnert's memory seemed all at once defective, and his powers of understanding too, seemed to have been greatly weakened; but this was of little avail to him, and he had to admit that he had heard and knew that Opitz had traded in 1886 under half a dozen different names, that he had been connected with notorious long-firms, and that he finally became bankrupt. Lehnert grew more and more fidgetty during this part of the cross-examination, and tried to escape answering the awkward questions, by constantly referring counsel to Opitz, in exclaiming: 'You better ask Opitz himself, he will tell you.' But Mr. Mathews assured Mr. Lehnert, 'he wanted to have it from him, that he heard Opitz saying so, and what impression these admissions had made on his mind with regard to his employee.'

Lehnert: At that time I had no knowledge of it.

Mr. Mathews: Do not say so, because I have something in my possession what may prove very disagreeable to you.

Lehnert: The sooner you bring it forward the better.

Mr. Mathews: Wait your time. Did you hear him say that he opened his third banking account under the name of L. L. Clark, and that the maiden name of his wife was Louise Lancaster Clark?

Lehnert: I could not say.

Mr. Mathews: And do you remember that he filed his petition on the 28th of January, 1887.

Lehnert: That is so.

Mr. Mathews: Were you not shown at the Police-court a number of cheques which were signed by him in the name of L. L. Clark & Co., and signed after he had filed his petition?

Lehnert: I could not say.

Mr. Mathews: Go on, Mr. Lehnert, go on! I think that would have been sufficient to convince you.

Lehnert: You are always asking me about the business of other people, ask me about my business.

Mr. Mathews: I am asking you about your confidential man, the secretary of your company, who is signing your name with your consent.

Lehnert: You seem to think a man ought not to be permitted to do honest work again, when he had the misfortune to fail.

Mr. Mathews: You are still believing him to be an honest man?

Lehnert: Certainly, or he would not be in my employ.

Mr. Mathews: In spite of the bankruptcy, and the different banking-accounts he opened in fictitious names, and using them for his dubious operations? Before leaving this matter—you know his handwriting—(handing the witness a document) is this his signature?

Lehnert: Yes, G. Opitz.

Mr. Mathews: Look at the back of this letter, what names are given there as references?

Lehnert: Mr. Hume and L. Lehnert, 14, Trinity-square. I described him as a respectable man.

Mr. Mathews: Look at the other document. In whose handwriting is the signature 'Walter Arnold & Co.' Is it that of Opitz?

Lehnert: I am no expert in handwriting. It may be his, and it may not. (A third document, bearing the signature of L. L. Clark, is handed to Lehnert, who gives a similar answer and adds: You are always asking me about matters which I do not know, you better ask Mr. Opitz himself.)

Mr. Mathews: Ah! But you heard Opitz swear at the Police-court that this were his signatures?

Lehnert: I do not remember.

Mr. Mathews: I must say, that is very strange indeed.

Lehnert: If I had known that you would put such a great stress on that what Opitz said, I would have made a study of his depositions; but I did not pay attention to what he said. I had quite enough to do with my own affairs.

Mr. Mathews: That's just to what I want to draw the attention of the jury. There were bankruptcy proceedings against him, writs, summonses, and finally he was declared a bankrupt in February, 1887.

Lehnert: You know it better than I do, you have the official documents before you.

Mr. Mathews: Why did he fail? What were his liabilities? Were they not £6,377 1s. 6d.?

Lehnert: I could not say, but I think they were about £6,000.

Mr. Mathews: And you heard him say so under oath? And now tell me, Mr. Lehnert: you knew quite enough about this bankruptcy; did you know who the creditors were?

Lehnert: Yes, I saw the list, and I had even to support a claim of one of the creditors.

Mr. Mathews: I thought so. He purported Morris Brandt & Co. were his creditors. Did you know that according to his statement his own liabilities under the name of G. Opitz were

£2,000; and that for the remainder of £4,000 he had been made liable, as he says, as partner of 'Martin Cohen & Co.' and 'John Mouat & Co.' Did you know it? Did you know it, or did you not?

Lehnert: Well, really—

Mr. Mathews: I suppose you cannot remember!

Lehnert: It may be as you say.

Mr. Mathews: Do you know of his leaving England from Cardiff in a coal steamer for Bombay towards the end of 1886?

Lehnert: Yes.

Mr. Mathews: Do you know that he never attended his public examination, and that he never got his discharge as a bankrupt?

Lehnert: (After a deal of fencing) I think I know.

Mr. Mathews: You think you know. But you know, and we know now already Mr. Opitz up to his bankruptcy as Gustav Opitz, Martin Cohen & Co., John Mouat & Co., Walter Arnold & Co., and L. L. Clark & Co. Did this not shake your confidence in the man?

Lehnert: No. He always tried to lead an honest life.

Mr. Mathews: Your confidence was not shaken in the least, neither through the names nor dates I mentioned? I leave it to the jury what to think, that you have promoted this man from the position of your manager to that of secretary of your company.

Lehnert: Yes, I did so (correcting himself)—that is to say the shareholders did.

Mr. Mathews: Of course, the company and you are two different things, as far as I know the law. But I suppose we shall hear more of that bye and bye. For the present I am quite satisfied with having Mr. Lehnert and Messrs. Liman & Co. in one person before the jury. I want now your full attention, for I shall put you a very important question: you are an honest man, Mr. Lehnert?

Lehnert: I cannot give information about myself, but I think I am.

Mr. Mathews: You think you are, but you are rather shy to say so publicly; you are modest, Mr. Lehnert, but you think you are an honest man; we may say so in your presence without fear that you would contradict it?

Lehnert: Certainly.

Mr. Mathews: Would you recommend Mr. Lehnert, if you were asked as Messrs. Liman & Co. for information about him?

Lehnert: Why not?

Mr. Mathews: And if you were asked as Lehnert about Liman & Co., then you would recommend the latter?

Lehnert: You are asking questions which I cannot answer. All depends on circumstances.

Mr. Mathews: Quite so, Mr. Lehnert. Take your time to answer my questions, but tell me: if a man would come to you and propose to you to order goods from a foreign manufacturer, to seize them after their arrival and to sell them, so that the manufacturer loses his money, would you listen to such a proposal? Yes or no?

Lehnert: Well, if a man would come to me—

Mr. Mathews: What? I wish you to estimate your own honesty, that is what I want you to do, and I ask you once more: if a man, living in England, would come to you and propose to you to obtain goods from a foreign manufacturer, to seize them after their arrival and to sell them, so that the manufacturer is cheated of his money, would you listen to such a proposal?

Lehnert: Well, let the parties settle the matter between themselves.

Mr. Mathews: Would you participate in such a transaction?

Lehnert: Such an occasion would never arise.

Mr. Mathews: I challenge you: yes or no; would you do it, and do it for money? You say, you would have no occasion to do it. Do you mean to say that you have not done it? Yes or no?

Lehnert: I am unable to tell you; all depends on circumstances. If you will put before me a particular case—

Mr. Mathews: Ah, Mr. Lehnert! Did a particular case occur to you? It looks like it.

Lehnert: It may be. You seem to know more than I do.

Commissioner Kerr: May be you can refresh his memory.

Mr. Mathews: I can, my Lord. First of all, Mr. Lehnert, is this your signature? (Handing a letter to the witness.)

Lehnert: Yes. (Opens the letter to read it.)

Mr. Mathews: Stop. Do not read it yet.

Lehnert: It is very interesting to me.

Mr. Mathews: I have not the slightest doubt, it is. Well, the signature is yours. Now look at the date. Is it the 15th of August, 1893?

Lehnert: Yes. Can I read the letter now?

Mr. Mathews: You can. Now, did you come to an arrangement on that 15th of August with a Mr. van Raalte to obtain some goods from a German manufacturer. Did you or did you not?

Lehnert: I know Mr. van Raalte.

Mr. Mathews: I know you do. That is not the question. Did you make arrangements with him to obtain goods from a manufacturer in Teplitz. Well, Mr. Lehnert, well?

Lehnert: He intended to order some goods.

Mr. Mathews: Say order goods, if you prefer it. This van Raalte had obtained goods before that from the same manufacturer?

Lehnert: I cannot say, without asking first Mr. van Raalte.

Mr. Mathews: You cannot say? Had he not goods for which he never paid?

Lehnert: No, Mr. van Raalte pays everybody.

Mr. Mathews: He did not pay the Teplitz manufacturer, who had to sue him, and at Raalte's motion the manufacturer was ordered as a foreigner to give security for costs, and when, by an oversight, deficient security was given, did not Raalte manage to get the action dismissed and obtain thus judgment for his costs?

Lehnert: He had a judgment against the manufacturer.

Mr. Mathews: And then he came to you, and you arranged with him to get more goods from the manufacturer under another man's name?

Lehnert: No, no, no!

Mr. Mathews: Did you arrange to induce a Mr. Worlitschek to order goods from the manufacturer?

Lehnert: I think he required some goods.

Mr. Mathews: Did you arrange with van Raalte, that his name should not be mentioned to the Teplitz manufacturer, but that the goods should be ordered in the name of Mr. Worlitschek?

Lehnert: I did not arrange anything.

Mr. Mathews: Was not the plan to order the goods through

Worlitschek, to seize them after their arrival in the name of van Raalte, to sell them, and then to divide the proceeds between you, van Raalte, and Worlitschek?

Lehnert: You better ask the others.

Mr. Kemp (Lehnert's counsel, severely): Answer the question, if you please.

Mr. Mathews: Did you make such an arrangement, yes or no?

Lehnert: No.

Mr. Mathews: Will you swear to it?

Lehnert: You are asking me questions, which to answer I am not prepared.

The Commissioner: You must answer the question.

Mr. Mathews: You are an enquiry-agent, and I remind you of your responsible position; the Continental manufacturers are putting their trust in you. I put now a transaction before you, in which you played a dishonest part. Will you deny that?

Lehnert: Yes, I deny it.

Mr. Mathews: Now you may look at your letter, and then you will permit me to ask you whether I was right to say that you played a dishonest part. Is this letter addressed from you to Mr. Worlitschek?

Lehnert: It is written by one of my clerks.

Mr. Mathews: But you signed it, and it reads thus (reading the translation):

'I regret that you, in spite of my repeated requests, did not come to see me. I was now not able to postpone any longer the business in question, and accordingly I have referred Mr. van Raalte with a card of mine directly to you. He has a manufacturer in Teplitz who brought an action against him in London last year, but as the former had not given sufficient security as foreigner for costs, he lost the case, and is now indebted to Raalte with nearly £90. Now Raalte should like to get this money, and this should be done in this way—that he puts you forward to give an order in Teplitz, and that, as soon as the goods arrive in London, they be seized by the Sheriff for Raalte on the strength of the English judgment. R. is willing to pay £10 for our trouble, which we would then divide between us. I had liked to confer with you about this matter personally, if I knew when and where to meet you.'—Is this the visiting-card you gave to van Raalte, to introduce himself to Mr. Worlitschek?

Lehnert: Yes.

Mr. Mathews: And at the back of it you wrote in your own hand: 'Introducing Mr. van Raalte to Mr. Worlitschek in the matter I mentioned in my letter.'—If you can explain the matter, I ask you to do so now, before you have an opportunity to take advice. Explain the matter, if you can!

(I feel bound to state here that Mr. Worlitschek refused to have anything to do with such a swindle, and that Lehnert in consequence to have his revenge did his best to ruin the honest man, in slandering and denouncing him at the German firms Mr. Worlitschek was representing, causing him thus the loss of all his agencies.)

Lehnert: I cannot explain this letter. It is not the letter I would have written.

Mr. Mathews: You said under oath, such a thing did not happen. Did you speak the truth?

Lehnert: I remember now. There was some talk about this matter.

Mr. Mathews: I put it to you, that you said a little while ago it did not happen, and that you did not speak the truth when you denied it.

Lehnert: What have I denied?

Mr. Mathews: That transaction which you planned in your letter.

The Commissioner: He, in fact, denied any transaction of that kind.

Lehnert: I did not deny anything. But you are putting things—

Mr. Mathews: One question more. Is that letter written by an honest man? Answer—yes or no.

Lehnert: No. The clerk did not write the letter carefully enough.

Mr. Mathews: I am quite satisfied with this answer. And now, Mr. Lehnert, do you say still, that you are an honest man?

Lehnert gave no answer. The court adjourned now for lunch, and Lehnert left the witness-box with an unsteady step. What would happen next, was the question eagerly discussed during the luncheon-time, and the opinion gained ground that the action would not last as many hours as days which were adjudged to it. Everybody felt the end was at hand.

When the court met again, *Commissioner Kerr* turned to the counsel of the prosecutor and said in a sympathising, grave manner: 'Well, Mr. Kemp, what about this case *after this letter?*' *Mr. Kemp*, who appeared a little irritated, answered: 'I do not see much in it, my Lord.'—'I have no right to be surprised at what my learned friend says,' *Mr. Mathews* put in. *Commissioner Kerr* remarked drily: I do not know what the Jury will think of it.' Mr. Mathews, concurring, said: 'Yes, it is quite for the jury to decide.' *Mr. Kemp* fell in protesting: 'This matter has nothing whatever to do with the justification of the libel.'

Mr. Mathews: My learned friend will excuse me, but does not the incriminating article say that Lehnert was the confederate of people in England who were obtaining goods by fraud from foreign manufacturers? When the goods arrived here, the proceeds were divided between these persons and Lehnert. That is the incriminated assertion.

Commissioner Kerr: Ten pounds are mentioned which should have been divided between these persons.

Mr. Mathews: Proceeds from the sale of goods obtained by fraud and swindle, and that is '*the libel.*' (To Lehnert): Did you hear Opitz cross-examined in the Police-court?

Lehnert: There you are coming with Opitz again! Why don't you call him and let him answer for himself!

Commissioner Kerr: Answer the question and do not make speeches.

Mr. Mathews: Did you hear Opitz swear at the Police-court that he was from February, 1890, to January, 1892, secretary to the Eastern Exchange?

Lehnert: I did, and to the best of my belief it is true.

Mr. Mathews: Now, what did he do since then? Did he remain in London?

Lehnert: I am not responsible for Mr. Opitz.

Mr. Mathews: Of course not. But do you know whether he remained in London since he left the Eastern Exchange?

Lehnert: Yes, he did.

Mr. Mathews: Then I can take it from you that Opitz was in London from 1890 to 1895.

Lehnert: Yes. He was first at the Eastern Exchange, and in 1892 I made him manager in my business.

Mr. Mathews: Had he done work for you before that?

Lehnert: Yes, for a few months before I engaged him, at the close of 1891.

Mr. Mathews: Did it come to your knowledge that Mr. *Bernard* Opitz, not *Gustav* Opitz, addressed some foreign manufacturers offering to represent them as agent at a tour to the East, on which he was preparing to start?

Lehnert: Yes, I had some enquiries and I gave the informations.

Mr. Mathews: And you said of him he was a most trustworthy person.

Lehnert: And that he is.

Mr. Mathews: Let us draw your attention to a certain correspondence that passed between you and Mr. Opitz, and between this Bernard Opitz and the *Manufacture Liègeoise d' Armes à Feu*. I shall take the letters as they follow each other, for they appear to me very instructive. First of all you sent in January, 1890, a letter to Messrs. William Schmeisser & Co., in Berlin. I must first of all inform the jury who these gentlemen are. They are enquiry-agents in a very large way of business in Berlin. Is it so, Mr. Lehnert?

Lehnert: I cannot tell you. I do not know.

Mr. Mathews: Are you in earnest, Mr. Lehnert? Are not Messrs. Schmeisser & Co. a great firm of enquiry-agents in Berlin, and did you not act for many years as their London agent?

Lehnert: Yes, unfortunately. I had a lot of transactions with them up to 1892, when I resigned.

Mr. Mathews: You resigned? Messrs. Schmeisser & Co. declare they dismissed you in consequence of a trick you played upon them.

Lehnert: I do not know anything about it.

Mr. Mathews: Were you in correspondence with Messrs. Schmeisser at the beginning of 1890.

Lehnert: We were very diligent correspondents; we exchanged about 7000 letters.

Mr. Mathews: 'That looks like correspondence. Did you send this letter of the 21st January, 1890, to Messrs. Schmeisser in answer to an enquiry? (The letter is handed to Lehnert.)

Lehnert (in looking at it, sneeringly): I thought that was a confidential report. They are writing here from Berlin: 'strictly confidential.' Is that the way how they treat confidential letters?

Mr. Mathews (gravely): Messrs. Schmeisser & Co. have to perform here a public duty. Please to follow me. Is this your answer to the confidential enquiry of these gentlemen? (Lehnert admits it, and the letter, which was reprinted already on another page is read).

Mr. Mathews (continuing): The letter is signed G. Opitz, not Bernard Opitz. Was he your correspondent at the time as you say in your letter?

Lehnert: Yes.

Mr. Mathews: Now listen. You write: 'My reporter has spent the last 20 years in the East.' Was this true?

Lehnert: Yes, it is true.

Mr. Mathews: But we have it from yourself that he was in England in 1885 and 1886, and that he never left England since 1889. Accordingly what you stated was not true.

Lehnert: But he was a very long time in India, China, and Japan.

Mr. Mathews: What was he doing in 1890?

Lehnert: He tried to find twelve manufacturers, to go for them to the East, and to sell their goods.

Mr. Mathews (reading): He is now with his family on a recreation tour in England. Was this true?

Lehnert: Where is that written?

Mr. Mathews: In your letter, written by yourself. (Reading again.) 'In the following pages you will find an excellent report how business is transacted in the East?' Was to your letter affixed a report which, you said, came from your correspondent?

Lehnert: I could not say, after such a lapse of time. I know Opitz was here and wanted to go back. Do you see the reasons why he wanted to go back?

Mr. Mathews: No. But we shall come to that. I am dealing now with your statements. How was it true that he spent the last twenty years in the East, and that he was at a pleasure trip in England?

Lehnert: Well, his family was living in England, and they came over here and went back again. You better ask Mr. Opitz. I am not answerable for these statements.

Mr. Mathews: Do not say so. I am not speaking now of Opitz's letter, I am speaking of the letter signed with Lothair Lehnert. You say, he spent the last twenty years in the East.

Lehnert: And so he did.

Mr. Mathews: And you say further: 'He is now with his family on a recreation tour in England.' I have given you an opportunity to explain. This letter with the affixed report of your correspondent Opitz you sent to Messrs. Schmeisser & Co.

Lehnert: Yes, unfortunately.

Mr. Mathews: I agree with you. Now let us pass on to the 20th of March, 1890. Did you know at that time that Opitz had not paid a single farthing to his creditors?

Lehnert: I knew he was an undischarged bankrupt.

Mr. Mathews: You knew it, and yet you said in your answer to an enquiry of Messrs. Schmeisser regarding this Bernard Opitz, who you knew to be Gustav Opitz: 'The man is clever, experienced in business, and enjoys the fullest confidence of the first-class English firms who have engaged him.' The fullest confidence—an undischarged bankrupt! Did you enquire from these English firms he mentions in his letters?

Lehnert: Yes.

Mr. Mathews: From all of them?

Lehnert: Not from all, from some.

Mr. Mathews: Name them.

Lehnert: I cannot. I do not remember more.

Mr. Mathews: I put it to you: you did not enquire.

Lehnert: Yes, I did. I remember now, I asked Mr. Barclay.

Mr. Mathews: Be careful what you are saying. You are under oath. I have Mr. Barclay here in court. I shall call him as a witness. Do you still adhere to it, that you saw him?

Lehnert (looks nervously round the court): Well, it may be that I did not see him.

Mr. Mathews: Now go back to the first page of this letter; you will find there that Messrs. Schmeisser ask you: 'What is his past?'

Lehnert: Well, he was actually for many years in Japan.

Mr. Mathews: Well, why did you not say what you knew of his past? This great Berlin firm are making enquiries with you and pay you for it.

Lehnert: Yes, a shilling. They got their shilling's worth of information!

Mr. Mathews: Do you mean to say, that an information for a shilling can be a false report?

Lehnert: Would you write more for a shilling?

Mr. Mathews: No, less, Mr. Lehnert, much less—at least, about Opitz. Now, you knew that Opitz received in June, 1890, from the Liège firm £50.

Lehnert: Could you assist me with the date?

Mr. Mathews: I should prefer if you would assist me. Try to remember. When did you hear first that Gustav Opitz received under the name of Bernard Opitz from the Liège firm £50 on account of his travelling expenses?

Lehnert: Well, let us say in 1891.

Mr. Mathews: Did Opitz leave England in 1890?

Lehnert: As far as I know, he did not. I saw him very often in 1890. He told me he did not get a sufficient number of firms to represent, and for this reason he could not start on his tour.

Mr. Mathews: Did you inform Messrs. Schmeisser & Co., that Opitz had not gone to the East?

Lehnert: I do not know, I do not remember.

Mr. Mathews: Well, on the 9th of April, 1891, Messrs. Schmeisser and Co. wrote to you and enquired about Mr. Bernard Opitz. Take your time, Mr. Lehnert.

Lehnert: I am trying to remember.

Mr. Mathews: I quite believe it.

Lehnert: I come to think now, that Mr. Opitz was on his travels in 1890.

Mr. Mathews: No, no. You heard him swear in the Police-court, and you said so yourself, that he was in England from February 1890 to January 1892.

Lehnert: Would you not call Mr. Opitz? He could put me right. I cannot be responsible. May be I told you an untruth.

Mr. Mathews: That is quite possible. You cannot get out of this affair so easily, Mr. Lehnert. Look at this. It is a letter Messrs. Schmeisser & Co. wrote to you on the 5th of April, 1891. I will read the translation. Follow me. (Reading.) 'Under the date of the 5th of April of last year, you gave us under the number 8006 an information referring to Bernard Opitz, London, S.W. You told us that this honourable man would travel for some first-class houses to China and Japan, and that he received from each firm a collection of samples and £100 travelling expenses. In consequence of this information a Liège gun-manufacturing firm sent to him a valuable collection of sample-guns worth 1,200 francs, and they enquire to-day whether we are not in a position to inform them how the gentleman is doing, especially whether he has spent their money in comfort in London, and whether he has flung away their guns, for they never heard a word more from him. You can certainly hear from the first-class houses whom he was to represent to what end this man has come?'—That is Messrs. Schmeisser's enquiry. On the other side you will find your answer. It is in your own handwriting.

Lehnert: Yes, I ascertained, as I say here, that Mr. Opitz had gone in 1890 by steamer to Colombo.

Mr. Mathews (smiling): How? Mr. Bernard Opitz, who was at that time Secretary to the Eastern Exchange in London?

Lehnert: Did he not go out for the Eastern Exchange?

Mr. Mathews: No, you know very well, he did not. And you were the man to protect these foreign firms! (Reading from Lehnert's report.) 'It is said, he resigned the representations which he had accepted in order to be enabled to devote himself exclusively to the representation of a Manchester firm, for whom he has to conclude contracts for the fitting of spinning-mills in the Colonies, and who guaranteed the whole of his travelling expenses of £1,000.'—Was this true?

Lehnert: Yes, that was true.

Mr. Mathews: How could you tell to the jury only a few

minutes ago, that he did not start, because he was unable to get some more agencies?

The Commissioner: He wanted a thousand pounds, and got only fifty.

Lehnert: He could not get the money together, and so he travelled for one firm only. If you would permit me to call Mr. Opitz—(he looks in a helpless manner towards the door).

Mr. Mathews: It is your letter, and not his. I ask you for an explanation.

Lehnert: What I wrote was true at that time. I cannot say now after a lapse of four years, how that happened.

Mr. Mathews: You heard he was seized with fever in Burmah. Who told you so?

Lehnert: Captain Bateman.

Mr. Mathews: Why did you not ask Opitz? He was in the house.

Lehnert (confused, gasping for breath): No, no, they were his relations. He was living with them.

Mr. Mathews: How far is the Eastern Exchange from Queen Victoria-street?

Lehnert: Three or four minutes' walk.

Mr. Mathews: You swore that he was there. (Reading again from Lehnert's report.) 'In Burmah, it was said, he was seized with fever, and, according to reports from there, he left directly for Australia. His samples, it is pretended, are deposited with a firm at Colombo.'—They were not!

Lehnert: I do not know. I was told they were.

Mr. Mathews (reading again): 'Opitz intends, as it is said, to bring them with him at his return from Australia. His relations are not possessed of more detailed news. Judging from his last letter, which arrived here a few months ago, it is thought that the samples probably are already on their way back from Colombo.'—Why did you not ask Opitz himself?

Lehnert: Because he was not in London at that time.

Mr. Mathews: You swear that?

Lehnert: I do. I have not seen him at that time.

Mr. Mathews: Will you swear that he was not in London? Be careful, that is a direct statement of facts. Will you swear that

Bernard Opitz was not in London when you wrote this letter in April, 1891?

Lehnert: I cannot swear to anything more after such a long time.

Mr. Mathews (reading again): 'The samples are already on their way back from Colombo.'—That is not true, they were not in Colombo. They never left London.

Lehnert: Would you not better ask Mr. Opitz?

Mr. Mathews: Are you charging a fee for these false reports?

Lehnert: I do not admit it is false.

Mr. Mathews: Is it true?

The Commissioner: They say you are not libelled.

Lehnert: They are always bringing forward one or two cases which concern Opitz.

The Commissioner: They say, not only what was written about you is true, but they say you were not libelled at all, because you cannot be libelled.

Lehnert (in a wimpering voice): But they always talk about Opitz.

The Commissioner: The gentlemen of the jury must gain the conviction that you were libelled.

Mr. Mathews: Will you swear, that you did not see Opitz within one or two days after this letter was written?

Lehnert: I told you already, I cannot swear to anything. If you will refresh my memory, I will answer to the best of my knowledge.

Mr. Mathews: Just answer what concerns yourself. Bernard Opitz, whose real name is Gustav Opitz, was recommended by you to Messrs. Schmeisser; on the strength of this recommendation he received money and goods from Liège. I put you the question: At the same time, when you said this man was travelling in the far East, in Colombo, in Australia—

Lehnert: I beg your pardon, not at the same time. I wrote he was in Colombo in June or July, 1890, and my letter dates from April 12th, 1891.

Mr. Mathews: Quite so. 'In Burmah he was seized with fever, and according to reports from there he left directly for Australia.' That is, what you told at the time when you were meeting this man in London nearly every day. This I ask you to explain one way or the other.

Lehnert: Without knowing the dates, I cannot do so.

Mr. Mathews: Here is the date in your own handwriting.

Lehnert: Very likely, I saw him a short time afterwards.

Mr. Mathews: Did you see him a short time before you wrote this letter?

Lehnert: I could not tell you; I do not remember.

Mr. Mathews: If you saw him, Mr. Lehnert (with impressive energy), *then this letter is a tissue of lies.*

Lehnert: Well, you are always picking out one or two things. I tell you, I cannot remember.

Mr. Mathews (with great force): This letter is from beginning to end a tissue of lies! You are very cautious not to give a direct, straightforward answer. You are asking then for a power of attorney, and you write in your letter, that the samples are on their way back from Colombo. I suppose you asked Opitz about it when you met him two days later.

Lehnert: Very likely. I received the power of attorney, and I went there.

Mr. Mathews: And asked him about the samples and his speedy return from Australia?

Lehnert: Ah! I remember now. I did not go personally, I sent somebody.

Mr. Mathews (reading from the letter): 'His relations are not possessed of any more detailed news, judging from his last letter which arrived here a few months ago, it is thought that the samples are already back on their way from Colombo.'

Lehnert: To which letter are you referring?

Mr. Mathews: To the letter which you are holding in your hand. It is written by yourself. 'His relations.' Did you see his relations? You must have seen them. You say so in your letter. Where were they living?

Lehnert: In Brixton.

Mr. Mathews: Speenham-road, Brixton. Were you often there?

Lehnert: I did not call personally.

Mr. Mathews (quoting): 'His relations received the last letter a few months ago.'

Lehnert: His uncle gave me this information.

Mr. Mathews: The same uncle?

Lehnert: Yes, Mr. Bateman.

Mr. Mathews (reading): 'It is thought that the samples are already back on their way from Colombo.'

Lehnert: Where is it written?

Mr. Mathews: Here, this time in your own hand-writing. Ah, well! What tissue of lies!

Lehnert: In fact you are putting a false construction on my letter. I looked at it quite differently. I reported what I ascertained.

Mr. Mathews: Point out anything in this letter what I put in a false light.

Lehnert: Everything! You see my report was based on the information I obtained.

Mr. Mathews: Why did you not make the enquiries personally? You ask me, and I repeat to you your own words: that *you* called at the house, that *you* saw his relations, that *you* heard he had gone to Colombo, and I say it is no' true.

Lehnert: I reported at the time what I ascertained, and what was told to me.

Mr. Mathews: Is this the way how you earn your money?

Lehnert: For a shilling.

Mr. Mathews: It is the old story. The prices were so low that the information could not be true. Do you remember that something of the kind was said in the incriminated articles?

Lehnert: Yes.

Mr. Mathews: It is something what caused you to bring this action. You say it is libel, and you complain of it.

Lehnert: Yes, I do.

Mr. Mathews: Is that the best what you can do for a shilling? There is also a delightful touch of humor in your final remark, which I cannot pass by unnoticed! 'That really is a cheap way to make a tour round the world! What clever ideas some people have!'—What did you mean with that?

Lehnert: Well, that I had liked to travel myself, and to represent the manufacturers.

Mr. Mathews: In the same manner as Opitz? And under the same conditions?

Lehnert: No, I am very fond of travelling.

Mr. Mathews: But what was the meaning of your remark?

Lehnert: Nothing. It was a joke.

Mr. Mathews: You must have meant something. Did you not want to say with it to Messrs. Schmeisser & Co.: 'This Opitz is a clever fellow! It is a nice way to make £100. What clever people there are! What clever rogue this Opitz is!'—That are your informations for Germany.

Lehnert (anxiously): No, no.

Mr. Mathews: That is for Germany, good enough for the poor people over there!

A dramatic pitch was reached, the influence of which was felt by all present. It was evident, the catastrophe was near at hand. One of the jurymen remarked quite audibly, 'What that gentleman in the dock has written, is true; he was justified in doing so.' For some moments a general commotion prevailed. 'Silence, silence,' the ushers called, and *Mr. Mathews* turned to the jury, saying:

'There is still more of it, if you wish to hear it, gentlemen. It quite depends of you. If you want to hear more, there is still plenty of it (pointing to a large heap of documents before him). But it depends of you. If you should think you heard enough—' (The jurymen are consulting together). *Mr. Mathews* continuing: I should not, but I did hear, my Lord, if I am not mistaken, that the jury are of opinion, there is no case more for the defendant to answer.

A Juror: That is so.

Mr. Mathews: Yes, I think I was not mistaken. If you are agreed, gentlemen, then matters will be considerably shortened. (Turning towards Mr. Kemp.) I am quite sure my learned friend will raise no objection, if this be your opinion.

The Commissioner: The jury has always the right to stop a case, if they wish to do so.

The Foreman of the Jury: We are of opinion that the articles published by the defendant were justified. The evidence brought before us leaves no doubt about it, and we are agreed he is not guilty.

The Clerk: You find the defendant 'Not guilty,' and the incriminated articles justified?

The Foreman of the Jury : Yes.

Mr. Mathews applied for costs, which were granted by the judge as 'a natural consequence of the verdict.' Proceeding

The Commissioner said :. This letter ought to be forwarded to the Public Prosecutor, if else the whole of the case is not put before him. (Considering a while) I order that the solicitor of the defendant submits the documents to the Public Prosecutor.

Mr. Mathews (seeing that the court was to rise) : There is still another action to be tried. The prosecutor in this case is Mr. Opitz, who complains, too, of having been libelled by the articles published in the 'Cologne People's Gazette.' I am prepared to justify.

Mr. Kemp : We shall not produce evidence.

The prosecution being thus withdrawn, the jury, by the direction of the judge, returned also in this case, a verdict of 'Not guilty' for the defendant.

Mr. Mathews applied for costs in this case too, remarking 'We pleaded justification. We had called a great number of witnesses from the Continent at a great deal of expense to us, and a great deal of inconvenience to the witnesses, who came not only to prove the truth of our assertions, but also to disclose a scandalous state of affairs.' The application was granted, and thus the trial came to a rather abrupt end.

In accordance with the judge's directions, the documents were submitted to the Public Prosecutor. But, as his decision takes always some time, the danger was within measurable distance that Lehnert and Opitz would escape justice by exporting themselves to a milder clime ; and to prevent their flight, and frustrate their renewed scheming from somewhere else under a new firm, we, that is the 'Cologne People's Gazette,' caused at our expense a prosecution for conspiracy to defraud to be instituted against the two 'gentlemen.' Our suspicion was soon justified. Both were arrested, but liberated on bail in a very small amount, and after the first remand Opitz only put in an appearance. Lehnert did not appear ; he had decamped ! Opitz, after due proceedings in the Lord Mayor's Court, was committed for trial at the Old Bailey, where he was tried, found guilty, and sentenced to eight months' hard labour.

The matter has cost myself and Messrs. Bachem (nominally the 'Cologne People's Gazette') a tremendous sum of money, which we sacrificed in the interest of trade. It was rather hard on us, but we did it with good cheer. All we wish is, to see our troubles and our sacrifices turned to good account. I say, my experiences ought to be useful to the whole commercial community: to the German manufacturers by using greater caution, and supplying less of their goods on credit, contrary to the present practice, so damaging to the English manufacturer. The English manufacturers, again, should put pressure on the Government to put a stop by legal enactments to the doings of the international gang of long-firm swindlers in London. I propose that a commission of English and German manufacturers be formed, whose business it would be to make a thorough and searching enquiry into the nuisance of the guild of modern highwaymen.

I should regret to find my revelations rendering the position of honest agents more difficult, but there is no help for it. I have to consider the other part, the numberless honest manufacturers who have been ruined by these heartless swindlers. Who is not possessed of sufficient capital, ought not to start business on his own account; then he will never come into a position that these lines may apply to him.

* * *

An interesting contribution to this 'literature' is a letter of Opitz, dated July the 15th, 1886, and addressed to a firm at Hainichen. Opitz writes:

'In answer to my letter of the 10th inst., I received your favour of the 13th, and I find to my regret that you will not accept my offer for the 396 pieces at 9d. The difference in the price is a small one, but I am not empowered to raise my offer, even if I should feel disposed to do so, and my profit at this transaction is restricted to the 4 per cent. discount you are granting, and this is not enough to permit me to add another penny to the price I offered.

'I leave my offer open to Monday next, and should you decide until then in accepting it, please write or wire. . . With regard to the other contents of your letter, I am, as a cautious man of business, far from being offended at your enquiry; but on the other hand, I am rather surprised to hear that the firms I gave you as references, have given you unsatisfactory answers, for with two of them I am connected for years, and have done considerable business with them.

'Until now I have done very little with Germany, because I bought here what I wanted. I name to you

Messrs. Armstrong, Wild & Co., 17, Great St. Helens, E.C.

„ Bernard & Co., 4, Bury-street, E.C.

„ Holm & Greetham, 66/67, Milton-street, E.C.,

who will give you information about my firm and my way of settling accounts.

'But if you prefer a perfect independent information, you can address yourself to any large enquiry-office, represented in London, for example: *(Opitz gives here the names of four enquiry-offices, who at that time, were represented by Lehnert; he mentions too a German forwarding firm, for whom Lehnert acted as agent, and Louis Lœwy & Co., a firm who was no-one else than Opitz himself. With the other firms he mentioned, he was closely connected.)* But you need not be afraid to deal with me; you are finding in me a straightforward and honest countryman, who knows his business, and by his fifteen years' stay in these transatlantic countries, the customers too.'

The manufacturer who received this letter writes to me:

'I lost with Gustav Opitz £431 4s., that is by his own acceptance of £154 6s. 7d.; by an acceptance of Morris Brandt & Co., drawn by Opitz, £138 7s. 5d.; and by an acceptance of Walter Arnold & Co., also drawn by Opitz, £138 10s.

I made my enquiries at the references given by Opitz, and the replies of the enquiry-offices were all similar and to the same purport, that Opitz had a considerable exporting business according to the official shipping-list, but that he seemed rather short of working capital, as his payments were often far from being made promptly.

'I, accordingly, did not enter into the offered connection; but a fortnight later I received nearly simultaneously from all four enquiry-offices the information that Opitz's father had died (I ascertained later on that this had happened in 1884 already), that he had left to his son considerable property, deposited with the Agra Bank, and that it would be most advisable to enter into business relations with him. (*This gratuitous advice emanated from Lehnert.*) I followed the advice with the result mentioned.

'I went personally to London, and I will just give you an idea of the artful arrangement of Arnold's and Opitz's joint-office.' (*D.* means door, *W.* window, *E.* exit.)

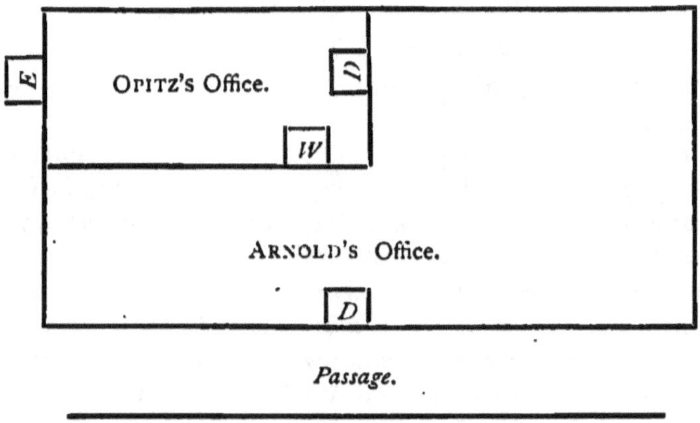

'Opitz's office, as will be seen by this rough sketch, was divided from Arnold's office by a wooden partition. The window, giving from Opitz's office in the other one, was covered by some kinds of blinds, permitting Opitz to remain unobserved, and to see who was entering. From his office he could escape unobserved by another exit and over another staircase. When I enquired after Mr. Walter Arnold, I was informed he was a very old gentleman, who could not attend any longer personally to business.

'The proprietor of Morris Brandt & Co. was certainly the most dangerous of the whole gang of swindlers. He wrote out an acceptance to any amount for a commission of 1 or 2 % in the name of his or any other firm. He shew me a letter of a Swiss firm, ordering a bill for 100,000 francs, and offering 1¾ % commission, and he produced this letter, very likely with the intention to induce me to avail myself of his services 'in this line,' which, as he explained, 'was his favourite,' and it was always a pleasure to him to 'procure' acceptances of highly respectable firms.'

I must add that the above mentioned bill of £138 10/-, dated from 1886, signed and indorsed by G. Opitz, is drawn and accepted in the name of Walter Arnold & Co. by Lehnert *in his own handwriting*, and, knowing that Opitz was Walter Arnold & Co., this is a clear proof that Lehnert & Opitz were swindling together already at that time.

In his bankruptcy Opitz did not account for this debt £431 4/-, which shows what kind of bankruptcy it was.

NEW REVELATIONS.

THE abrupt collapse of Lehnert's and Opitz's action at the Central Criminal Court, has deprived me of the possibility to disclose in a court of justice the devices of the swindling fraternity to their full extent. The evidence produced at the trial was, as shown already in this book, a small sample only of the material in my possession. If all should be published, I would have to fill volume after volume. It is sufficient to indicate the abundance of the material, in stating that my defence rested on 5374 documents, and that from these for the action in London so much was put in the hands of my solicitors, Messrs. Osborn and Osborn, that they had to employ, besides of their usual staff, 18 copyists, to make the copies required for the court and my three counsels. In spite of this drain on my 'resources,' and in spite of having heaps of material untouched and undisturbed in my archives, I was still enabled to put 1000 documents into the hands of my solicitor in Germany, who is conducting my case in the libel-action which I brought against the 'Rhenish Westphalian Gazette' in Essen.

It is, therefore, not difficult to undertand, that the whole of the documents in my possession will never become publicly known. There are so many side-issues connected with it, that I could mention them only at the risk of rendering this book quite unintelligible. For an illustration I shall adduce the affair Max Matzdorff from Landsberg, who is serving now a term of penal servitude for fraudulent bankruptcy. He had also transactions with Lehnert, and it was not the merit of Lehnert that he and Matzdorff avoided to come into a bad scrape with the customhouse. I shall give the outlines of the story only. But before doing so, I just remark that Lehnert would have been helped to some years rather unpleasant work by the English custom-house authorities, if Matzdorff had had time and money to entertain Lehnert's proposition. Considering how experienced Lehnert was, it is impossible to suppose that he would have run such a risk, and it is more likely that he intended to cheat Matzdorff, a surmise that was expressed too at the latter's trial.

The facts of the case are the following: Max Matzdorff had sold to a London firm 3000 boxes of Brandy with a spurious label of the well-known 'Martel' brand. Each box contained 12 bottles, and the total of the invoice amounted to 48,000 marks. The first shipment of 1500 boxes was seized by the English custom-house officials, under the Merchandise Mark's Act, Sec. 3 and M. J., 1887, on the ground of 'false trade description.' Matzdorff came in January, 1894, personally to London, and tried to obtain a release of the impounded goods, in which he failed. Somebody brought him to Lehnert, and this versatile enquiry-agent offered to 'arrange the matter with the custom-house,' for a consideration of 1000 marks (£50). From a letter of Lehnert's to Matzdorff, it is evident that he pretended he could 'bribe the officials,' and the same assertion he repeats in a second letter, dated January 20th, 1894, which runs as follows:

'In receipt of your favour of the 17th inst., I beg to thank you for your communications, and I can but assure you once more that you can depend on my loyal collaboration and the guarding of your interests in this most important business, if you show yourself prepared to pay me adequately for my trouble, expenses, and loss of time. At any rate, I am prepared to assist you in this important and difficult matter with my services and my experience, that you may be saved from the great loss threatening you. The matter has reached an acute state, when energetic, politic, and especially immediate action is required, and I had liked very much to see you personally, to consult about the steps which must be taken. Unfortunately this cannot be done, for you will understand that your appearance in London could have unpleasant consequences for you under the prevailing circumstances. Until now you have made but a sparing use of my services; you have initiated me partly only into the matter, and given preference to correspond with me. This must come now to an end, and if I shall be of any use to you, I must have your confidence, and the power to act and to mediate for you.

'First of all I must speak with you about many things, *which I cannot and will not put down in writing*, and as you cannot come here, I do not see another way but that we meet at a place conveniently to be reached by both of us, for example Calais or Ostend.

'Of course, I could do so only under the condition that you pay not only my travelling expenses, but also an adequate fee, and remit me the amount in advance. I would charge you for coming to Ostend or to another place, similarly distanced, £10.

'If required, I could even come to Landsberg. But as this would necessitate an absence of a week, I would have to charge you at least £20.

'You must do something, and this at once, if you will prevent the matter ending in a total loss for you. How matters stand, you have not to lose a single day. Fortunately neither R. nor the General Steam Navigation Company, nor anybody else, *myself excepted*, can get the brandy, but, as matters are to-day, I shall be very careful not to teach anybody *how* the thing is to be managed. *But without the necessary 'grease' nothing can be done.* In London the goods are absolutely unsaleable, and it is useless to make further offers. But I have a relative in Bombay, who could do this business, and could afford to pay what R. offered. But more about that at our meeting. Without an immediate interview and consultation, nothing is to be done, and you are rid of your goods to see them never more. Therefore act with promptitude.

Yours faithfully, (Signed) L. Lehnert.'

The careful reader will have observed, that Lehnert speaks of a 'relative' in Bombay, a figure who makes his convenient appearance in many letters, and on many occasions, when the able conjuror requires it. The fact is, that Lehnert had no relations in India, but Mrs. Opitz had, and it is a strange sign of identification, going so far that even in their private life, Lehnert and Opitz considered themselves one and the same person.

Lehnert's letter to Matzdorff, however, was of no avail, for Matzdorff had meanwhile been declared a bankrupt, and his creditors recognised in Lehnert a bird with whom they would not have any dealings. They preferred to bear the loss, to preventing it by bribery and by other dishonest tricks, which even Lehnert wanted the courage to 'put down in writing.'

Such secondary matters I have in great numbers in my documentary evidence. But this example will suffice.

My publications had 'taken' and at once undermined the confidence to the famous enquiry-office 'L. Lehnert' and 'Liman & Co.' This, of course, raised a great anger in the sledge-driving community, and especially in the office of 46, Queen Victoria-street, where Lehnert and Opitz were living like in a robber's castle, and never thought that anyone would dare to attack them. I need not have regard towards anyone in the world, and I could afford to do it, and the honest trade is obliged to me for it.

But not to deviate from the matter, I must publish still in this chapter some interesting documents, and I hope I am not tiring the reader with it. I, personally, do not like to read letters in books and newspapers, but in this case I have no other escape, and have to do myself what I do not like in others, if I want to show the reader how Lehnert was driving his sledge.

After the publication of my articles against Lehnert, he circulated some 'Declarations and Explanations,' in which he, putting on the mask of an honest man, tried his best to clear himself of the accusations raised against him, and create the impression, as if he was enjoying the fullest confidence on the part of his customers, and that 'Rollo' was the only one who was speaking badly of him. But it was strange that to his thousands of applications for testimonials, only about a hundred of his customers acceded, and many of these in very colourless letters. As Lehnert published the letters only which were in his favour, I will just look for once at the reverse side of the medal. It is, of course, impossible to publish more than a few of these adverse letters, but I can supply any amount of them.

First of all, Lehnert wrote on the 17th of November, 1894, to one of his customers, as he had written to many before that: 'Last year you made an enquiry regarding a firm B. Arnold & Co., who later on failed, as I duly informed you. As you will see by my 'Rejoinder,' and by articles in the German Press,

(Lehnert referred there to the articles published at the instigation of Lehnert and Opitz by Adolph Stein, alias Adolph Semansky, alias Herbert Winter, in the 'Rhenish Westphalian Gazette'), the London swindlers, who of course are hating me furiously, are using Arnold's case to deprecate my trustworthiness, very likely for the purpose to hide their own guilt in this matter.

'Among other things I am accused of having given such a favourable report that a number of manufacturers, who received exactly the same report as I supplied to you, were induced to credit considerable amounts to the firm mentioned.

'You being a highly esteemed customer of mine for many years, I should be greatly interested to hear your opinion. I think I can take it as granted, that you gave no credit to Arnold, because you did not answer the supplementary information I sent out in June. I should like to have it attested by you, that you refused to credit anything to the firm in consequence of my report.'

The answer of the manufacturers, who supplied me with a copy of his letter, was the following:

'In receipt of your letter of the 17th inst., we should advise you to read the 'Cologne People's Gazette,' which will give you a perfectly satisfactory explanation with regard to your enquiry. Not your information was the cause that we did not enter into any connection with the firm of B. Arnold & Co., but the information we received from a highly reliable German enquiry-office.

'How could you state in your information that the proprietor of the firm was a Mr. Arnold, when his name was De Groot, and if he was a Mr. De Groot from Amsterdam, then he was certainly the same fellow who swindled us of a sample collection worth 200 marks.

'You further describe in your information this Arnold as the salaried buyer of four Indian firms, the names of whom you gave, but who, in fact, were not existing. Why do you not bring an action for libel against the 'Cologne People's Gazette,' who have exposed you in such a manner, that there cannot be any longer a question of confidence to your firm.'

This letter was answered by Opitz, signing himself as 'L. Lehnert.' He wrote:

'I am rather surprised at the contents of your esteemed letter of the 21st inst. I have read the 'Cologne People's Gazette,' and if only half of their contentions were true,* then, certainly, I should be a great swindler. But circumspect people know that many things printed by such dirty rags and 'party-organs,' are not true. Please take therefore notice, that directly after the publication of the libellous articles in the 'Cologne People's Gazette' proceedings were taken against the paper by my solicitor in Cologne, and that I instructed him to include in the action all further articles, if such should appear. I have also instituted proceedings against all other papers who have reprinted, as far as I know, the incriminating article; finally the authors, Hesse and the famous correspondent of the 'Cologne People's Gazette', *Rollo*, are summoned and will have to appear to-morrow before the magistrate to answer in the dock for their miserable lies. Who could do more for his justification?'

It is surprising where these fellows learned to utter such bold lies! The statements made in this letter were untrue, and the result of the action they brought later on, is already known.

The reason why the firm just mentioned did not suffer a loss at B. Arnold & Co., was therefore not the information given by Lehnert, but information received by a Trade Protection Society, given at the same time when Lehnert sent out broadcast his favourable reports. The contents of this information were simply: 'Rotten, keep aloof.' This was supplemented by a private letter, dated the 18th February, 1894:

'*Re B. Arnold & Co.* I have tried my best in this matter, but nobody has to say anything in favour of this firm. Everybody dissuades from having anything to do with these people, excepted they pay cash before delivery of goods, and these terms B. Arnold & Co. will hardly accept, in spite of their protestation that they are buying for cash only.

'From a manufacturer in Lienbach B. A. & Co. bought also goods for cash at delivery, but since then two months have passed, and the manufacturer is still waiting for his money, and, very likely, will never see it. I, therefore, cannot advise you to execute the

* Not only a half, but the whole was true, and a good bit more.

order and wired to you yesterday: *only for cash in advance*, a message, which I beg to confirm with this letter. Be very careful if you do not want to lose your money. I just receive your telegram: 'Does Arnold consent?' Of course not, if you mean cash before delivery. I do not want to make any other arrangement with him, because I know, if he has once possession of the goods he will humbug you and find constantly new excuses for delaying payment. I am told he is a man who promises everything and keeps nothing.'

That is clear and unmistakable. Now let us compare what Lehnert is writing at the same time: 'Orders to the value of some hundred pounds sterling can be executed with very little or no danger.' And this advice he is giving after serving up the tempting story of the three Indian houses, the £1200 salary and 2½ per cent. commission they are paying to Arnold, the 'good banking account,' and 'the excellent recommendations' given to this 'experienced man who understands his business.' To disclose fully this miserable conspiracy, I ask permission to publish one more of the many letters in my possession.

A German firm to whom Lehnert had given his stereotype information about B. Arnold & Co., had in spite of this some doubts, and before delivering the goods ordered, they made another enquiry, to which Lehnert replied in a lengthy voluble letter in which he also says: 'Some time ago I had occasion to call *personally* at this firm, and they produced some 50 invoices with the cheques they had paid in settlement, and it appears that until now all transactions passed off in a satisfactory manner.' This letter was written on the 2nd of April, at a time when the City Bank had already closed the account of B. Arnold & Co., because the business of the firm left no doubt about its swindling character. The '50 invoices and cheques' Lehnert parades with so much ostentation, are an invention of his; he never saw them, because they never existed. As B. Arnold & Co. had an account at the City Bank only, these cheques would appear in their banking-account; but, with the exception of a few small cheques paid to German manufacturers, all the withdrawals were in favour of Mr. Ernest Schreck, Mr. Arnold's dear 'self,' Mr. Lehnert (£20), the landlord, and two 'numbers'—mysterious cheques, that, very likely, could tell a tale, if they could. But the '50 cheques' were never written out, and never paid.

The firm, who had made the two enquiries at Lehnert's, executed Arnold's order, the value of which amounted to £205 4s. 5d. No payment was made, and asking for it did even not elicit an answer from the debtor. The manufacturer wrote finally to Lehnert, saying: 'As these people absolutely will not pay, I do not find confirmed what you said in your informations, viz.: that B. Arnold & Co. are prompt payers. I have sent them repeatedly my statement, and I advised them finally that I have drawn on them the £204 4s. 5d. at sight. I enclose the draft with the request, to collect the money, and to remit it to me. But, if the people should not pay, I expect to have your advice what to do, to see my claim satisfied.'

Lehnert answered a few days later, on the 6th of June, 1894: 'I thought it best for your interest to call personally at B. A. & Co. These people admit that they gave you the order to ship the goods on the 10th of April, but they say that cash after 30 days meant cash 30 days after receipt of goods, and not after shipment. B. A. & Co. are quite willing to settle the matter in this way, and to pay your claim on their next pay-day, that is the 20th inst.' Lehnert finished his letter with some re-assuring remarks, and the manufacturer's surprise was therefore the greater, when he received eight days later the following communication from Lehnert: 'In receipt of your favours of the 9th and 12th inst., I have to supplement to-day my former communication regarding your claim against B. Arnold & Co., with very disagreeable news. I received yesterday from another firm a draft at sight on B. A. & Co., and calling there repeatedly, and finding always the office closed, I enquired at the housekeeper's, and heard to my immense surprise that the proprietor of the firm had gone to India, and that the office would remain closed during his absence. The rent, which was not due yet, he has paid in advance, and he left an address in Calcutta, whereto all letters are to be forwarded to him. I am not able to draw definite conclusions from this sudden departure, but I have strong suspicions, and these are increased, as not only in your case, but also in that of many other firms, Arnold had fixed the 20th inst. as pay-day for considerable amounts.'

'As many of my customers are concerned in this matter, I am firmly decided not to spare either troubles or costs to bring Arnold to book, and, if need be, to proceed against this dubious individual even in India, where I can succeed better than anyone else—thanks to my long stay in that country, and the relations I have living there.' (What tissue of lies! as Mr. Mathews said. *The author.)*

'I enclose a formular of my customary power-of-attorney, and if you wish to entrust your interest in this matter to my care, please to fill out and to sign the formular, and to return it to me *with the stipulated preliminary fee.*'

I need hardly remark that this letter is signed by Opitz in the name of Lehnert. The manufacturer answered by return on the 16th of June:

'I have received your letter of the 14th inst., and am surprised at its contents. You call now the proprietor of the firm B. Arnold and Co. a 'dubious individual,' but according to the wording of your first information of 27/2/94, I was bound to think that you were well informed regarding the position and character of the man. How else could you have said that he was for many years in the employ of the Indian firms, who had sent him as buyer to London? You named the salary and the commission he is receiving. According to your statement his income was larger than that of a Prussian prime-minister, and on the strength of this, I entered into connection with this firm. If matters are as you report now, then B. Arnold & Co. was not a commercial firm, but a long-firm—a 'sledge-driver' as they are called—and you must have known it, and you ought to have reported accordingly. Before I sacrifice another shilling for the prosecution, I want to know what steps you intend to take in this matter.'

Lehnert answered, saying he pardoned the manufacturer's rather suggestive letter by the vexation he must have felt at the loss he suffered, and explained what he would do to secure Arnold's person and to help the creditors to their money, and wound up, that the manufacturer may do what he thought best; but if he wanted to make common cause with a large number of other defrauded manufacturers, who had put the matter in his (Lehnert's) hands,—(an assertion which was true for once, and brought

Lehnert a nice lot of money, who thus turned also the 'smash' of Arnold's firm to a profitable account. *The author)*—he would have to sign the power-of-attorney, and to pay in advance the principal fee of 44 marks.

This the manufacturer did after some more correspondence, and in exchange he received two circular-letters of Lehnert, and—nothing more. Referring to one of these circulars, the manufacturer wrote on the 14th of August, 1894, to Lehnert:

'Your circular in matters of the *famous* firm B. Arnold & Co., has come to hand. I have told you already, that I entered into connection with this firm on the strength of your information only. You stated, they were buyers for Indian firms, whom you named, and to show how well-informed you were, you stated also the salary B. A. & Co. were drawing. Who was vouching to you for this information, which you supplied to the commercial world, causing thus great loss to myself and many others? It is hardly credible that an enquiry-office would give such frivolous informations, and state as facts what never existed. Or do you want to maintain still that you really believed Arnold to be as what you represented him? You even were not able to ascertain who he was. According to German law, you could be held responsible for the loss you caused, but this, unfortunately, does not apply to England.'

To this Lehnert answered (the Italics being ours): 'My informant for this report was, as usually, my clerk, who is making the enquiries for me in the City, and he has taken great trouble in this matter. I reported to you faithfully what he reported to me, as result of his careful researches *(but the 'trap-doors' at least were added by Lehnert).* I named to you the three firms whom Arnold pretended to represent. But, as I did not know them, and as Arnold was newly established and quite unknown in the City, I recommended you to supply him with goods for cash only. *(This is absolutely untrue. In the information given to this manufacturer, Lehnert says distinctly: 'It is thought, a few £100 can be credited.' The belated assertion that 'Arnold was quite unknown in the City,' is simply incompatible with Lehnert's former apodictic declaration that 'the man is highly respectable, experienced, knowing his business, and possessed of some means of his own.')* Why did you not enquire about these Indian firms *(who never existed).* You ought to have done so yourself, or through my office, before trusting such people with goods to the value of many thousands of marks. For my fee of 1/9 I give, as you know, informations only about that what may be gathered here in England. *(But B. A. & Co. were in England, and it was Lehnert's duty to ascertain here the truth of his statements.)* If I shall make enquiries in India, I require a special fee. *(But Lehnert received 300 enquiries regarding B. A. and Co., and that brought him over £26 in fees—quite enough, to be sure, to make on his own account an enquiry about these three firms, before parading them in such a manner, as he did. Besides, so many enquiries about a new firm, who had a small office only, furnished in true sledge-driver style with one table, one chair, a directory, and a copying-press, ought to have made him suspicious, as it did in the case of the manager of the City-Bank.)*

The manufacturer gave him on the 23rd of August the following appropriate answer, one of many similar and even sharper ones Lehnert received from Arnold's victims; he wrote:

'You have not the slightest understanding of a manufacturers business, else you would not reproach me with a want of following your advice to transact business with B. A. & Co., for cash only. You must have copies of the informations you gave me. Just read them, and you will find, that you could not have given a better report about a thoroughly honest and accredited firm, than about this Dutch swindler, whom you did not know personally.' *(Wrong; Lehnert knew 'Arnold' as Mr. de Groot, and they often had a quiet game at cards together.)* 'You have supported this experienced swindler indirectly, *(it ought to be: directly)* and you helped him thus to success in his frauds. With all your sophistry you will not alter my opinion, shared by all my colleagues in misfortune, that you are the cause of the loss we sustained, and that your informations are cheap, but works of fiction.

'If you had said: B. Arnold & Co. *pretend* they are the buyers for these and these Indian houses, we could have made an enquiry, and the swindle would have been detected. But you stated positively: They *are* the buyers, and you have made yourself guilty by this of culpable negligence, for which you would be answerable in Germany.'

On the 22nd of September, the same manufacturer sent Lehnert a cutting from a newspaper, according to which a Mr. G. had been arrested in Amsterdam, and enquired whether this was not his Indian buyer Arnold.

Lehnert answered on the 24th of September, that this paragraph did not refer to de Groot but to a Guttmann, 'who was the soul of a firm Barnard & Co. in London, who had become bankrupt a fortnight ago. This firm opened as cloth dealers about eighteen months ago with a capital of £250, and failed now with liabilities amounting to £32,900, the principal creditors being English firms. The assets are put down with £5,000, but will hardly realize one third of this amount. Not enough with cheating the manufacturers who supplied them with goods, they cheated also their customers and confederates in London, among whom was also a certain van Praag, who appeared also in a very dubious light in Arnold's matter. To him the Guttmanns sold a parcel for 1,800 florins and there was a deficiency of not less than 1,200 yards. This swindle led to the arrest of Guttmann. Regarding Arnold, *recte* de Groot, absolutely no information was to be obtained, excepted that he had not been seen either in Calcutta or in Bombay. In both seaports and in Rangoon firms are existing whose names are very similar to those Arnold mentioned *(the German consul in Calcutta wrote however, as we know already, that these firms do not exist)*, but they all declare, that they never heard until now of B. A. & Co., and had not authorised him to make use of their names.'

Finally after the publication of my revelations, the same manufacturer wrote on the 15th of November the following 'testimonial' to Lehnert:

'You did not answer my enquiry regarding Colmann. Without doubt this firm belongs also to your protégés, as Arnold did. Much is said about your firm, and still more may be read about the queer manipulations of your enquiry-office. What I suspected for a long time, I find it now confirmed: You are the procurer of the sledge-drivers! What you are saying to your defence is simply foolish. What interest should these swindlers have to slander you, after this de Groot, alias B. Arnold & Co., whom you and your Mr. Opitz knew so well, enjoyed your vigorous and effective support in his miserable frauds. The impudence to obtain money from the victims by pretending that you are prosecuting the swindlers, is the crowning of the edifice. Such a perfidious action is really unheard of. I am now putting together the material to recover from you the 44 marks which I sacrificed for the pretended prosecution of your friend, de Groot, and to render you liable for my loss of £205. I expect to hear from you by return, otherwise I shall take proceedings against you, and I hope to find the matter ripe for the public-prosecutor.'

It is a great pity that Arnold's victims did not take common action directly after the appearance of my revelations, and had Lehnert arrested as a confederate. The fellow did not deserve any pity, and this view guided me when I finished him off with a few strokes of my pen. But the preceding correspondence is quite sufficient to show that the firms who went so far as to support Lehnert with their testimonials, had no suspicion of the real facts of the case.

Sledge-Drivers, who are a Common Danger.

IN this concluding chapter I intend to show that the sledge-drivers are not only cheats and swindlers, but also directly scoundrels. The one quality certainly includes the others, but the criminal laws make differences, and these are observed too in the practice of the judicial proceedings. If somebody obtains goods and does not pay for them, the loser can proceed by civil action only, excepting the debtor had incriminated himself in some secondary particulars, as it usually is the case with the German sledge-drivers. But matters are different with those sledge-drivers, who form a common danger (and to these B. Arnold & Co. must be reckoned), and intentionally cheat by swindling their fellow-men.

The first case that I will mention as an illustration of this theme, is a most instructive one. It deals with the swindler Jackson, a London celebrity, who formerly was carrying on his nefarious trade under the name of Hansen in Kiel, and later on in Hamburg, 49, Wilhelminenstrasse. Of this scoundrel no manufacturer was safe, whether English or German, and I am informed by a most reliable voucher that Hansen even succeeded to swindle a shipowner of a fully-equipped steamer. A similar, but still more daring trick was played by the famous international Knight of Industry, Hoffmann, on a celebrated Scotch firm of ship-builders, with whom Hoffmann lodged an order for a steam-yacht for a well-known and sadly-remembered 'crown-prince.' The swindler, who introduced himself under the name of a Hungarian magnate in the best London society, pretended to act as plenipotentiary of 'his friend' the crown-prince, produced credentials (forged, of course) and drew over 10,000 pounds sterling on account of commission. The yacht was nearly finished before the fraud was detected. 'Friend' Hansen, alias Jackson, fared better. He steamed away on board his ship, rounded Cape Horn, and succeeded in selling it at the port of a South-American Republic, where people are not very particular with regard to ship-papers. In spite of the new coat of paint, and the new name the steamer bore, she was traced, and the buyer had to fight a hard battle for her possession; but Hansen was not troubled with it, for he had brought himself and his booty safely to England. This 'stroke of business' I am unable to prove to him by documentary evidence; but it is different with his sledge-drivings in London. It is not worth speaking of his long-firm swindles to which so many Continental manufacturers fell victims, for they are mere trifles in Mr. 'Jackson's' glorious career, to which he turns only for a change, if no 'great matters' are occupying his precious time and fertile mind. At present his principal occupations consist in defrauding honest people who managed to save something by hard work, and are anxious to secure some kind of employment for their old days. These kind of people are his victims, and with the help of a shady solicitor and some experienced forgers of documents, he succeeds wonderfully well in the most hazardous and difficult transactions without transgressing the line that would bring him within the clutches of the law. It is always 'a close shave,' but until now he managed to escape.

In a newspaper, given to me by one of Jackson's victims, I read the following advertisement: '*Manager and cashier wanted, on trust; cash deposit, £25.*' The man who fell a victim to this catch, was an old soldier, and as the procedure in his case was the same as in the next following case, I shall not enter into particulars. The advertisement in the next case read as follows: '*Man and wife wanted to manage a house of trust and business. Cash deposit, £25.*' To this advertisement quite a number of applications by respectable married couples were received, and they were *all* engaged by Mr. Jackson, and *all* defrauded of their £25. According to the documents handed over to me by one of these victims, the matter was done in the following manner:

Jackson was living in a house of imposing appearance in the swell-part of Kentish-town. Rich curtains, and beautiful flowers on the window-sills betrayed a richly furnished interior, and who drew this conclusion was—betrayed indeed. For, in fact, the house was empty. The swindler slept with his family in a bare room on some paliasses, and a ground-floor back-room only was furnished as a kind of office. There he received his victims to rob them of their hard-earned few shillings. A table in this office was covered with piles of properly red-taped documents, especially leases, creating the impression of a solicitor's or land agent's office in no small way of business. Who would have suspected that these parchments were either forgeries, or obtained by fraud?

My informant applied for the situation, and was received in this office in a most formal and condescending manner; he was very close questioned about his past, his state of health, his references, and everything had the appearance of a *bona fide* matter. The applicant was informed, he would have to look after some house-property, and collect the rents and some debts, and for this services he would receive a weekly salary of 30 shillings with the free use of two rooms and a kitchen in the house. As security, he would have to deposit £25 in cash, for which amount the lease of No. 12, Eversham-road, Kentish-town, would be given as security into his hands. 'Jackson made inquiries at the references, and 'these having proved satisfactory,' he wrote to my informant, that his offer was accepted, and he would be appointed to the place as soon as the security was deposited. Pleased of having succeeded to obtain the berth, my informant, who was in the employ of a coal-merchant, called and deposited on account £14. Mr. Jackson favoured him at the same time with an order for 10 sacks of coal and six sacks of coke, and told him to call next week, when at payment of the remainder of the deposit, he would receive the lease as security, and enter on his appointment. The coals and coke were delivered, the remaining £11 paid, and 'the next week' definitely named as time when my informant would be installed in his new dignity, the day when he could move in, to be communicated to him by letter. The next week came, but no letter, and my informant called therefore at Mr. Jackson's, who received him very kindly, and put him off for another week. Calling again, he was told Mr. Jackson was out, and waiting for his return in the street, he met another man, apparently on the same errand. Pacing up and down like sentinels before the house, they got into conversation with each other, and my informant heard, to his great surprise, that his companion was also appointed housekeeper, had also deposited £25, and was also promised the lease of 12, Eversham-road, Kentish-town. My informant did not say anything, but, on 'Mr. Jackson' not turning up, he returned home, and wrote him a very plain-spoken letter, in consequence of which 'Mr. Jackson' called the next day on him and produced the lease, saying he would give it up if another five pounds were paid. My informant took it, without paying the additional five pounds, put it in his pocket, and told 'Jackson' to be gone, a polite request which the latter thought advisable to obey without much ado.

The new possessor of the lease went to 12, Eversham-road, and being admitted there, introduced himself as the new landlord, and wanted to come to arrangements with the occupier. The lady, who received him, seemed surprised, but said nothing more than that he may be good enough to call in the evening when her husband would be at home, who, she had no doubt, would come to an understanding with the visitor. The 'new landlord' called, of course, as he had been requested to do; but it was now his turn to be surprised, for, after having produced the lease in the presence of three gentlemen, one of whom declared he was a solicitor, and the other, a detective, the 'new landlord' found himself given in charge for trying to obtain possession of the house on false pretences, the lease being a forgery. My informant explained, and, after the police-officer had ascertained who he was, he went with the latter to the station and laid information against Jackson. A warrant was applied for the next morning; but when the police came a few hours later to execute it, the bird had flown, and had left the empty nest. Even the coals and coke, which had not been paid for, were gone, and only a pair of tapestry curtains remained as bequest of Jackson-Hansen, who had got wind of what was going on, and had left the country in a similar manner, as his great model Opitz had done in 1885, when he took his pleasure-trip to India in a coal-ship.

Another swindle belonging to this category of sledge-driving, that came to my knowledge, deserves also to be mentioned in this place, for it equals, and maybe surpasses in audacity of conception and execution all what I related until now.

A great drawback, especially to the stranger, who comes to London, and a source of much trouble and inconvenience is, that so many streets in all parts of the vast town are bearing the same name. There are Queen's-roads and Queen's-streets, King-streets, Prince's-streets, Broad-streets, and so on, by the dozen. A less favoured, but nevertheless frequent name, is also Liverpool-street, and this conformity of names was made use of in a most ingenious manner by one of the sledge-driving fraternity.

In Liverpool-street, E.C., just opposite Broad-street Station, there is established for many years the well-known restaurant of Messrs. Moretti Brothers. The proprietors are highly respected, and, if they would require it, purveyors would be only too pleased to supply them with goods on credit.

In June, 1894, the firm of Carlo Antognini, in Magadino, in the Tessin, received from 'Moretti, 7–15, Liverpool-street, London,' a letter, enquiring, whether they would give the London agency for the sale of their Gruyère and Emmenthal cheese and Italian salami, to the enquiring firm. The letter was signed 'Moretti,' and the nicely printed letter-heading read :

'Moretti's Cafe and Restaurant,
Refreshment Rooms supplied, 7–15, Liverpool-street.'

The omission of the postal-district in this address shows at the first glance the fraudulent intentions of the sender of the letter. Nevertheless, nobody would be suspicious about it that the *E.C.* was omitted, and, who knows London, would take it as granted, that Moretti's Restaurant, Liverpool-street, E.C., was meant, in spite that the number was given with 7–15, instead of 7–11.

Moretti's letter closed with 'To save a deal of useless correspondence, I mention that our firm is very well known in the trade, and that you may enquire about us wherever you like.'

Enquiries were made, and the reports received were, of course, highly satisfactory. Signor Antognini had a friend in London—a Mr. Maschini—and to be quite on the safe side, he asked his opinion about Moretti from Liverpool-street, and was informed that he (Mr. Maschini) knew the Morettis personally, that they came from Riva San Vitale, and were highly respectable and prosperous. A banking house said 'Moretti Brothers, Café and Restaurant, Liverpool-street, are very respectable and hard-working people. They are Italians, possessed of means, and prosperous in business.' Another business-friend confirmed that the Morettis came from Riva San Vitale, and that they were good for any amount.

On the strength of such reports, Mr. Antognini wrote on the 14th of June, 1894, to Messrs. Moretti, that he was willing to supply them with goods against three months' bills—conditions that seemed very acceptable to 'Moretti's,' for they gave an order for 23 boxes of cheese and two boxes of salami, an order which was executed without delay by Mr. Antognini and invoiced—the cheese with 5254 frcs. 95 c., the Salami with 303 frcs. 90 c., together 5558 frcs. 85 c., Moretti being informed at the same time who the forwarding agent was.

The letters of 'Moretti' came to him in the *printed envelopes* which 'Moretti' had enclosed with each of his letters, and this trifling manœuvre contributed principally to the success of his game, as we shall see presently. 'Moretti' lost no time to give the forwarding agent his directions where to deliver the goods at their arrival, and he gave as addresses 117, Westminster Bridge Road and 94, Portland-street, W.C. On the 10th of July, 1894, 'Moretti' acknowledged receipt of goods, and remitted to Mr. Antognini their acceptance in settlement of the invoiced amount.

Some time afterwards Mr. Maschini, the gentleman already mentioned, paid a visit to his friends, Messrs. Moretti Brothers, at 7-11, Liverpool-street, E.C., and in the course of the ensuing conversation, he inquired, whether they had been content with the quality of the goods obtained from Signor Antognini. Messrs. Moretti were surprised, and said they did not know Signor Antognini, and they had not ordered and not received any goods from that firm, and they ventured the opinion that there must be a mistake, or that a swindle had been perpetrated. Mr. Antognini was communicated with, and at his enquiry at the forwarding agents, he was informed that the goods had been delivered in accordance with the instructions received by Messrs. 'Moretti,' 7–15, Liverpool street. The matter became quite inexplicable, and yet the solution of the riddle was as easy as possible. I shall just say what I ascertained.

Opposite St. Pancras Station, turning out from Euston-road, is Liverpool-street, *W.C.*, as officially described. The absence of all traffic forms a sharp contrast to the busy life of Liverpool-street, *E.C.*, where Messrs. Moretti's celebrated restaurant is situated. The Liverpool-street, W.C., does not belong to, let us say, the fashionable part of the West-central district. No. 7 is a private hotel; the proprietor, Mr. Wood, never knew a Mr. Moretti, and he certainly was never living there. No. 8 is a similar house, the 'Derby-Hotel,' and no Moretti is known there too. Now comes Derby-street. Crossing this street we pass on in Liverpool-street, the Nos. 10, 11, 12, 13, 14 and 15—all strictly private houses, each of them tenanted separately, and in no connection with each other. There is no trace, and never was, of a 'Moretti's Restaurant.' At No. 15, a highly respectable French family are living, who are letting appartments to single gentlemen.

In May, 1894, a 'gentleman,' who said he was a restaurant keeper at 117, Westminster-bridge-road, came with another young man, whom he introduced as Mr. Moretti, a man of about 35 years of age, of fair complexion, with a 'very funny' fair moustache, pretending not to know English, and his friend explained, he had come to this country to learn the language. The conversation was carried on in French, spoken by Moretti with a slightly foreign accent, that proved him not to be a Frenchman or native of Switzerland, but caused the landlady to think he was a German, and even roused her suspicion that his assertion of being unacquainted with English, was an untruth. However, a bargain was concluded, and the 'Mr. Moretti' engaged a bedroom at a small weekly rent. He was not many days in the house, when letters arrived with the printed address: 'Messrs. Moretti's Café and Restaurant, 7-15, Liverpool-street. They bore unmistakable traces of having travelled through many postal-offices, before being delivered at their ultimate address at 15, Liverpool-street, W.C. Very likely they were first presented at the real Messrs. Moretti, but the *printed* address with Nos. 7-15, instead of 7-11, induced this firm to decline to accept them, and thus the letters reached finally their goal. The landlady remonstrated with her lodger with the 'very funny moustache' about the 'very funny address,' and declared her house was a respectable house, and she would not have such things. He explained it was a mistake, and he would have the matter rectified without delay.

A few days later another letter with the same printed address, and a small parcel arrived from Switzerland. The landlady remonstrated again, and warned her lodger that if such a thing occurred again, she would ask him to leave at once. From this day 'Moretti' was waiting for the postman in the street, and took his letters from him. A few weeks later 'Moretti' came home drunk one night and overslept the morning delivery, which brought to the house a letter, addressed as before, and bearing on the envelope, that apparently had been opened, a remark, that the letter did not belong to 'Messrs. Moretti, Liverpool-street, E.C.' The landlady was thoroughly disgusted, gave her lodger notice, and he left a week afterwards. During his stay at 15, Liverpool-street, W.C., no goods had been delivered to him (the small parcel excepted), and he also could not have stored them in his small bedroom. A long time after Moretti had left, that is on the third of October, 1894. an acceptance of his, amounting to £222 6s. 9d., was presented at the house through Lloyd's Bank. No cover had been left, and the bill consequently went back protested. It was, of course, the bill of Mr. Antognini, who never received a farthing for his cheese and sausages.

In prosecuting my researches, I further ascertained that a part of the goods had really been delivered at 117, Westminster-bridge-road, where Moretti, with another man of dark complexion were constant customers. The 'News-rooms' in Bedford-street, the 'Café du Nord' and Capalli's Restaurant, then No. 94, Portland-street, and the clubs and German Public-houses in and about City-road, were the favourite haunts of the two swindlers; and following these traces, I was finally able to collect unmistakable proof, and to convince myself, that 'Moretti' was no other than the notorious scoundrel Lewin, alias Popert, to whom I helped in 1886 to eight months hard labour, and whose career as Popert, and lucky escape to justice has been related in a preceding chapter. Directly after the great haul of cheese and salami from Signor Antognini, Lewin, alias Popert-Moretti, went last year to New York, but came back from there a short time afterwards to Europe, landing at Antwerp, and very likely he is staying now in Holland, in a convenient distance from England, where he is certain to be seen again as soon as his last exploit is forgotten, and the storm has blown over.

His confederate and partner in this transaction, the man with dark hair and moustache, is, if I am not greatly mistaken, at present well secured. What I ascertained about this fellow, points to his identity with a criminal who appeared under the alias of Domenico Moretti on March 28th of this year at Bow-street under a warrant for extradition to Germany, for frauds committed there. The demand was granted, and it transpired that the man, whose real name is said to be Ossacino, had just served a term of five years penal servitude for defrauding a clergyman in South Kensington of £2,000 by means of the 'confidence-trick.' Let us hope that the now prisoner in Germany and Lewin's confederate is one and the same person, and that he will meet his punishment. But the cheese and salami have shown that even the most cautious business-man is not safe before the ingenious tricks of the sledge-driving fraternity.

* * *

On the arid plains of a South-American Republic are strewn the bleaching bones of many thousands valorous sons of the German fatherland, who were killed in the battles of two rivalling parties. This fact is well known to the authorities, and if I am not mistaken the press was not silent at the time to the traffic going on between London and the said Republic, that amounted to nothing more nor less than slave-dealing. If I do not mention the name of the Republic who employed agents here for 'enlistening' soldiers, it is easily explained by stating that I do not want 'a war' with that State in an English law-court, because the poor fellows, who were actually kidnapped and pressed into the service of these South-American Hidalgoes, cannot appear as witnesses before the day of general reckoning. Dead men are silent! But one question I shall answer: Who were the scoundrels who acted as agents for the Republic, and who sold the young lives for slaughter? They were the countrymen of the poor victims—the German sledge-drivers of London. Who did not know the 'star' of the sledge-drivers and sharpers and smugglers, ***Venediger***, who, after a long and prosperous career, sinned against the 'eleventh commandment,' and was caught at a most daring fraud by the excise-officers, and sent to prison, where he died? He was the *matador* of the whole fraternity, and supplied the un-named Republic with the fighting material at £5 per head. Who does not know his confederates—the brothers ***Frantz***, who are still serving a term of penal servitude; ***Holm***, who died in prison; the miserable scoundrels ***Drucker***, ***Hermann Arnold***, ***Goetz***, and ***Ritsch***, who are all at present in safety in one or the other of H.M. prisons. But none of them deserved his fate better than their *matador* Venediger, who was not satisfied by ruining wholesale striving manufacturers and merchants, but sold and sent into death thousands of his German countrymen, for whom many a mother and sister and many a German maiden are crying to this day. All these poor young fellows were engaged under false pretences as clerks, stewards, and ship's cooks, with good salaries and better prospects, and a 'free passage' to their new home, and when on the high sea they were informed of the truth, and forced to become soldiers, and to fight the glorious battles of the miserable Republic. They were not permitted to communicate with anybody, and treated as prisoners. Like cattle they were driven into death, and the bleaching bones of these poor fellows in the distant plains of the Andes are the appropriate monument of the German sledge-drivers in London—a monument that cries for vengeance!

PRESS OPINIONS.

'The Cologne People's Gazette' *(Koelnische Volkszeitung)* has rendered a signal service to the German export-trade in exposing a considerable number of London 'Sledge-drivers.' In bearing the tremendous costs of the prosecution, amounting to fully 40,000 marks, and in taking the great trouble of collecting evidence, the paper has made a sacrifice in the interest of German trade and manufacturers, deserving gratitude, and of which it is to be hoped that it was not brought in vain.'

'*Neueste Nachrichten*,' Leipsic, 27/4/95.

'By their energetic proceedings in this matter, the '*Cologne People's Gazette*' have earned the gratitude of the whole trading community of Germany, and all we wish is, that the great sacrifices were not brought in vain. There are certainly existing still in London some more of these companies of swindlers; but to trace their dealings and to disclose it to the public, means so much trouble, danger and expenses, that it cannot be undertaken by a single individual or a single newspaper. There other factors must come to the rescue, and there the chambers of commerce seem to have to fulfil a duty, for it is easy to them to take the necessary steps and to find the means to protect German trade against these rogues and swindlers.'

'*Mercuria*,' Berlin, 14/4/95.

'The Cologne People's Gazette,' one of those solid papers who are not tainted by any kind of corruption and have to thank their prosperity to their high character, combined with commercial honesty and intelligence, are publishing, for some years already, most interesting revelations by their London correspondent 'Rollo,' regarding the fraudulent doings of the London 'Sledge-drivers,' who have swindled already the German trade for many hundred thousand marks. By disclosing the dangerous dealings of these London swindlers, hailing mostly from Germany, the 'Cologne People's Gazette' has rendered a really great service to German trade, that deserves greater appreciation still, as it involved the paper into costs of 40,000 marks. The 'Cologne

People's Gazette' intend to go on with their activity in this regard, and it is to be wished that there were more papers who would recognize and fulfil their ethical and practical mission in an equally thorough manner.'

'*Icaa*' (Organ of the Int. Corresp. Ass.), Vienna.

'It is the merit of the 'Cologne People's Gazette' to have unmasked quite a nest of dangerous impostors who have systematically swindled the German export-trade.'

'*Neueste Nachrichten*,' Düsseldorf, 9/4/95.

'As an extraordinary proof of German enterprise and public spirit must be regarded the action of the 'Cologne People's Gazette' (the leading organ of the Centre party), who have expended 40,000 marks on the criminal prosecution of some members of the so-called 'Sledge-drivers,' a gang of German and Austrian swindlers in London, who are systematically victimising respectable, but too confiding German manufacturers. The action ended with the total defeat of the rogues. These 'Sledge-drivers' have for many years past defrauded, and often even ruined countless firms on the Continent, by obtaining goods under false pretences, and selling the same at any price by the help of their equally dishonest confederates. The 'Cologne People's Gazette' deserves the greatest praise for expending such a sum to bring for once to justice this swindling rabble. The chief swindler, a respectable looking jubilee-rogue named Lehnert, has taken to flight.'

'*Abendpost*,' Chicago, 29/4/95.

'The 'Cologne People's Gazette' has rendered a great and meritorious service by checking these nefarious dealings. The paper spared neither trouble nor costs to disclose the tricks and secret doings of these swindlers.'

'*Confectioner*,' Berlin, 4/4/95, and
'*Post for Commercial Travellers*,' 11/4/95.

'The German trading community is under the greatest obligation to the 'Cologne People's Gazette' for their energetic proceedings which cost the paper the enormous sum of 40,000 marks.'

'*Manufacturist*,' Hanover, No. 14, 1895.

'The paper has spent a large sum to disclose the dangerous doings of this swindling fraternity, who were robbing German manufacturers year after year. We hope that these proceedings will prove a salutary warning to German firms not to enter so easily into transactions with unknown firms in England.'

'*Eisenhändler*,' Bunzlau, 13/4/95.

'By exposing this dangerous gang of swindlers in England, who have inflicted great losses on German manufacturers, the 'Cologne People's Gazette' has rendered a signal service to the German export-trade.'

'*Zeitschrift für Deutschlands Buchdrucker*.' 18/4/95.

'The brave organ of the Centre party, that is guarding so energetically the interests of German trade in exposing the swindles of the 'Sledge-drivers,' deserves general recognition. It is the merit of the 'Cologne People's Gazette,' of having brought to justice quite a number of arrant rogues who were systematically defrauding and swindling German merchants without number. We congratulate our Rhenish colleague to this success.'

'*Niederrhein. Volkszeitung*,' Crefeld, 1/4/95, and
'*Reichspost*,' Vienna, 9/4/95.

'The 'Cologne People's Gazette,' who spent 40,000 marks over this prosecution, deserves the greatest praise for having rendered this important service to German trade.'

'*Badischer Beobachter*,' Karlsruhe, 9/4/95.

'The influence of the Centre party, not only in the political, but also the practical and economical life of the nation, has received a further illustration by this signal victory of the 'Cologne People's Gazette.' Supported by an excellent correspondent in London, the paper has waged for many years a merciless war against the 'London Sledge-drivers.' The energetic action of the 'Cologne People's Gazette' in protecting German trade deserves the greater praise, as the proceedings in English courts of justice are very troublesome and expensive, and have cost the paper not less than 40,000 marks. To the victory gained in these unselfish proceedings, which involved so great a sacrifice, we tender the organ of the Centre party our heartiest congratulations.'

'*Neues Mannheimer Volksblatt*,' 7/4/95.

'The 'Rollo-Articles' of the 'Cologne People's Gazette' caused a tremendous and justified sensation. Mr. Reuschel is himself a man of business, and is in direct touch with the commercial life of the great English metropolis. He has made the doings of the 'Sledge-drivers' his journalistic speciality. His revelations in the 'Cologne People's Gazette' will, undoubtedly, save the German export-trade from further incalculable losses. Next to Mr. Reuschel the merit belongs to the 'Cologne People's Gazette' and to the English judges, who grant to the journalist the right to discuss the dangerous dealings of others, even if they do not concern him directly—a view that is a honour to England. It seem desirable that the judges of other countries would be converted to these salutary views.'

'*Kosmos*,' Nürnberg, 7/4/95.

'Whenever possible, there is no better or more satisfactory defence in a libel action than a justification of the incriminating statements. Had Heath Hellier prosecuted 'The Draper's Record,' we should have justified our application to him of the epithets rogue and swindler. A similar course was followed at the Old Bailey last Monday, when two persons, named respectively Lehnert and Opitz, prosecuted Mr. Reuschel for having published in a German paper the statement that the prosecutors are, and have been for some years past, connected with long-firm swindlers, and also that they have been guilty of frauds and giving false references. After the cross-examination of Lehnert, the jury stopped the case, and declared that in their opinion the libel was justified. Of course, the defendant was immediately discharged, and Opitz's case against him was not proceeded with, Mr. Commissioner Kerr remarking that the documents in the case ought to be laid before the Public Prosecutor. This was afterwards done, with the result that both Lehnert and Opitz were arrested, brought up on the Mansion House Police Court on Thursday, and remanded for a week on bail. Thus it would seem that justice in on the track of long-firm swindlers in London as well as in Amsterdam. The trade generally will welcome the news, for it is an undoubted fact that of late years these knaves have been growing both in numbers and in assurance.'

'*The Draper's Record*,' 30/3/95.

www.ingramcontent.com/pod-product-compliance
Lightning Source LLC
Chambersburg PA
CBHW032101220426
43664CB00008B/1094
* 9 7 8 3 3 3 7 2 8 0 7 2 7 *